The Granville Hermit

The Granville Hermit

Robert S. Foster

Burlington, Vermont

Onion River Press
191 Bank Street
Burlington, Vermont 05401

Note: This book is peopled with men and women who perhaps truly existed, and many who were created out of the author's imagination which implies all names, livelihoods and interactions of folklore within these pages. We bear and intend no reference to anyone or any company that was or is part of Granville or its historical and founding inhabitants through our timeline, and, of course, current citizens and ancestors.

Cover photos: Catamount photo: ID 6220776 © Ultrashock | Dreamstime.com Woods photo: Johannes Plenio. This work by Johannes Plenio is licensed under a Creative Commons Attribution 4.0 International License. https://j.plenio.de/index.php/all-free-images. Historical photos and maps from the Granville Town Archives and used with permission. With special thanks to Mike Eramo for the Ford farm photos.

Book and cover design by Kitty Werner, RSBPress LLC

ISBN 978-1-949066-39-5

Printed in the United States of America

Publisher's Cataloging-in-Publication Data

Names: Foster, Robert S., author.
Title: The Granville hermit / Robert S. Foster.
Description: Burlington, VT: Onion River Press, 2020.
Identifiers: LCCN: 2019919121 | ISBN 978-1-949066-39-5
Subjects: LCSH Morse, Carl. | Granville (Vt.)--Biography. | United States--Vermont--Granville--History. | Granville (Vt.)--Social lives and customs. | Folklore--Vermont. | BISAC HISTORY / United States / State & Local / New England (CT, MA, ME, NH, RI, VT) | BIOGRAPHY & AUTOBIOGRAPHY / General
Classification: LCC F48 .M67 F67 2020 | DDC 974.3/092--dc23

Dedication

So many manifestations stem from those who inspire.

Out of so many friends and acquaintances who have inspired this writing,
Bob Foster, my father, provided the deepest of inspirations, the most unique
experiences and adventures. If it weren't for him, I would not have learned
the woodsmanship necessary to navigate the hills of Granville, Vermont.
By drawing from those experiences and teachings, I was able to create and
enrich this story.

Thank you, Dad!

Contents

Preface

I would like to express much thanks to the folks of Granville and surrounding areas who gave me so much of their time and knowledge allowing me into their present and past, with their memories recollections and folklore.

Of course this story is not an account of history per say, but more of a teaching of how folks made and used implements and utensils from the earth's resources in the period, then utilized a barter system in times of national monetary duress

Intention throughout these pages is to awaken folks of today to the pristine beauty that fills the eye at every glance; a sleepy mountain community nestled in the ancient "green mountains" seemingly lost in time. Feel and enjoy the forest's energy, views, and vistas; walk, hike, or camp along the ancient trails and cart-ways that the town of Granville has proudly reclaimed.

Experience the historical sites and mystique of the original farmstead foundations now sleeping in the national forest, and all four seasons of outdoor activities along the ancient trail systems and White River. Take in its abundance and natural beauty. It is a place to regain one's spiritual connection and imagination of a simpler time and interact with its energy.

A secret, magical and mystical place that I, and many others, can attest and hold sacred.

Robert S. Foster
Granville, Vermont
November 19, 2019

Acknowledgments

Special thanks to a host of folks who contributed a wealth of information in the preparations, along with historical accounts and events that inspired, formulated, and nurtured this town of Granville historic archives

Kathy Werner, Town clerk
Town of Granville Trails Committee
U.S. Forest Service at Rochester
U.S. Forest Service at Rutland
U.S. Army Archives
Mike Eramo
Steve Werner
Norm Arsenalt
Bill and Petey Parish
Denny Beaty
Kenny Beaty
Wilma Washburn
Jean Sergent
Eleanor Norton
Ruth Newton
Lori Twitchell
Bob and Jean Foster
Larry Miner
Ed and Wendy Eramo
Howard and Sue Estes
Ron Mallard

And a special thank you to my wife, Mary, for her endless support and encouragement.

Introduction

I actually met Carl Morse when I was only about nine years old one fall day at the Granville general store as he stood there with his long beard and steel grey eyes of wisdom. We did not speak, but the connection we made inspired me to tell his story.

We could find no record of the Granville Hermit's (Carl Morse's) death. With that said, according to all accounts and remembering of folks, legend and beliefs remains as such that he actually returned to his cabin off of Texas Gap Trail and faded his life journey into nature's grasp.

In its heyday, 1880 to 1900, the town of Granville was a timber and logging community. The diversity of local farmsteads provided a network of tradesmen, wood crafts, livestock, and smith works, all working, bartering and sustaining its fluctuating population of over 1100 folks, during these times.

With the exception of the Granville "burrow" nestled in the valley alongside the White River, mostly all of the farmsteads and unique characters reflected in this story were located within the lower ridges and upper elevations, as they bustled, flourished, and even failed their endeavors during this era. Route 100 as we know it today did not exist.

Census reports from 1950 mention a Granville population of only 280 folks. By 2007 it rose to 287. Today it remains at 298, all still very unique folks of character still applying their skills and trades.

Recently some of the folks took great pride in reclaiming Granville's ancient trails and roads that supported the bustling timber town era of the 1800s and early 1900s.

These roads and trails have been mapped, revived and remain open to public use for hiking, camping, ATV and cross-country skiing, horseback access, mountain biking, and snow traveling. One can enjoy all forms of outdoor activities in all four seasons on Granville's trails that meander through and intertwine with the state and U.S. Forest Service road systems.

The old homestead and schoolhouse foundations still remain very close to the trails and ancient roads, and they emit an enchantment and history of the bustling era gone by in these hills. The natural views and vistas, along with the fall foliage of natural beauty that fills the eyes and centers the soul add to the mountains enchantment. We leave to you, the reader, only your imagination of the lore of Burke's Buried Cache of gold and silver coins, and the lure of placer flakes and nuggets of gold in Granville's streambeds that can and will create an adventure and sense of mystical magic of this special place.

We would like to honor the story of one man's life trials and travesties as a teaching for some. He became known in Granville's folklore as a wise mystical healer for animals and people. He was the "seer in the mountain."

Perhaps one can now understand why Carl Morse, the Granville Hermit, chose to live for more than fifty years in the solitude of Granville's magical Green Mountains.

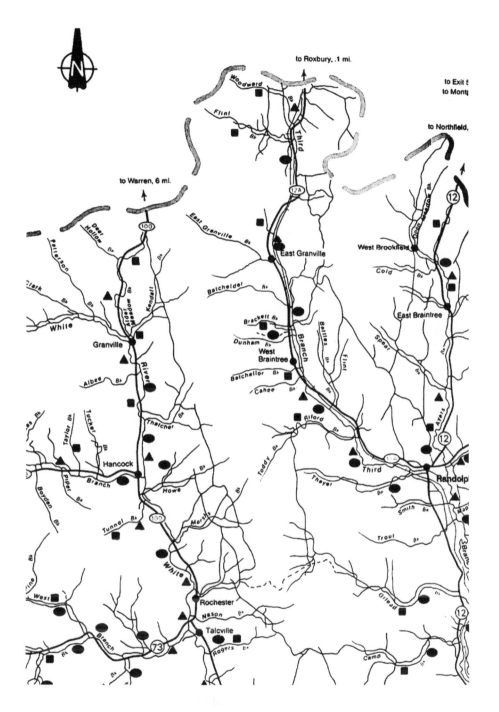

The headwaters of the White River begin in the western section of the mountains just off what is now known as West Hill. The area is now part of the National Forest.

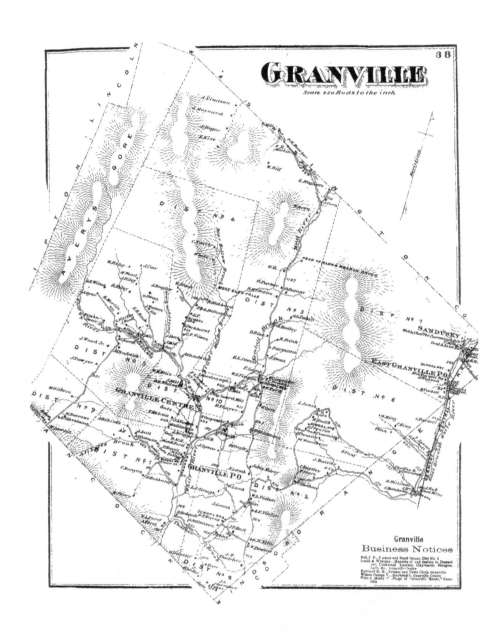

from *The Beers Atlas* 1871

1 Sands of Time

We begin our story in northern central Vermont, in the sleepy town of Granville, nestled in the mists of the Green Mountains, so named from the French for green *verde*, and mountain *mont*. Neighboring townships include Hancock, Rochester, and small communities now a part of Addison County, Vermont.

Before our story, only Native American tribes inhabited and sustained their culture harmoniously, living with the earth's rhythms and cycles.

These indigenous people were known historically as the Abenaki with smaller clans living in villages along the brooks and riverbanks throughout the upper valleys of Vermont. One Abenaki clan was known as the Hasani, who inhabited the upper valley area where our story takes place.

While the Hasani natives often migrated with seasonal changes to the south from this area, their spring and summers were spent here fishing and foraging in the green rich valley floor and hunting in the ancient forest, thriving in the mountain hills and hollows that loomed up to peak elevations of 5,000 feet.

In the early 1400s, the wildlife that inhabited this area was diverse. Black bear, wolf, cougar (also known as catamount), bobcat, and coyote were abundant carnivorous creatures. Hooved animals including elk, moose and deer roamed the terrain. Also, turkey, beaver, rabbit, quail, partridge, squirrel—the list goes on and on. This ecosystem provided much of the food supply for the inhabitants.

The Green Mountains provide a pristine lush forest, with crystal clear mountain streams beginning high in the steep lush hills, with tributaries that merge and cascade ever downward, bringing nutrients, minerals and silts into the green fertile valley floor. Like fingers of a hand forming into a wider arm, the rivers rage in the springtime as vast snow melts occur, yet meander gently during sunny summer days and cool evenings.

Here begins the White River, a prominent landmark in Vermont's geography. Flowing southward through the mountain valleys, gradually winding through the gentle hills of southern New England, she becomes ever broader, winding more than 250 miles, ultimately reaching the southern coast of New England and joining the vastness of the Atlantic Ocean.

The eddies and pools of the White River teem with native trout and salmon, luring wildlife to its banks. In the valley, these pools and eddies are sanctuary for the fish unrestricted all the way upstream into the foothills. Their spawning grounds were created by the looming mountain forest, where the White River narrows to just a brook and to even narrower finger streams. Small pools of crystal waters formed by the clutches of boulder till and crags of bedrock created their protective spawning grounds over the centuries.

The natural evolution of this place hosts a topographical creation of unsurpassed beauty. The valley itself was formed millions of years ago. Glaciers gouged the earth's crust, pushing and dragging billions of tons of aggregate over the bedrock floor and carving out the erratic landscape.

The subsequent raging torrents of glacial ice melt, along with hundreds of years of seasonal winter snow melts, formed deep gores. The White River carried these aggregates and rich silts in vast layers to the valley bottom floor, providing Granville with abundant vegetation, berries, crabapple, grains, and forage.

At the higher elevations, a forest flourished of immense red and white oaks, beech, and white birch. The softer hemlock, spruce and white pines grew in their best-suited terrains, with preferential soil type and desired elevation.

Flourishing undisturbed for thousands of years, withstanding only nature's weather rhythms and ecosystem adjustments, these trees knew only to reach higher toward the nourishing sunlight.

Hundreds of years of undisturbed growth had created vast areas of immense timber, trees reaching over 100 feet tall, with trunks five to six feet in circumference. The gentle sloping hollows and sun-drenched slopes balanced each species of tree grove and dictated their height based on the elevation near and above the harsh winters' frost lines.

From the early 1500s to the late 1600s the French Europeans began to migrate into the region along the Champlain valley.

French-Canadian settlers climbed over the steep Green Mountain range, which is much like a backbone that runs centrally along the territory's natural spine, claiming the region that is now called Vermont, as French territory.

As they migrated, the colonists brought with them the European way of life, at the same attempting to integrate with the indigenous tribes.

Around 1666, France claimed the territory as "New France." This region drew French, Dutch, and English settlers alike. The 1758–1763 French and Indian War, also known as King George's War, changed the dominance of the territory. It was now being vied over its natural resources, fur trades and proximity to Lake Champlain. Land titles and claims to the territory were bantered and annexed, creating opportunities for the early American settlers to claim land grants under certain conditions and contracts.

Colonists made their "pitch" and "claim" on their parcel or allotment of acreage, with the expectation to create prosperity from the land claim within an agreed number of years.

The population in Granville (then called Kingstown, after the many settlers with the name King) was moderate. With prospects of a good living from the natural resource of timber, the homesteads and settlements of early Kingstown grew rapidly into a bustling lumber town.

In the early 1800s the name Kingstown was changed. Prominent folk took umbrage with the name King, and after a few town meetings the settlement name was, by majority vote, changed to Granville. The settlers agreed that the township should be named after its land-grant origin.

The first names under consideration were Grantville, Grant, and Gran. In 1833, a final agreement made the name Granville.

Timber resources were abundant in Granville. Its mountains had elevations of 2,500 feet at lower ridges and up to 3,500 feet at the extreme ridges, with many gentle sloping hollows and dells.

The inhabitants of the areas known as West Hill and North Hollow were predominately farm homesteaders in the late 1700s through the 1800s.

They prospered from timbering and making Vermont wood products. The village of Granville, located at the northern head of the valley, hosted many diversified lumber town support enterprises, along with cottage-style homes.

The farmsteads were in the vast forest acreage on both lower and upper elevations. The farmsteads spanned both east and west of the valley, and the farmsteaders eked a living off the land. These neighbors and enterprises formed their own support and barter systems.

Local trades consisted of raising livestock, turkeys, horses, cows, etc., also blacksmiths, teachers, store owners, and loggers. Loggers at the time dragged their harvested logs by sledge downhill to the village or the lower ridge mills.

A network of cart roads was established along with ten or eleven school districts for the families and children of the town to attend schools within a reasonable walking distance—a few miles from most farmsteads.

Here our story begins.

2 Catamount

As Leslie Carl Morse (Carl as most people called him) was walking to school, he looked down at the rough Texas Falls Gap road ahead. He never looked forward to the arduous three-mile walk to school and most certainly not to the walk back uphill to go home again.

This morning, however, the excitement of interacting with other kids his age encouraged him. He was accomplished in reading and writing. Learning about the outside world and its history fascinated him enough to pursue the path.

Carl was careful to pick his footing along the slick rocky trail that late September morning, as an inch of light snow had accumulated overnight. At first, he didn't notice the paw prints overlapping deer tracks, as deer tracks are very common.

The tracks first indicated walking. Then he noticed a torn-up area churned with leaves and snow in a ten-foot round diameter with clear tufts of deer hair in the mix.

A good tracker, Carl curiously followed the deer tracks about 20 yards and began to unfold the story of the tracks. They left the trail running and leaping into the side woods, and then down the trail another 30 yards or so leading to another torn up area of leaves, snow, and hair tufts.

Catamount, cougar, or fisher cat, as they were called then, were subjects of folklore, legends and fantasy. No one had ever caught or shot one, not in the entire state of Vermont of any record, and certainly not in the mountains of Granville.

These creatures, as big as any knee-high large dog, with a paw print in the mud or snow as round as three to four inches, boasted a long "S" curved tail. They were to be feared as carnivorous predators that hunted game year-round, surviving the harsh winters.

A cat of this size could and would take down moose, deer, and domestic livestock. Nor were small boys excluded from the menu, according to his dad and other hunters.

These tales told around the fire at various social gatherings or hunting camps flashed through his mind.

Mesmerized by the unfolding story, Carl continued down the trail, noticing the pinkish spots of blood mixed into the leaves and snow. He quickened his pace, not thinking much about school or even about his footing.

As he rounded a slight knoll in the trail, he came upon the dark silhouette. Instinct took hold, and he dug his heel into the muddy leaves and snow. The adrenalin surged into his chest. His lower backside hit the embankment just as the cat jumped to a startled stance over its kill.

What happened next is only lore to which woodsmen and skilled hunters can relate. A moment when time stands still, one's essence and inner being is abruptly forward in consciousness, the body moving not from mindful commands but purely on instinct.

Hardly six feet from this large cat, Carl assumed a defensive stance, as did the catamount.

As Carl's eyes fixed on the cat's, the sound of his own heartbeat calmed him. Through some ancient wisdom, he did not allow the emotion of fear to well up, for the emotion of fear will be sensed immediately by the cat, or any animal. Instead, Carl surrendered to the moment and took in the beauty of this magnificent and powerful creature.

In his mind's voice he thanked the cat for this experience, and in his mind's eye 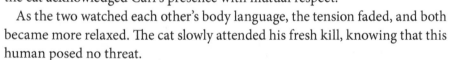 the cat acknowledged Carl's presence with mutual respect.

As the two watched each other's body language, the tension faded, and both became more relaxed. The cat slowly attended his fresh kill, knowing that this human posed no threat.

As the catamount prepared to heft his game, Carl sensed that he would encounter this cat again, a knowing that came from the cat's essence. At that, the catamount picked his limp kill in his powerful jaws and carried it with ease off the trail downhill into the thick undergrowth.

The last half mile to the schoolhouse seemed like just a few feet, as Carl's legs and body seemed to float over the rugged road. He burst through the schoolhouse door, finally catching his breath. Totally out of his timid character, he shouted in stuttered words to his friends and teacher as to what he had seen.

The few acquaintances, boys and girls of various ages, gathered around at the lunch break to hear about his escapade with the cat.

Leslie Carl Morse was considered by some of the older boys a little slow because of his quiet character and cautious behavior with groups of people. They sometimes teased him and pulled tomfooleries.

Carl did not always take the razzing too well but would hold his emotions inside and lived with distrust of getting too close to others. As he retold the tale of the cat, a few older boys interrupted, accusing him of making it up.

For fear of ridicule he left out the part about the mental communication with the cat. The younger kids were mesmerized by his story, however, and wanted to hear more, which made him feel accepted.

One girl, from the Hubbard farm, a few years younger than Carl, always caught his attention. Whenever she made eye contact, he felt a deep connection to her—a familiar bond that he knew she also felt.

Mamie Hubbard never understood her insights and connection to Carl; she just liked him.

As the small group of kids walked home from the schoolhouse, one by one the others would bid farewell, splitting off the main road onto the various side trails towards their own farms.

Mamie and Carl were the last two walking or sometimes riding along. Carl lived the farthest out, up on Texas Falls Gap road. It was a good mile and a half farther from the main through-way where Mamie's trail split off.

As they walked along physically quiet, her hand brushed his. She stopped and looked at him, smiling, took both his hands in hers and said, "Tell me what the cat said."

Off in the distance, just past the Ford's farm, they could hear the timber loggers working up on the slope. The sounds of their axes and shouts coaxing the horse and ox teems along echoed across the hollows.

It was just a little farther before the old trail road split where Mamie would head towards her family cabin. A small clearing of green grasses about thirty yards off trail was situated on a gentle slope with eight to ten sugar maples. Here they always liked to stop for a rest, have a chat and take some shade on a hot summer day if it wasn't raining. The first time, Mamie took him by the hand, excited about investigating the grassy clearing. A single pine stood in the middle of the grove of old maples, and under it in the softer pine needle bedding they sat holding hands.

Carl didn't mind. Affections were very limited at home due to the chores demanded by his Pop since he was about six, maybe earlier. In his early memories of childhood, fun and games seemed nonexistent, and affections were only vague remote memories of bedtime stories from his Mum.

This time while holding her hand, he felt a much stronger connection to her, a nurturing bond that made him not want to let go of her hand, but then also, feeling awkwardness and apprehension of what was to happen next.

Carl had no experience in these matters of the heart and did not understand the new emotions welling inside, so he just smiled, content with the moment.

In the next minute Mamie nestled her head on his shoulder; then slowly, without speaking, she kissed him. The awkwardness of this new realm of life naturally gave way to their passion. From that day, for him, that clearing under a solo pine tree in a sugar grove became a special place, a sacred sanctuary.

As Carl arrived home to the simple cabin, he could hear his dad muttering from behind the barn. The moon was already rising in the hot evening sky. He was a couple of hours late for his chores. Carl knew he was in for a reprimand, but nothing this day was going to allow his new experience to evaporate so fast, despite his Pop's criticism.

The catamount story—the only part of his day's experience he was willing to share as the cause of his delay getting home—temporarily satisfied his Pop's cantankerous disposition.

The only thing that ever seemed to make Pop happy was his getting the chores done, with no show of gratitude. Day in and out, chores were repetitious, with the seasonal tasks varying, the shorter days, and heavy winter snows adding to the challenge.

Many nights, diner conversations were limited only to what tasks needed to be done, what needed to be planted or harvested, and always how to earn some money or barter for the store-bought supplies.

Occasionally some exciting event like a bear hunt or some gathering that they could go to would come up, but for the most part with Pop it was always about prosperity or the lack of it.

There didn't seem to be any joy for Carl. His Mom had stopped smiling a long time ago, going through her daily routines with her jaw set. Laughter was nonexistent.

Pop was a good, hard-working man, obsessed with making the farm prosperous. Being a good woodsman, he taught Carl how to hunt and fish and track game at an early age.

Navigating the mountainous terrain was not just a skill, but an inborn sixth sense that only few men possessed—not so much as a skill taught, but as an acquired or honed instinct.

In the woods, Pop was always the efficient teacher but he never praised his son's accomplishments. Carl's first deer was a doe, shot with Pop's single-shot rifle while Pop was off cutting timber with Rob Ford and his crew of Frenchmen. Meat was scarce in those times, and Pop always said, "Son, if the opportunity arises, do not hesitate to take advantage."

The young deer meandered into the small meadow behind the barn grazing the grasses that early evening, Carl remembered the loading procedure of the old 44–40. Taking careful aim as he was taught, his shot was true to vitals of the deer. Carl hung the deer up in the lean-to shed and waited smiling for his dad to come home.

As Carl's dad approached the cabin after a hard day's work, he heard the shot in the distance and knew it was his son. His thought process always leaned to the negative side of things—something he was aware of but never learned to control.

Anger was his first reaction, imagining that Carl was playing with the rifle instead of performing his chores, or worse yet, that a predator was in the chickens or the garden and his wife was shooting his limited resources of cartridge shells!

He muttered to himself that he should have brought the rifle with him.

Upon his arrival, tired and anxious as to what the shot was about, he found Carl and Mother sitting on the stoop smiling. "Dear!" his wife exclaimed, "Leslie has something to show you!"

Carl proudly took his dad to the lean-to and showed him the hanging deer.

Pop just nodded with approval. Then after a brief moment, he said, "We'll need to get to the gutting and cleaning right away before the heat causes spoilage, so go get the carving knife." Then he turned around to check the rifle and the box of cartridges.

Carl expected a much more enthusiastic response! He wasn't sure if he should explain the circumstance. Pop didn't seem to care or acknowledge his first deer.

He just said, "Yes, sir, I'll go get it." As he turned, deflated, he muttered, "It was about a 40-yard shot."

With fresh venison for dinner that night, a little later than usual, because the other chores still needed to get done, they ate the meal with quiet contemplation.

His Mom, a resourceful cook and farmstead wife, smiled briefly to herself as she admired her son recognizing his day's accomplishment. She enjoyed the moment of satisfaction with her family and their humble home, watching her man and son eating their fill, an infrequent occasion.

Her mind flashed back to her late teens when the excitement of their journey to Vermont for a land grant was all she and her husband could dream about, it seemed to be an adventure beyond imagination.

The prospect of building their own homestead on acreage for clearing and grazing with only the challenge of making the land prosperous was a great opportunity for a young couple starting out in life. They did not anticipate the challenges nor foresee the hardships that could occur in the Vermont climate.

Through the years of hard work and toil building the homestead, she slowly withdrew due to the constant demands and routines. With fewer and fewer social events to break the monotony, she was often solemn, and after Carl was born her husband became less affectionate, multitasking all the time with a self-imposed urgency to create a living and to provide for his family. He was not a bad husband or father; he just didn't realize how his focus and ambitions overwhelmed the simple joys of life, and he forgot how to recognize them. As young Carl went through his adolescence Pop taught him about the chores and ways of the woods. But there wasn't much difference between necessity and enjoyment, and Carl was scolded many times for not performing a task to the standard that Dad wanted.

This scolding caused some loss of Carl's self-esteem, but he never showed it outwardly and he could not express it to his Mom or anyone else for lack of understanding.

His dad knew about his own mistakes, and on this day at dinner he thought to himself quietly how well Carl had performed today and how his imagination first created a negative thought when he heard the shot.

He sat there for a long minute with a half-smile of proud appreciation and camaraderie that only a father and son can feel without the words being spoken.

3 *Diana*

Snow flurries fell more often now in the cool September mountain eleva-tions, surrendering to the sun's warming rays during the day.

The sun warmed their faces as Carl and Mamie sat under their favorite tree just off the beaten trail. Sharing deep feelings, their tender touches took them into the afternoon hours.

Suddenly aware of the time, Mamie kissed him passionately one last time. Then reluctantly tearing herself from their embrace, already late, she rushed off towards home.

Carl stowed the wool blanket back into the hollow tree to keep it dry for their next rendezvous. Though she was barely gone five minutes, Mamie was all he could think of, her soft touches, soothing voice, that half smile, and her starry eyes.

He could only think of how she completed his thoughts, how their soul-mate connection became stronger with each encounter, at least in his mind. His day-dreams consumed and filled him, seeing her as his loving wife and best friend.

Fixated on Mamie, he rounded the sharp bend in the road and almost walked past Elwin standing there.

"Good thing I wasn't a bear!" Elwin shouted, jumping off the stump, star-tling Carl.

Elwin was one of Carl's only real friends, deeply bonded since they were young boys, sharing not only school sessions, farm and town events, social functions, as well as hunting and fishing with their dads, working for old man Ford logging timber, or, in Mr. Shirley's case, from trades at the general store.

Both Carl and Elwin were to report to Mr. Ford's farm this day to perform chores, for pay of real coin—an arrangement their dads had made to teach the boys some hard-earned values.

Manure from the pigs, horses and cows needed to be shoveled directly from the pens and or from the stockpile outside the barn onto the long manure wagon. It later would be spread into the pasture or meadow to fertilize the hay lots or crops.

Once a week they performed these tasks, which neither of them really cared for, but to earn 75 cents a week was good pay when grown Frenchmen would gladly do it if given the opportunity.

Just before Elwin's dad became involved with the general store, he and Carl's dad were both foremen at Ford's logging camp operation, managing the cutting and skidding of timber from the mountain slopes down to the staging areas for old *Diana*, a steam-driven track engine, to haul it down to the lumber mills in the valley.

They would spend sometimes a full week straight at the timber camps supervising the teams of Frenchmen. Harvesting the timber was all done by teams of long-saw men and axe men, and horses and oxen would skid the logs down the slope to stage in stockpiles.

The summer season entailed long days from sunup to sundown.

Old Mr. Ford did them a favor by hiring the boys over outsiders, to teach them work ethic and build their character and self-esteem.

While their dads were proud of their positions, the boys saw it a little differently.

"I'm tired of shoveling shit!" Elwin muttered as they put the last of the pig manure on the wagon.

"Yeah, especially this pig crap, but it's the smell I'm getting sick of," Carl said.

"Well it's easier to load than the damn turkey manure at Farr's, which we gotta do again next week!" Elwin replied.

"Yeah, but this job pays better than old man Farr, and he yells too much, like we can just magically load it and spread it in the same hour!" chimed Carl.

"Well, it takes me two days just to get the smell out, and then we gotta do it all over again," Elwin said.

Just as Carl was throwing a dried chunk of manure at Elwin and laughing, Burke poked his head in the stall. "You boys about done with this?" he asked.

"Yes, sir," said Carl, as Burke came full in to inspect a bit closer.

Burke was what everybody called him. The boys did not know his first name, but out of respect they called him Mr. Burke. He was the senior farmhand at Ford's homestead operation.

Burke oversaw most daily routines as well as breeding livestock, planting, milking, and tending wood and supplies for Mrs. Ford's household tasks.

Burke was a new resident who spent two days on and two days off at his own small shack about two miles down West Hill Road.

"Now on Saturday, you boys need to hitch Sally and Bart up and spread this out over the upper meadow so we can till it in before frost." Burke directed.

"Yes, sir, Mr. Burke," the boys said simultaneously.

As Burke walked to the front step of the house, he turned to look around.

He instructed the boys to close the stall doors. Then they could head for home. Oddly, he took another look in all directions again, as if he were checking for something. At that, he opened the front door and walked into the Ford's ranch-style house.

The boys were just finishing loading the wagon from cleaning the horse stalls. Elwin put the wheelbarrow back against the tool shed and said, "Now I get to go home and do it again for Pop."

"Yup, me, too. 'Cepts I don't have to shovel today. Mum needs wood brought in. So, I guess I'll see you here on Saturday morning?" Carl asked.

"Yeah, you can smell me coming! Say about the usual time?" replied Elwin.

At that moment, they both heard a horse whinny and snort at the back of the barn. Mr. Ford had just arrived, surprising the boys because he was usually at the log camp until Saturday.

"You boys seen Burke?" Ford asked.

"Yes, sir," they both said at the same time.

"He just went in the house," Carl added.

"We're set here and ready to spread it out on Saturday," Elwin chimed in.

"That's good, fellas," Mr. Ford said, as he just stared at the house, paying them no mind. His intent was obviously not on what the boys were doing or saying. It was a little strange that he was back this soon, but they both had learned not to question an important man like Mr. Ford.

He could be intimidating at times just by his cold steel stare. A staunch realist, Ford knew the answer to his question well before you could stutter out your response. He demanded proficiency and results from all his employees.

His posture and demeanor were all authority, and he respected others for their experience or expertise in their trade. Still, his outward composure and stone-cold demeanor were intimidating to folks who did not know "Old Ford" personally.

His trust and respect came hard earned, nevertheless. Ford's religion was to use others as they would like to be used, pay his bills, and mind his own business. He ran a 1,000-acre farm with 100 dairy cows, raised fine horses, and grew corn, grain, hay, and poultry. Ford's son, Ted, was just a few years older than Elwin and Carl. Ted had some tough shoes to fill with his dad's stature in the community, and Ted had to work a little harder to gain respect from the workforce men.

Mrs. Ford, Mabel, was a very quiet woman, not as sociable in the community functions as one would think. While she had more luxuries in her household compared to other farmsteaders, she still did the home chores and met the demands her husband placed upon her. Timid when Ford was around, Mabel was gentle, giving, and kind of heart when he was off at the log operation. She would offer sweet tea or lemonade on the hot days and hot soup on the cold days to the farm helpers, but her smile was a forced effort when she could manage it.

The Fords would host apple paring and corn husking bees, card parties, straw rides and dances in the wintertime. The music was always accompanied by Mr. Ford, a good fiddler and harmonica player. These events were held dear by most people of the community as West Hill's good times.

Being acutely intuitive, Carl noticed immediately Mr. Ford's focus on the house as he gazed at the front door. His arriving home a day early meant that something was not right. Carl dismissed his intuition and turned to Elwin.

"Well, I'm gonna just head home now unless you need anything else from us, Mr. Ford," Carl said.

Ford turned to the boys. "Could one of you just break the saddle down and water and grain Pete in his stall for me? Then we'll see you fellows on Saturday to get that manure spread under."

"Yes sir, that's what we just set up with Mr. Burke," said Carl.

Ford just stared at the house again and muttered "Yeah. Mr. Burke." He walked toward the house. Carl and Elwin just looked at each other. Elwin shrugged, and Carl just raised one brow, and they led Pete into the stall.

It was a harsh economic time, to say the least. The country was reeling from the war of the rebellion, which had just ended, and the beginning of the economic trouble known as the "great panic." Most farmer folks bartered for services and supplies. The system worked well in the neighbor-helping-neighbor way of things.

Some folks lucky enough to have paying jobs had to compete with the Frenchmen from Canada for the labor services that the logging companies and mills offered.

Granville was a bustling community of about 1,100 year-round residents. This number could double in the summer season with the transient workers from Canada and neighboring states. The main industry in this area was logging timber from the steep mountain slopes. National Paper Company was paying good money for pulp logs, and the various clapboard and bowl mills demanded their own varieties of timber. Land was still being cleared for grazing meadows at the farms, under the land grant agreements.

Timber was skidded down slope to the staging depot where agents would compensate with currency. Farmers who did not own teams of horses or oxen would lease out their timber lots to men like Rob Ford, who ran crews and teams. He was one of the few who had direct contract with the paper company and mills. A loading dock was located at the White River's edge.

Diana, a steam-powered skid tractor, made two to three runs per day. Her steel tracks could pull three times the volume of logs mounted on hardwood sledges with steel runners. She was more proficient than any horse or oxen team. ("Diana" was named after a beautiful French girl who worked at the Granville hotel.) It took three men to run her engine and steer. She was, for that day, a revolutionary piece of machinery, developed and manufactured by Lombard Log Hauler Company of Waterville, Maine.

Diana was quite the sight to behold on any given day whether she was under power or just sitting idle in her shed. Three times a day Diana would effortlessly haul, drag and skid her payloads off the mountain to the roll-off ramp just uphill from the man-made flood pond just off Puddle Dock Road, now referred to as just Puddle Dock. Ice and snow would sometimes accumulate on the skid road overnight, reducing traction for Diana's steel tracks, so workers would lay loose hay ahead of the engine to insure non-slippage of the tracks.

A pond nearby was flooded naturally by the brook running off the eastern slope of North Hollow. Twice a day, after the sun warmed the ice and it broke up, the dam or sluice gates would be opened, and a select number of logs would be floated into the White River. The surge of water once released would carry the logs downstream approximately 30 miles to the town of Bethel, Vermont.

The floating logs were navigated by talented French-Canadian teams with their "caulk shoes," who guided the logs down river, keeping them from jamming. They camped in tents along the river's edge at night during the three- or four-day voyage. They would then travel back to Granville to do it all over again—a very dangerous higher-paying livelihood better left to the Frenchmen.

The farmsteaders endured challenges as well. With uphill and downhill runs by horse and oxen, teams raced against the clock in difficult conditions to get their final loads in before winter.

Warm days would cause a melt, but in the upper elevations, cold was steady. Old Diana, still hauling log loads, had to rely heavily on the hay laid down to keep traction on the icy steeper inclines.

October snows would soon come in fast this particular year. By mid-month up to a foot or more could accumulate up on West Hill and Texas Falls Gap Trail. The same accumulation was expected across the White River on North Hollow and Puddle Dock, while in the lower elevations of the valley only a few inches was likely, a depth still maneuverable by horse and wagon.

Winter brought a slower pace in the village of Granville. The mills still buzzed along producing clapboard, lumber boards, beams, bowls and other wood products. And the National Paper Company continued to haul logs by horse and oxen team out of the upper stage areas to Bethel. But the overall pace

Skidding logs with *Diana*

was much slower, and it soon came to a halt as the tundra cold bore down on the steep mountain terrain.

Carl missed his secret rendezvous with Mamie. Now that it was getting colder and the snow was deepening, the travel time to and from school became much longer and more arduous. Most days in early winter her dad would bring her down from their farm to the intersection, or by horse-drawn sleigh on his way to town on the logger's road. Sometimes she would miss school altogether if the snow were too deep. Their brief encounters were limited to the short walks after school, only holding hands until the road split towards their trails home, with just a short departing kiss.

4   Barn Dance Social

The October Fest dance held at the Ford's farm allowed Mamie and Carl to be a little more social, and more than a few noticed their attraction for each other.

"Ya know, it's gonna be a cold winter, Mr. Morse! Good you have a woman to keep you warm at night!" said Elwin.

Carl acknowledged Elwin's presence.

"But what's your dog gonna do, now that you got her?" Elwin laughed as he drew another cup of hard cider from the spigot of the barrel from last year's batch. Old Ford kept a few barrels on hand, especially for these functions, so the ladies and the younger folk could sip, while the imported stock was savored by the older men and foremen of his crew.

Rob Ford fiddling

"Yeah, well at least I got me a girlfriend. You're the one snuggling with the dogs this winter, Shirley!" Carl laughed as he drew some cider for himself and some to bring over to Mamie across the barnyard.

Mamie was in a circle of six women, including her Mom and Mrs. Ford. Some older girls from school huddled in their own gaggle. The first group consisted of the closer neighbors, while the other women from North Hollow were gathered in their own groups. It was like the pecking order of a large flock of hen turkeys. The dominant hens of each group were clearly in charge of the conversations. The mere gesture of bringing cider to Mamie, as subtle as it was, caught most everyone's eye. All the female folks from the West Hill side of the valley, including Mrs. Hubbard, were now alerted to the possibilities.

"I guess I'll see you at school on Monday?" Carl said.

She just smiled with approval, and they walked across the barnyard towards the fiddle and banjo music that just started up in the big barn. He continued, "… unless you can meet me on my way to Ford's chores on Saturday?"

She looked at the ground, speaking softly, "You know that won't get to happen unless we have to deliver some hay to the logger's road—and even still, my Dad or Mom will be driving the horse wagon, so I won't be able to stop 'cept to say Hi."

"I know" said Carl, "but I was just hoping 'cause I been kinda missin' you." The whole time he was looking at the ground and kicked the dirt with his foot.

The music started seeping in as well as the ciders and drink, and feet began tapping. As the moon came up, first the older folks started the dancing in square formation; then the younger folk joined in. Just as Carl got up the courage to ask Mamie to dance, Georgie Farr grabbed her by the hand and yanked her into the line.

"Looks like you're back with the doggies," Elwin said as he sidled up to Carl, not once taking his eyes off the dancers. "Maybe it's because you still smell like horse crap from yesterday's shoveling!"

"Or maybe she saw you heading towards me!" Carl retorted.

"Aw, she likes you. You just got to be a little quicker on your feet, like this!" Elwin reached out and grabbed Lola by the hand and headed toward the line. She was from down in the village by the White River valley shops. Her dad was one of the woodworking shop owners who made bowls from birch logs that Old Ford harvested and delivered.

Carl finally got a few dances with Mamie and then socializing with some friends in their own corner of the barn. But it was their holding hands that made it obvious that they were attracted to each other.

Afterwards Mamie kept glancing at Carl from wherever she was in the barn throughout the event. As the night began to wind down, Mamie's dad and mom were ready to leave for home, but they both could not help but notice Mamie's good-bye kiss with Carl. It lasted slightly longer than just a friendly handshake type, or a see-you-later peck on the cheek.

Her dad stared straight at Carl with a look of what seemed like disapproval and surprise. As Carl met his gaze from across the room his whole essence flashed and he felt a kind of dread, or fear—an embarrassment he had never felt before. His keen gift of intuition spoke in his core and in his mind's eye, he flashed Mamie with tears pouring, reaching her hand to him as if she were being pulled away by some unknown force. The vision passed and he regained his composure, still holding her hand.

"Looks like we have to go," she said, "so I'll try to see you Saturday." Carl slowly let go of her hand, stood just a little straighter and smiled.

"I'll wait for you at our place." He wanted to just hold her close but there were too many gossipers, so he stood there and watched her perfect shape walk across the barn and out the door, unaware of everybody around him.

Mamie's Mom and Pop were silent most of the way home, commenting only on the night's events, and some of the women's gossip, and men folks, and other work-related things.

To this day, a favorite pastime in human nature is to talk about other people, good or bad, and to question people's motives, actions and personalities.

In the women's circle at the party, just after Mrs. Ford had left the group, she went immediately over to Burke. After a few moments of small talk, she ever so slightly reached and touched his hand—a small gesture, but not to the keen eyes of the gossipers in the circle.

More than one of these cougars thought to themselves that Mrs. Ford was not as timid as one would think! So, it was just a short time before the whispered innuendos about her and Burke began.

But to start a rumor about an influential member of the valley's society such as the Fords could have repercussions if it were untrue. Rob Ford was a dominant force in the town's business affairs, employing and supporting many of the men and their families directly or indirectly. Most of the savvy women would dismiss the whispers as soon as they left the circle, or even reprimand the gossiper right off.

Mamie's Mom knew all too well that the affections between her daughter and Carl were also noticed. In these times, marriages and dowries between young ladies and men were still arranged by the parents whenever it was practical, usually by the dominant figure in the family.

Although they had never discussed it, Mamie's parents had different visions of Mamie's future. Because the Morse family was of similar status to their own, and Carl was known to be a little "off," they had an understandable concern about his being close to Mamie. They hoped that she could do better. Now the gossip circles were going to be even more focused.

"That was not very ladylike of you, Mamie!" Her father exclaimed.

Mamie was puzzled. "What, Poppa?"

"Well, I saw you kiss that Morse boy, Carl."

"Oh, Poppa, we're just friends, and he's really nice once you get to know him."

In her defense, Mamie's Mom cut in, "Oh, Father, let her be! Mamie and I will be speaking of these matters of the heart and a young lady's social conduct." With that, Mrs. Hubbard claimed her territory and pecking order of handling matters of womanhood within the family.

Poppa just looked at them both, knowing he was outnumbered. Eyebrows raised, his jaw was set as he relit his pipe.

5   Pe'leg Bear Hunting

Winter storms in the Green Mountains form quickly at the upper elevations, dropping four to six inches of snow with each squall. By late October, darkness rolls in at four in the afternoon. The air is scented with each farm home's wood fires.

A dry cold air at night can keep the mercury low in the teens, and daytime sun can bring it to a comfortable 25 degrees at this time of year. It's the time of year for black bears to forage heavily before heading up to their winter dens. Men folk would organize bear hunts mostly in groups; others would specialize in hunting alone.

One such fellow, known for his skill hunting bear from horseback, was called Pe'leg, as he had lost part of one leg in the Revolutionary War. Despite his handicap, John Pettis built a farm and raised his family using a handcrafted wooden peg as a replacement. Pettis was one of the earliest settlers in the township of Kingston prior to its becoming Granville. He made his pitch to claim Lot No. 17 from the original allotments, bargained for and bought a reasonable tract of acres. Like many settlers, he had chosen a steep hillside due to the greater ease of clearing the logs of beech, birch, and maple without the use of oxen to roll them downhill, oxen being expensive for most poor settlers.

To traverse the mountain terrain on foot was a difficult task for Pe'leg. Through trial and error, he soon trained his spotted grey mare to navigate the woods and terrain and not to spook at the scent or sight of the indigenous black bear or timber wolf.

He and his trained mare frequently traversed the mountain terrain up in bear wallow. They became very good at this form of hunting because the bears were never "spooked off," as the horse's scent and size were the same as a moose.

Black bear, moose, deer, and smaller game like turkey, partridge and rabbit were abundant back in those early days of settlement. Pe'leg in some seasons had plenty of bear meat for winter stores. He was happy to share it with those in need or friends of the family to barter with.

One particular bear hunt secured Pe'leg Pettis's reputation. He was digging his meager crop of potatoes and other garden "sass" on a fall day when he heard off in the distance bear "hoots" echoing from the south hill across the steep gorge and brook from his cabin.

He kept on for a while digging "taters." He had only one bullet left for his black powder rifle, as he'd dallied on the process of melting down the small quantity of lead into balls. But the bear hoots finally got on his nerves and his hunter spirit took over. With the one bullet and several charges of powder in his "possibles" pouch, he and his mare Old Spot made a wide birth of the impassible gulch, then rapidly rode into the wallow from whence the bear hoots and howls emanated.

He found a large bear along with two cubs nosing beechnuts from the carpet of fallen leaves. With the one bullet now rodded into the muzzle, and still mounted on Old Spot, he aimed at the vital part as the bear stood upright in awe of the spectacle of horse and rider and tried to identify the scents of each.

The shot echoed through the hills. The cubs had already clambered up into the birch trees and the mama bear was wounded on the ground. Now, this part of the hunt differs from the version of the story written by Mr. J. R. Flint titled *Pe'leg's Bear Hunt* and archived as folklore in the white book at the Granville town hall.

Pe'leg was without a doubt practical. With a black powder rifle and a couple of separate powder charges, many types of projectiles can be used so long as they can be fit into the rifle bore. Pe'leg cut a straight switch from a nearby beech, sectioned it to fit the bore, and fired again to put the still-thrashing larger bear down and out of its pain.

Three hundred pounds of bear meat will feed a few families for quite a while, but also it requires a lot of help to haul that large an animal from the woods. Pe'leg let the large bear lie until he could acquire such help for the task.

In J. R. Flint's version of this story, it is said that the beech shaft projectiles were discharged on the two treed cubs, Pe'leg perhaps reasoning that they would not survive the harsh winter. He slung them over his mare's rear, their rear legs lashed together with a beech limb bough. Being too small to survive, the cubs were also needed meat for his family's winter stores.

Word quickly sent to the other settlers nearby to retrieve the larger bear. It provided a great shared bounty for the poor settlers—a Thanksgiving feast of roasted bear steaks and a pot roast stew.

The story of this unique bear hunt was handed down through successive owners of the land where the Pettis cabin once stood. Its foundation and the Pettis family gravestones nearby remain undocumented and grown over today off the old Rob Ford Trail about two miles north of the intersection of West

Hill Road. One can take the hike if so inclined, sit near the gravestones and the Pettis house foundation, and ponder the family's lifestyle and events they may have endured.

Any bear hunt and subsequent kill always required quite a group effort. Most bear kills took place in the backcountry areas up in higher and snowier terrain. It took three or four strong men or a horse, if available, to drag a 250- to 300-pound bear a long distance. It was an all-day chore just to get a dead bear out of the woods. Well worth the work when its meat was seasoned and prepared properly. It made a savory meal when accompanied with fixin's as a pot roast. Carl Morse always enjoyed helping to bring a bear out and its flavor of the roast.

6 Venison

His breath misted with every exhale, as he trudged through the three inches of snow. He took notice of the fresh bear tracks that crisscrossed his deer tracks four times in a hundred yards, but it was not the bear he was focused on, even though he took a moment to reflect on the stories handed down of Pe'leg Pettis who'd lived up here some 80-odd years earlier.

Tracking this big buck through the hardwoods and now down slope along the edge of the remote beaver pond, Carl was sure this deer was under the pine grove just ahead, were the snow was spotty and the beech buds were not yet browsed off. As he came closer to the stand of pines, he saw the silhouette of this monster buck.

The rack had to be at least ten points! Carl's heart already pounding from the workout began to pump harder from the adrenaline rush as he aimed the open sights on the deer's neck. He moved the sight just below the deer's ear and feathered the trigger of the Springfield rifle.

The shot at first seemed to resonate a crack sound then in a millisecond a secondary muffled tone quickly deadened by the dense trees and contained in between the surrounding hills. Startled, the deer snapped to attention, then leaped directly behind the snow-covered pine tree while the snow fell from its limbs; Carl was covered instantly in a whiteout as snow fell from the pine boughs next to him as well.

Regaining his senses and vision, he strained to see if the deer was still running. No movement! The way he leapt, I must have missed! Okay, okay, he didn't go far. Now he's spooked—reload! Reload!

As he reloaded, and with slow fluid movement focusing on the tree line to his left Carl made his way to tree where the deer was nibbling. As he found the tracks, he slowly looked out in all directions for movement or silhouette, which takes a keen eye because deer are like ghosts in the forest and can disappear or just melt from view while remaining just a few yards away.

As Carl stepped backward next to the pine, he stumbled and fell backward into the two-foot-deep powdery snow. Saving the rifle from getting buried, he got back to his feet and dusted off the snow to regain his focus.

It was the buck he had tripped over! He couldn't believe it! The ten-point buck was completely covered in snow from the boughs of the pine he had leaped into! Proud of this kill, Carl was even prouder when he noticed the shot went just behind the ear at the base of the skull! "A perfect shot from forty yards!" he said to himself with the mist coming from his breath in the cold air. After field dressing, saving the heart and liver, which he put in his pack, he began the arduous task of dragging the deer out to the trail.

Dragging 185 pounds through two feet of snow will test a man's mettle. The 15-degree temperature felt good as he sweated under his coat and woolen pants and shirt. It was a good kind of tired, after he finally got the deer home and hung to cure for a few days. He did cut the back straps out for dinner that night, as tenderloins always go good with some potatoes and pumpkin. Mother was pleased to cook and serve the meal, as they were all a little tired of tack and beans.

Pop wasn't feeling all that great lately and had not gone to the timber camp that day because of the cough he had developed. He figured if he just rested for a day, catch up on some light chores around the cabin, and prepare a few things for the long cold winter. The log camp was winding down anyway, and the men were just finishing skidding the last of the lighter stock to the staging area for *Diana* to collect and haul down to the valley. Suppressing his cough all day he thought he could shake it off, and after a good night's sleep, the next day he would be like new again. After dinner, sleep overcame him very early as fatigue took him over.

Carl said to his Mom, "Better make him some soup. That'll knock it out of him." As he recounted the deer hunt with Mom in whispered tones, fatigue from the work all day claimed him, too.

December and January temperatures caused the folks to concede. Temperatures dropping below zero most nights and into the low teens during the day kept the wood fires burning constantly. All work and progress tended to slow to a crawl as the snows accumulated to more than three to four feet just in the valley. On the upper ridges of West Hill, Puddle Dock, and North Hollow, the roads saw six to eight feet on average. Horse-drawn drag plows kept some of the through-ways passable so folks could get to the schools and churches. Most of the roads leading to the village of Granville were kept clear, or more often, packed down to run a sled over. Under these conditions, people did not travel to and fro as much, which often caused some cabin fever.

The morning sun feels good on one's face as it shines through the window at daybreak, sort of an alarm clock, saying time to wake! Carl lay there half debating on jumping up to get blood going, or to slumber in a while longer to plan his day.

He didn't need to be doing anything right away except to stoke the fires for mother and feed the livestock. Feeling good with the warm sun on his face, he lay in just a little longer. A short daydream about Mamie followed. The prospect of seeing her later in the day when he headed down to Ford's would be great! Everything seems to be going well, he thought to himself. As he closed his eyes for another cat nap, he could hear Pop coughing in the next room and Mother's muffled tones.

After stoking the two stoves and the fireplace on mother's request, and tending the animals, he grabbed the rifle, saddled up Ol' Sadie and headed down to Ford's for an "earn day."

Mother had asked him to come home earlier due to Pop's condition and to relay the message to Mr. Ford that Pop was feeling poorly and would be away from the log camp for a couple of days.

"I'm going to make a nice stew with the Dutch oven. That should be a couple days' worth of eating and get Father back up. See if you can trade for some honey to put on the bread. That would be a nice change; the syrup is getting low anyway!"

Carl cut of a slab of venison for the trade. Barter and trades were the most common form of monetary compensation in the mountains when it came to common goods and wares. Usually a luxury, honey was kept in the form of cut comb; it never goes bad unless it gets wet, and the bees cap the wax cells, so it keeps naturally, and you can eat or chew the wax also.

The wild bees lived in hollow trees. Old man Twitchell, known as the beekeeper, lived down off Patterson Road just past Farr's turkey farm.

Carl heard tell of how Twitchell could follow the beeline through the woods straight to the hollow tree. Then he would cut the tree down, cut out the section where the nest was, take that log back to his farm, and set it up on a stump to cut the full honeycomb out.

Once when he was little, all the kids got to taste and chew honeycomb wax that ol' Twitchell brought out for treats. He remembered seeing six or eight logs set up on stumps back there, but he was told the bees can sting, so little kids should stay clear of the hole in front of the logs were the bees flew in and out.

Maple syrup was a little more common, though just as precious because of the labor involved. Who would have thought that the sap from a maple tree that only flows in early spring during 35- to 40-degree temperatures could taste so good! Well, it doesn't, as Carl found out one day when he chopped into a maple with his ax and tried to taste the sap straight from the drippings. But if you collected a substantial quantity in a pail and boiled it down to a thick syrup (requiring tedious hours of methodical labor and preparation) then it did become a treat for the tongue. Many homesteaders boiled down syrup to keep in stores for the kitchens, and some made it their livelihood, as many did throughout the state.

Carl always enjoyed helping to tap the trees, haul in the sap, and work the fires during the boil-down process. It always cured the cabin fever at the end of the cold winter months.

He nudged Sadie gently with his heels and she reluctantly trudged through the snow. By horseback the travel time was reduced a lot, so Carl had a little time to slip up the trail that led to Mamie's house. The honey barter was a good excuse to stop there and inquire, and to see her, too, he hoped.

"Mornin' Mr. Hubbard," he said as he dismounted. Mamie's dad was just coming from the woodshed with an armload when Carl rode up.

"Oh, mornin', Mr. Morse," he said, surprised that he didn't hear him prior to backing out of the shed. Though he knew instinctively why Carl was there, he asked, "What brings you by today?"

Carl replied, "Well, Mother asked me to see if anyone had some honey because Pop's feelin' poorly and you were on my way to Ford's." Taking advantage of a new helper, Mr. Hubbard replied, "Grab an armload and we'll head to the house and check with the missus!"

Carl grabbed an armload of wood, thinking that this could be a win-win situation. Sure that Mamie was inside, he thought helping her dad out a little could put him in good standing.

"Seen that catamount lately?" Mr. Hubbard asked.

"No, sir, not since that morning heading to school. He was big though—picked that deer kill up like it was a squirrel. I got a big buck yesterday. Took me all day to haul him out. I got some backstrap to trade for honey if you've got any," Carl said.

As they came inside the door, Mr. Hubbard said, "Just set that in the wood box over there. Ladies! We've got company!" As Mamie's eyes focused from across the room on Carl who now was standing there smiling, she jumped up from her reading, looking at him and then at her dad a few times, trying to figure how Carl got in, let alone on his good side.

"This young man would like some honey in return for some fresh venison. Do you think we can help him out?" he asked.

Getting up from her chair, just as surprised, Mrs. Hubbard said, "Well, I believe there's just a bit left in the cupboard—let me check." As she headed for the small pantry, she glanced back at Mamie and Carl a few times.

"Please sit down," Mr. Hubbard offered, pulling out the chair nearest the kitchen table. "Your father's not feeling well?" he asked.

"No, sir. He's been coughing and my Mom's cooking up some stew from the buck I shot yesterday," he said, showing off a little for Mamie as he said it. "So, she sent me out for some honey because it's to help stop the coughing. Pop should be back to the logging camp in a couple of days. I gotta tell Mr. Ford when I see him after I leave here."

Just then Miami's Mom came from the pantry closet with a four-inch square of the golden yellow comb and placed it in a tin. "There you are, Carl. I hope it's enough."

"Oh, thank you!" Carl replied. "And here's that tenderloin. I can bring you more if you need some in a couple of days." He looked at Mamie.

"Where are you going now?" Mamie asked.

"I'm supposed to go to Ford's to help feed the stock and clean some stalls for pay chores, but that won't take too long. Today I got Ol' Sadie tied outside. If you're not doin' nothin' you can come along, and I'll drop you back on my way through, if it's okay with you all?" Carl said questioningly.

Mamie looked at her Mom and Pop for the approval while putting on her boots. "I was just reading some for studies, but I can finish later. I wouldn't mind getting outside today!" She breathed in and held it waiting for the answer from her Mom, who had the final word anyway.

"Before you both run off," her Dad said, "I could use a couple more arm-loads of wood in here!" With that and a reluctant nod from her Mom, they both headed out double-back on Sadie.

"Seems like a nice boy," Mrs. Hubbard said softly as she recalled the women's talk she had had with her daughter.

"Yes, he seems resourceful," he agreed.

7 Foreman Burke

As they arrived in Fords' barnyard there was no sign of anyone. Normally Mr. Burke or Burke, as everyone called him, was tending the animals, shoeing a horse, or fixing a wagon somewhere close by.

Carl explained to Mamie that he just needed to clean the stalls quick-like; then they could skip out early if Burke didn't show up with something else for him to do.

So, with a little excitement she pitched in to help it go faster. Carl would shovel the manure into the wheelbarrow and dump it into the wagon, Mamie would spread the fresh hay on the stall floor, while making small talk about her Mom and Dad letting her go off with him alone, unchaperoned for the first time.

Just as they were finishing the last stall, they both heard the door at the main house close. Within a few moments Burke rounded the corner, startled to see Mamie standing there with a bundle of hay. Then Carl came out of the stall with the pitchfork.

"Hey, Mr. Burke!" Carl said. "You remember Mamie Hubbard? I looked around for you, but you were off, so we just started in with the stalls." Burke stuttered something about putting wood in the main house for Mrs. Ford, then he just looked at the ground for a second and asked, "How long have you two been here?"

Carl replied, "Long enough to finish muckin' out these five stalls. Hopin' that's all you needed today, 'cause we want to head down to the village store while Pop's letting me use Sadie."

Burke just nodded in approval and walked back toward the farmhouse.

As Carl and Mamie were coming out of the barn, Mrs. Ford was sitting out on the porch and Burke was standing near her. They both watched as the youngsters mounted Sadie and headed out. There were no good-byes nor instructions from Burke for Carl's next set of chores, which seemed very odd. Carl's inner instinct was that Burke was distracted in some way and out of character.

General store

"Wow! I think something was wrong with Burke!" Carl said, as Sadie turned onto the main road towards town.

Holding on to Carl's waist, Mamie added that Mrs. Ford looked a little upset, too. "Well, I'll be stopping back tomorrow," said Carl. "Sure as rain Burke will have a long list for me by then!"

Mamie hugged on just a little tighter.

As they trotted into the village, even Sadie seemed excited! Very few snow patches were here and there. The smell of wood smoke from the bowl mill and the stoves filled the air.

The general store was their only destination, and it was a great treat to come off the mountain and view all the different luxuries and staples displayed in every nook and cranny. "Old man Shirley" and his wife, Elwin's Mom and Pop, just took over the store. The store was the haven for folks to congregate. The town clerk's office was nearby, and the store hosted meetings for the new community. The Post stops where mail and packages were delivered or sent out by the daily stage was also part of the central hub. Folks would trek in from their homesteads up on the ridges and the upper valley areas once every month or two to get supplies or order from the Montgomery Ward and Sears Roebuck catalogs for hardware and things that were not forged or made locally. Folks could also place orders or purchase, barter, and trade for custom locally made essentials like pots and pans, harrows, cultivators, horseshoes, pickaxes, and even a new style of plow at the Deere smith shop up on the Paterson Road.

Carl and Mamie were excited to be a part of the hustle and bustle. Along with the lists of things they were to pick up for their households, Pop's cough medicine was on top of his list, but Carl still made sure to pick out an assortment of sweets for him and Mamie to share.

"Heard about your escapades with that catamount, Mr. Morse!" Mr. Shirley said, longing to hear more directly from Carl about the experience.

"Yes, sir." Carl and Mamie sat in the chairs as he recited the tale to him. Mr. Shirley poured them both a birch beer soda from the fountain, as Mrs. Shirley came out from the back. She smiled and commented on Mamie's pretty features and how she had grown since she last saw her, then took her over to the fabric shelves displaying some new prints and designs. *Mostly girl stuff*, Carl thought to himself, but he was happy for her as part of this store visit.

As they were loading Sadie's saddle bags, Mrs. Shirley handed Carl a new type of cough elixir. "Make sure your dad takes some of this sample," she said. "It's new, but doc claims it to be a good relief for this new bug that's going around."

Carl replied, "Thank you. I'll be sure to get him to take it, even if I gotta hide it in his coffee!"

At that, Carl and Mamie mounted Sadie and headed back up the mountain. An hour at the store was not near enough time to explore it all! Hugging on to Carl's waist with her head resting on his shoulder, Mamie whispered, "Maybe we should stop at our spot! Or the hayloft at Ford's if Burke ain't around! It might be a lot warmer there." *Mmmm*, Mamie cooed, content with her whole day as the afternoon sun warmed their faces.

8 Shots Ring Out

As they pulled into the Fords' barnyard, they heard raised voices coming from the barn area. Still out of sight, Carl and Mamie stopped short of the yard just below the crest of the hill in the road, dismounted, and walked up to the crest a little further. Mrs. Ford was on the porch crying, as raised voices came from the inner larger barn. Well, so much for the loft idea!

"Guess Burke is in the manure with Old Man Ford!" Carl said. "Yeah, that's clearly his gravelly voice shouting something!"

"We best go. I don't want you to get caught up in that if it involves undone chores!" exclaimed Mamie.

"Yeah, I suppose you're right," Carl said. "I didn't think Mr. Ford was to be back this soon—according to my Pop he was coming down from the timber lots in two more days."

They remounted Sadie and headed towards the Hubbards', content with their day and the supplies and treats they had obtained. Their special place in the sugar maple stand was the next stop.

It was common at this time of year for muffled shots of shotguns and rifle reports to echo through the hills as hunters were harvesting deer, rabbits, and partridge. The sounds of hound dogs on a bear trail, off in the distant hollow, were also frequent. The dull muffled report that echoed and bounced off the surrounding hills as they plodded into Mamie's barnyard was no different from any other and went unnoticed except for a sudden queasy feeling deep in the pit of Carl's stomach.

As he shrugged it off, Mamie reached over to kiss him one last time while they were still out of view from her Mom and Pop. They went inside to display the supplies they'd picked up at the store. It was a good day!

The next morning Carl awoke at his usual time, thinking about the exciting day he just spent with Mamie. Then Pop's coughing brought him back to the reality of a new day of chores and commitments. Pop's condition seemed to improve a little overnight, with his Mom administering the elixir and hot tea.

"Carl, would you mind stoking the fire and relighting the kitchen stove?

I'm going to make some pancakes and oatmeal for you boys. Should be ready when you're done feeding the stock! We'll use some of the syrup this time. I think your father would like it this morning. He had a good night's sleep last night—the first in a couple of days!" his mother exclaimed. Carl looked over at Pop, still bundled up in his bunk slumbering. Pop was usually the first one up in the morning prepping the stoves for mother and doing other chores before heading off to the timber lots, sometimes for a couple days at a time. But not today. He was still overcome by the bug.

As Carl headed out to the barnyard, he thought of the workload he had waiting for him at Ford's, and the shot that rang out last evening. Then, for no apparent reason he had a sensation that made his stomach tighten into a knot, and a feeling of dread made him a bit nauseous for a moment. He shook it off, wondering why he thought that shot echoed strangely longer than it should have. He never understood these insights much, just that they occurred, and when they did the feeling or emotion it brought repeated rapidly.

As Carl was heading down to Ford's riding Sadie, about halfway there he got that same "pit" feeling in his stomach again. His thoughts strayed as he pulled up to the Fords' barn. Something deep inside said it wasn't going to be the usual day. He felt out of sorts and uncentered every time he thought of Burke and Ford's barnyard. It was as if something was trying to tell him not to go there today. Again, he shrugged it off and gave Sadie a nudge with his heel, clicking his tongue to encourage her forward. For some reason though, even she seemed to slow her pace.

He dismissed the feeling again and put his mind on Mamie's pretty face and holding her in the sugar stand at their special place. As soon as he was done with work, he planned on stopping by her place to see her before going home.

9 Something Amiss

As Carl entered the Fords' barnyard, Sadie just stopped in her tracks, and again Carl got the "pit" feeling. He nudged her forward, rounding the corner of the big barn. After hitching Sadie up and pitching some loose hay and a pail of water for her he headed to the main stalls where he would usually find Burke or a note for his daily tasks. Finding neither, Carl called out "Hey, Mr. Burke! You here?"

With no response, he headed towards the other section of the barn, which was an adjacent room with the horse stalls. Glancing in, he noticed Mr. Ford's gelding quarter horse, Pete, already in his stall—a little odd but it meant that Old Ford was indeed home early, confirming the voices he and Mamie had heard yesterday afternoon.

Just then he heard a rummage at the rear section of the barn near the manure wagon. If Burke were starting in on his chores, he figured he was in for it. Carl didn't care for Burke, but he could never put his finger on why—just something about him was always elusive, nor was he was an especially friendly guy. He was always angry about something, or just plain distant and aloof.

There in the manure wagon pitchin' manure into the front of the wagon was Burke? No, not Burke's features at all! But who? he wondered.

"Well, I think that's my job," Carl said out loud.

Who should turn around, startled, but Old Ford himself.

"Oh, I didn't hear you come in. You shouldn't creep on a person like that, you know. Could get yourself hurt."

"Oh, I'm sorry, Mr. Ford. I was expecting Burke. He's supposed to set my chore list for today. Didn't do it yesterday like he usually does. But I always clean the stalls first, so you don't need to do that."

"Well, young fella, I needed to load this one because it's a special load of manure!"

"Where's Mr. Burke?" Carl asked, now very perplexed.

"Oh, well, he's not gonna be around for a while, son. You know what your jobs are around here don't you?"

"Yes, sir, I do."

"Well then, you can just perform them as you always do, and you can set your own schedule from now on. If you got any questions you just talk to me directly," Ford replied.

"Okay, Mr. Ford, but I just got used to…"

"Rob! Please come in and talk to me now!" interrupted Mrs. Ford, entering the stalls.

As Carl turned and looked, he saw her flushed face, eyes red from crying, and he could tell something was very wrong.

Old Ford climbed off the wagon and stared at Carl with piercing eyes. "You know what the work is," he said to Carl. "I'll be back in a while to talk about a special job you can help me with."

To his wife he sternly replied, "Meet you up at the house!"

Carl's stomach went into another knot as Ford left the stall room. Every word Old Ford uttered was a directive. He never asked a question that he didn't already know the answer to.

Carl felt helpless and trapped and didn't yet know why. Sensing that something was wrong, he hurried through his tasks so that he could get out of there as early as possible. The negative feeling in the air was keen with his insights and the inner core of his being. He felt like he needed to escape. Yesterday's pleasures and joys were now far from his mind as he hastily shoveled the manure into the half-loaded wagon. Within the next few days, before the real frost and snow accumulated, the focus on the farm was an annual procedure that they performed during the last warm days of October—to till the manure lightly into the soil in the hay lots, for composting to replenish nutrients. This would ensure a good spring grass start and an early first cutting.

As Carl finished the last forkful, he stuck the pitchfork into the heap upright so it would be ready for the unloading up in the meadow as fertilizer to be tilled in. The fork felt like it hit something more solid than loose manure. The uneasy feeling in the pit of his stomach returned, and Carl felt an overwhelming sick feeling as if he wanted to vomit.

He sat down on the half barrel in the corner and wiped the sweat from his forehead. "That's it," he said to himself as the catamount experience flashed in his mind, suppressing the fear, which was what he was now feeling in his stomach.

The same sensations were occurring, but he didn't know why—only that something was wrong with the routines and everybody at Ford's was acting weird. Something was about to happen, and deep inside he knew it wasn't going to be good. He mounted up on Sadie and trotted her out of there, making a beeline for home. Even Sadie seemed glad to leave Ford's. Carl didn't even have to kick his heels to get her to trot.

Both relieved to be home, Sadie headed straight for her small shack stall as soon as Carl pulled off her halter. Carl headed straight into the cabin, grabbing an armload of wood on the way in. Sitting at the table with her knitting, his Mom could sense his demeanor.

"Something wrong?" she asked.

Carl looked over at the far corner bedroom curtain that separated Mom and Pop's quarters from the rest of the small cabin's living areas. Not knowing how to reply, he just asked "How's Pop? I really need to talk to him 'bout somethin'." His Mom replied, "Well, he's been sleepin' mostly since you left this morning. You want some soup? It's hot on the stove. I'll fix some with maple bread for dipping."

Hungry from the day's work, Carl replied, "Thanks, Mum. That would set good about now."

Overhearing their conversation from his bed, Carl's Dad murmured, "What's on your mind, son?"

Carl pulled up a stool and sat next to him. "How you feelin' Pop?"

As he spoke, he could see the tiredness in Pop's eyes. The fever and coughing had taken its toll. Even his voice sounded tired and weak.

"Well, it's about Ford's place," Carl said. "I don't know if I want to work there anymore." Carl handed him the warm cup of honey water as he sat up.

"What's this about now? You know Ford has been good to you and me both for paid wages. Soon as I'm on my feet we are back to Farr's timber lot to sledge the logs down to the stagin' area. Then it's winterizing the skid road with straw for traction so Old Diane can make it up the slope. I was gonna talk to Ford 'bout putting you on the crew. It won't set well with old man Ford if you up and quit him at the farm, now, would it?" Pop explained.

"Pop," Carl replied. "Somethin's wrong down there. Burke's gone, and Mr. Ford was actin' all angry, and Mrs. Ford was all crying, and I got some guts churning, and I don't know what's...."

Pop sat more upright, pointed his finger and said "Son, stop that right now!" Raising his voice, he continued, "He probably sent Burke packin', and you're up for a promotion. Old Ford is never happy, he's always griping about somethin'. If somethin' changed with him and Burke, then that's between them, and it must have put Ford into a worse mood than he's usually in."

Carl pleaded, "But Pop you don't know what I was—I mean something is really wrong or something's gonna happen down there, Pop. I don't feel right, I'm scared something's—"

Again, Pop interrupted Carl. Raising his voice even louder, he said, "Now you listen good, son. Old Ford will always take care of you if you keep your nose to the grindstone. You don't burn any bridges until you got a better job lined up! That's my final word on the matter." Exhausted from his own outburst, he then collapsed back to a lying position.

At that mother chimed in. "Carl, we need Mr. Ford right now with winter coming and father missing these last few days of work down at the lots." As she wiped Pop's forehead with a cool cloth, she looked Carl in the eye with a loving smile, knowing that he was feeling something deep but didn't want to upset father anymore. For her at that moment it was more important for father to get better. She would wait till Pop was asleep and then talk to Carl about his insights. His dad then went into a coughing session and started to doze.

Carl went to his loft after his soup, feeling alone and rejected. Pop never would let him get close enough for deep conversation. Even though his Mom was a better listener, he felt he needed Pop's ear on this problem. His insights were so strong he felt he needed a man's input on what he should do. How could he put into words what he was feeling? Even if Pop wasn't sick, would he even listen? He truly felt detached from his dad. He laid his head down with tears welling, feeling vulnerable and frustrated.

The Ford farmstead

10 Insights

He thought only of Miami, holding her and her essence, and the stress of the day began to wash away. Just being away from Ford's farm and its bad energy relaxed Carl. He felt great safety in his bed in the sanctuary of his home.

Mother came in and touched him softly on the head. As she noticed the dried tears on his face in the lamplight, she whispered, "Now tell me what's got you so down."

"Oh, Mum, I don't really know what it is, but somethin's not right at Ford's. Somethin' bad, Mum, really bad. I've been having these feelings and getting pictures in my head about Ford and Burke. Somethin' isn't right down there, and I know it deep in me."

His mother turned her head as she coughed, and then said, "Sometimes people get thoughts or fears or feelings about events that are about to happen. Some people are sensitive to those things more than others. My Grandfather was like that. He was a seer. He could see and hear things, messages about other people."

"What do you mean?"

"I'm not sure exactly, but when I was little, my Grandpa told me that he could see the light around people in colors and feel it if they were sick. He could sense where they were sick, and he could talk to their people from the 'other side' to help heal them or send messages.

"He could tell if a person was 'good' or 'evil' by these colors. Sometimes he could see their past lives and mistakes that they needed to correct in this lifetime." She paused and went on. "He said I have the gift in me, too, and if I wanted, he would show me how to See and Hear. He would teach me how to 'open it up in me' and understand it. But you can't tell anyone!" She quickly added.

"Why?"

She smiled a little and said, "'Cause regular folks don't understand it. They don't believe or they call it witchery. Grandpa said it was a connection with the earth and the stars, and it needs to be kept safe inside you and used only for love and good. People used to come to my Grandpa in secret when they or somebody close to them was sick, or if they had a problem. I remember the jar of coins he kept, and people would always drop off gifts for him," she reminisced.

Her eyes lit up a bit. "I think you have some of his Seer in you," she said.

"Did you take the teaching?"

She looked at him with loving eyes. This was the only time in her adult life that she could share her own insights, and she began to tear a little.

"I was only about ten when he told me. I would go to him when I had the pictures and he would ask me what the feelings around the pictures were, and the colors of the light around the folks. If you put it all together, it instantly gives you a knowing of the person or a situation. That's most of what I remember that he said. One more thing he said was that I should pay attention to those things when someone comes into my presence 'cause everything happens for a reason, or a synchronicity. He said I needed to choose to allow or focus the energy for that specific person or situation; that's when you go by the feeling. I had gotten very confused with it all, 'the gift,' and after we moved away, my Grandpa died. They said he just went to sleep one night and didn't wake up." She coughed again, "That's how God does it when you do his work, peaceful like that."

She continued, "I think you can choose how to use your gift, too. But right now, I'm worried about your father; his health light is not so bright right now." Carl looked over at Pop, and as he unconsciously stared, a faint light came into focus around him. Carl sensed and felt a knowingness—change was imminent. His Mom softly said good night and coughed again as she went to stoke the stove.

The morning sun warmed Carl's face as it peeked through the small window near his loft bunk. Laying there half-conscious, he thought of the chores for mother that need attending to: Stoke the kitchen fire stove and the pot belly; fetch hay, grain, and water for Sadie; feed the chickens; and bring up potatoes from the root cellar.

Then his thoughts moved on to Mamie, the way she just snuggled up and hugged him, the embraces at their secret place in the sugar orchard, her radiant smile. With that, he clambered out of bed and put on his wool pants, shirt, and boots.

As the cool morning air hit his face outside the door, he glanced at the sunshine again, drinking it in, letting it soak in a while. Taking pleasure with a moment of quiet time to regain a feeling of centeredness and connection with the elements. The smell of the fall leaves filled his lungs and the feel of the ground under his feet completed his knowingness that he expressed: "I am part of something bigger." With a half-smile of appreciation, he headed toward the stall, living in the moment, thinking fondly about his newfound understanding of the gift.

11 Schooling

Indian summer warmed the last few days earlier in the mornings except at the high elevations. What snow fell overnight melted away by mid-morning, leaving the fall leaves damp, wet and quiet. It was a good time to hunt deer because the bucks were in rut, acting all crazy with just one thing on their minds—does. The bucks were not so elusive when they were scraping and tearing up the ground, marking scent and checking their territories.

Last fall, Carl had seen two bucks locking horns, snorting and battling over the does and the domain of the herd. It was a sight as two big animals tore into each other with such force and thrashing. The rest of the herd watched the show to see who would be the victor. Quick as it began, the fight was over and the loser slinked off into the woods.

Carl thought that later would be a good time to walk in deer hollow, to see what kind of scrapings, rubbings, and signs were near the game trail in his favorite area of hardwood and pine. The terrain was gentle and easy walking. He knew he could make a loop on the way home. It would be even better while mounted on Sadie, so he prepped the saddle and the rifle.

Carl called out, "Mom, I'm heading out with Sadie to the schoolhouse, then to Ford's—be back by evening after I poke around the hollow!"

He heard her reply from the cabin: "Okay, son, don't be too late!"

At that, he mounted Sadie and they plodded down the worn trail road noticing the thick wet leaves blanketing the woods floor.

School sessions took place most of the year, except Sundays and in the very cold months, January and February, when most folks were hunkered indoors due to the extreme conditions. Heavy snow accumulated four to six feet deep in the high elevations, and temperatures dropped below freezing.

Based on its geography in the Green Mountains, Granville always got early snow accumulations compared to territories just twenty miles south and north and has been called The Snow Belt.

It was common here to shut the small school districts down for a month or two. Young people would attend school sessions whenever they could, but it was not mandatory. If they had chores or work to do to sustain the family, that was the priority and way of life in those times. Any missed session could be made up and or shared by the neighbors who did attend. Sometimes the instructors would trek to the student's home to help with the missed teachings.

Carl didn't plan on missing school today. While the learning was important, he wanted to see his friends and Mamie.

Smoke was wafting from the stovepipe that extended above the schoolhouse roof, filling his nose as he hitched Sadie to the post along with two other horses belonging to George Farr and an older boy that they called Twitchell.

He wondered if Mamie had walked in today. If so, he could give her a ride home later before heading to Ford's.

His teacher's voice broke his daydream. "Please be seated, Mr. Morse," she said, as he closed the door. "We are discussing world geography with the focus on the countries affected by the war in Europe." Mrs. Pettis, the teacher, looked at him with a slight sparkle in her eye. She was glad that her room was half full of students today, and she hoped more would show up.

Carl scanned the room but Mamie was not among the eight other kids. The spring school sessions were generally set up for the younger kids or grammar school age, as the older teenage boys were engaged in work chores at their own family farms or neighboring farms. The fall and early winter sessions were set up for the older teens, with a male teacher at each district to handle the older boys better and teach more advanced arithmetic.

The female teachers were usually local housewives and/or young women from the area whose teaching skills and credentials were provided by the semi-annual courses taught by the local male superintendent for all ten districts. By the age of 15 or so, most of the older girls or teenage students typically went off to a finishing school in Middlebury or Burlington if their parents could afford it. Those who didn't go became local housewives in the community.

As everybody did, Carl loved the teachings. They opened whole new visions, allowing him to imagine the outside world beyond Granville, and brought news of events from around the country. Newspapers were always brought to the classroom monthly at least, and from that all the folks living in the hills were updated about current affairs. Newspapers were shared gems amongst the townspeople. Even the farmers and homesteaders would trek to the schoolhouse for first-hand readings.

Carl took well to reading and writing. He tried to read everything he could. He went through the books that the teacher would let them borrow, flyers posted at the general store, grain sack labels, even the Webster's dictionary that his mother purchased at the Shirleys' store.

Carl's handwriting soon became meticulous due to his dictionary diligence,

Upper Village School

but his true love of reading included even the descriptions of goods in the Montgomery Ward and Sears Roebuck Catalogs. He would stop to study the pages whenever he came across one.

Carl always left enchanted by the schooling and truly could not get enough of the sessions and the shared experience with friends from the neighboring farms and homes in the area. The schoolhouse was more than just a place of learning; it was part of a social network not to be taken for granted.

Granville hosted seven school districts. Kids and young adults alike made up the student body. The more remote schoolhouses were set up throughout the town, in the hills or West Hill as well as North and South Hollows. The westernmost school was located farthest out on the Texas Falls road near the Hancock boundary. Two other districts existed north and south of Granville village. The southernmost school was also the northern one for the town of Hancock. At this time in Granville, 15 teachers were employed. The teachers were mostly part-time or volunteer residents, along with a few head teachers on a full-time paid basis who oversaw the school board.

Carl leaned over to Elwin Shirley as he opened his book and settled into his desk. He whispered to Elwin, "Goin' up to the hollow after Fords. You comin'?"

"Let me think on that," Elwin whispered back, which caused three other kids to turn around. Noticing the diversion, Mrs. Pettis stopped speaking momentarily and stared again at the two boys, this time without the sparkle.

Any one of the older boys with a horse attending a winter session would always drag the plow from his farm down to the next farm along the road networks in the community, to keep the road clear and packed hard for travelers.

Post and mail delivery worked the same way: whoever was down at the village would pick up the post at the general store, dropping it along the way back in the canvas mail bags that each farm kept hanging at their entrance post. A person carrying the mail would deliver to each post bag along the way until they got home, then leave the rest on their post for the next passerby to continue the deliveries.

Just outside the schoolhouse after sessions were over, as he was throwing the mail bag on his horse Elwin said, "Don't think I can go huntin' today. I got a pile of chores, and Pop needs me to put up more wood at the smoke shed for the bacon and hams we just quartered from the pigs. You're probably gonna hit Mamie's anyway, after Ford's, right?"

Carl pondered that idea then looked at Elwin and said, "Maybe I will, too bad you just butcher your girlfriends!"

With that Elwin replied, "Yeah, well I just replaced them girls with Lola from down in the village, and she's lovin' up the old "Ell." That's why I ain't been up your way so much!" Razing each other, as good friends do, was part of Elwin and Carl's bond.

"I'll catch you for huntin' in a couple days; we'll turn it into a full day hunt!" Elwin suggested.

"Sounds good to me. Bucks are just comin' into rut about now. I seen some rubs and scrapes down by Hubbards'."

Elwin got the last shot in, saying, "I seen some rubs and scrapes up by Mamie's. You better go re-mark your own territory!"

Carl laughed out loud. The two boys shook hands, mounted up, and rode off in opposite directions.

12   Entrapment

Carl and Sadie plodded along, heading to Ford's to hit the chores. He was hoping to rush through them. Stopping at the Hubbards' was better felt than burning daylight at deer hollow. It got dark a lot earlier these days, it seemed, and seeing Mamie was on his mind because she wasn't at the school today.

He felt again the bad feelings he got yesterday at Ford's and the talk with his Mom about the Seer. He compared the feeling of going to Ford's, then the feeling of going to Miami's. Mamie's felt better, but Ford's was paying, as his Pop put it to him last night. So, he trudged on. It was as if he had to force even Sadie to turn right on to the long trail that led to Ford's place, grabbing the mail bag off the post as he turned, bringing it up to the farmhouse for Mrs. Ford.

It was exceptionally quiet as Carl hitched Sadie to the post. He became aware of it as he went into the grain shed to grab a pitch of hay for Sadie to nibble while he performed his tasks. "About an hour here, then I'll head straight to Mamie's," he said to Sadie.

He headed straight to the porch on the house; smoke was coming out the chimney, so somebody was inside, he figured. Normally he would just hang the mail bag on the hook and go find Burke somewhere in the barnyard, but this time he decided to knock, loudly announcing, "Hello! It's me, Carl! Got your mail here!"

He could hear some voices from within and some shuffling of boots on the hardwood floor. Then the latch of the door opened.

Mrs. Ford appeared at the door. Her eyes and nose were red from crying, and her hair was in disarray. Her voice was fatigued as she said, "Thank you Carl," and took the mail bag from his hand. "Mr. Ford will be right out," she said in almost a whisper. Her hand was shaking a little as she opened the canvas bag to look inside. Then she clenched it closed and looked into his eyes. Her eyes spoke of a deep despair, fear, and pain. Then she abruptly looked down, turned and walked inside.

Carl stammered, "Guess I'll put some more wood on the porch for you, ma'am."

Rob Ford was a smart and focused man, an opportunist and entrepreneur, a self-made man with his business enterprises and farmstead. When he set out to a task or project, all his energy went into it around the clock until it was completed to his meticulous satisfaction. That said others, could never satisfy his demand for perfection.

All final touches to every job were performed by him; his employees were only tools to help in sequences to accomplish the goals. He was once quoted as saying, "Ya find a person's best skill and apply it to them. Use them as they want to be used and they will always perform." For Ford, this use of people was more like his religion and it worked very well in his favor.

Mr. Ford's nature earned him ultimate respect from those who sought employment as well as those who shared his status in the society of this small town. Success brought respect and at the same time intimidation and resentment. Mr. Ford did not believe he had any close friends; he only knew he had many acquaintances. By that, he figured people would only befriend him to get something they needed.

The closest people in his world were his wife and his only son, Ted.

Ted Ford was about two years older than Carl, so Carl never knew him well, only that he was now off at a private school and came home just once or twice a year during semester breaks.

The Ford farm supported more than 100 head of dairy cows and beef cattle. They raised and bred fine trotter quarter-horses, and poultry for sale. A sugar orchard could produce 25 big 50-gallon barrels of high-quality syrup. The flavor of the syrup comes not so much from the trees, but more so from the soil where the roots get their nutrients. Corn, hay, wheat, and other grains were all produced on the 1,000 acres of the Ford farm. Rob Ford employed many folks from the valley and hills to work the chores required in the seasonal enterprises including managing the timber lots on West Hill.

Apple orchards were abundant off Puddle Dock and West Hill. Sweet cider was a tradition in the fall, but hard cider recipes bubbling away in those barrels were the beverage prevailing at most social events. Rob Ford was known to get cantankerous when he overindulged in hard cider, magnifying his low tolerance of most people and his controlling personality.

"I'll be right out there, young Mr. Morse, soon as I git my boots on!" Old Ford yelled from somewhere inside the house. As Ford stepped on the porch, pulling his suspenders over his shoulders, he hollered, "Meet you in the stalls, got a list of new chores for you if you're up to it."

Carl stacked the armload he brought up just by the door. "Yes, sir," he stammered, not meaning it at all. Then that deep pit feeling in his gut came back, and he leaned against the porch post for a spell trying to quell it off. As he glanced over at Sadie to make sure she was hitched with enough hay and water, he noticed that she was looking at him with concern, too.

The manure wagon was still loaded, with the pitchfork standing up in it as he had left it the night before. Carl just stared at it blankly as he remembered that this load needed to be spread out over the upper meadow for tilling.

As he stared, old Ford came into the barn section. "Oh, there you are," he said. "I think we should hitch up the grey to pull this load up! So go get his bridle and pull Bart out of his stall."

Bart was a big-boned, well-tempered draft horse, powerful for pulling heavy loads and implements. As Carl coaxed him out of his stall, even Bart didn't seem eager about getting hitched up today, but he never did when he knew he would work without a teammate. Pulling the wagon was a single-horse task that Bart had done many times before, but he always liked to have one of the fillies like Sally next to him when harnessed up for a long day, so he kept looking over at the stalls for his teammate, reluctant to go it alone.

Cinching up the last buckle on Bart's harness, Ford climbed up on the buckboard, grabbing the reins. "Well, Mr. Morse, let's get this over with."

Carl started to climb up to the seat, but the wagon was already moving as Ford thwacked the reins on Bart's back, shouting "Hee upp! Hee upp!"

Carl barely got a grip on the side rail to pull himself up the rest of the way, thinking Ford wouldn't have stopped even if he hadn't made it!

The Ford Farm, barn on the right, home on the left in back

13   Devil's Deal

Spreading manure over the fields this time of year was common so long as there was just a little snow, but to do it in an afternoon with only two guys was not ordinary at all.

It usually started in the morning with three wagons loaded from the stockpile at the back of the barn with Bart and two other draft horses—six people, including Burke and four of Ford's migrant Frenchmen from the woodlots for a day.

Then they would reload the wagons two or three times until the manure pile was cleaned out. This was very odd to make only one trip late in the afternoon!

"Um, Mr. Ford, who loaded the wagon up today? The Frenchmen?"

"Son," Ford said, "This old man still has some steam left in him yet, and this is a special load that needs to be put back in the earth from whence it came! But I did have a couple of Frenchies come in late yesterday."

Ford slapped the reins on Bart's back, clicking his cheek just as they approached the bar way for the lower meadow and went right on by it.

Now Carl was very confused because the lower meadow was only half finished with the spreading and it was the only field getting it this season! Carl looked at Ford.

As he tightened his jaw, Ford said, "Son, we're headin' to the upper meadow for this one load, if that's what you're wonderin' by that look on your face!"

Carl's whole core knew everything was wrong. He felt trapped and uncentered, and he could sense that more of the same was about to come.

As they pulled through the already-open bar way for the upper meadow, Carl's eyes caught the mound of dirt piled up in the center of the two-acre lot with an inch and a half of snow all around, confirming his uneasy feelings. The wagon stopped next to a six-foot by three-foot hole about four feet deep.

When a pig or goat or a horse died from disease or age and was not usable for feed or parts, it would be buried so as not to spread the contagion to other stock. Carl felt a little relieved, thinking that this was the task at hand. "I guess the Frenchies dug the hole up here yesterday for you, huh, Mr. Ford?" Carl assumed.

"Yup, right you are son! Paid them well, and those two boys are headin' back to Quebec as we speak! Now let's get the shovels and get this done, we're gonna be burnin' daylight here pretty quick!"

It took only about three or four shovels of the manure at the tailgate of the wagon for Carl's world to come crashing down. As the pair of puffy swollen hands and forearms became visible under the pile, Ford said "Now, son, this is where you're gonna find yourself at a kind of a crossroad."

Ignoring how Carl had stepped back three paces with his mouth still agape, Ford continued, "Now old Burke here chose a path at a crossroad a while ago, taking advantage with my wife while we all were out at the timber lots. It's the worst kind of betrayal to take a man's pay, his trust, and his wife."

Carl saw the whole event unfold in his mind eye—split-second flashes of Burke, shirt unbuttoned, arguing in the barnyard with Ford; Mabel Ford crying out from the porch, collapsing there partially clothed, sobbing in shame; Ford grabbing the rifle from just inside the doorway of the barn; Burke obstinate and challenging with a violent arrogance, the rifle shot echoing through the hills and hollows; Burke falling in slow motion with a hole from the slug in his chest, Ford staring with his jaw set firm, then looking down at both his own hands shaking.

It was the first time Carl ever had this type of clairvoyance. He cocked his head slightly to one side, knowing this vision was truth.

The catamount flashed into his mind, and Carl suppressed and released the fear of it all. The catamount's eyes met his again and he felt the big cat's power become his own as his wholeness and centeredness returned, fully connected to the universe. In his mind, the whole earth flashed if he were above it looking down from a vantage point of space.

Then he felt his feet connected to the ground and the earth. He smelled the fresh dirt in the pile and became grounded, and the earth's vibration became his own. Like a magnet he was drawn back to the reality of the moment.

"So he got what he deserved," said Ford, finishing his spiel.

With a new demeanor and posture, Carl looked square into Ford's eye. Reversing the roles of seniority, Carl said, "Well, it seems to me, that you, sir, are the one at the crossroad. Now you're about to choose another rocky road by dragging me into your little mess!"

Feeling angry and empowered by Ford's body language, when he looked at the ground and leaned on the tailgate, Carl continued, "You have just violated my trust and respect in you! I'm thinkin' you should finish these chores here on your own." Carl then turned on his heel to walk away, feeling total disgust.

"This job pays 50 dollars when we're done tonight," Ford replied, "and we never speak of it again! You can say some words over him if you want, but I got no good words for this man. Your dad is a good man; he raised you right, so he gets paid for sick leave and gets a bonus and increased wages when he gets back to the timber lot. Two pigs each year for your family as long as you're workin,' and your choice of any yearling colt come spring—that's my offer for you to take, or you can keep walking. As far as anybody else knows, old Burke here just went off huntin' and we haven't seen him since." Ford then spit on his hand and held it out for Carl to shake.

Rob Ford was all business, and as savvy as they come, with a reputation of honor in any deal he made. He was generous with people he liked and unforgiving with people he did not. In these times of instability in the country and the talk of economic crisis in the news, the "great panic" was already underway.

Fifty dollars was a huge sum, equal to what a grown man could earn in a whole year! To have a job all year round for one member of the family was almost unheard of.

Carl stopped walking, still with his back to Ford, and looked up at the sky. Turning around, he put a look directly in Ford's eyes. He spit on his hand and squeezed Ford's hard and long. Still squeezing, he said, "It's your soul that's at the crossroad, Mr. Ford, sir."

The moon was bright and full that night. Bart pulled the two-furrow plow steady enough as it sliced and folded the topsoil over on the last row as they finished tilling up the 100-by-100 section in that upper meadow.

"Easy boy," Carl said calmly, as Bart's heavy hooves clomped along at almost a trotting pace toward the barnyard. As the work wagon bounced over the stony trail, he said, "I know, I know. I had a long day too, old man! Let's go home."

14 Cloudy Secrets

Carl slept deep and long, a sleep like none he had had in a while. As he came into consciousness he realized that he had left his body that night, and he was in a very peaceful place. He wondered what time of morning it was. The sun was not glimmering through the window, and he could hear the rain showering on the roof three feet above his loft bed. He had never heard his Pop get up and leave three hours before, nor his Mom rustling around the cook stove.

The event the evening prior rushed into his brain. Remembering that he would not speak of it, his eyes finally focused in the dim-lit room.

"Morning, Mum," he said softly as he rolled out of the bunk to put his woolen pants on before heading to the outhouse. His voice was still scratchy from sleep, and it took a second try for him to find it again. Then he felt the folded bills in the one rear pocket.

"I was wondering where you got side-tracked to last night. Thought you were down at the Hubbards for supper. I put yours into the stew pot over on the hearth if you want it for breakfast," she said. She then looked at him, slightly smiling, trying to get the answers in her subtle way. She was happy for her son in the thought that Carl was seeing Mamie, who was from a good respectable farm family.

"Where is Pop?" Carl asked, as he came back in barefooted 'cause it was too much effort to put his boots on.

"Oh! He felt a little better today, so he headed down to the timber lot to check on the men. Said he was going to be gone for most of the day. It should do him some good moving around and getting some good air in, but you know your father—he can't stay down for long anyway!"

"Yeah, Mum, but he sure didn't look too good last night. Well, I saw Mr. Ford the other night, so I sure don't think he's at the timber lots today."

His Mom just looked at him for a moment knowingly, then turned to the pot hanging on the fireplace hook, and with a ladle in one hand served a bowl for

Carl's breakfast. She already knew that he was there doing chores until late, but she didn't pursue the details, much to Carl's relief.

Carl's head pounded with a dull ache that day, plagued with the thoughts of the Burke event, so he didn't do much except for the light chores mother needed. He truly had no ambition to go anywhere, bothered by the commitment not to speak of it. About mid-day, the clouds moved in, the temperature dropped sharply, and snow started lightly. *There will be two inches on the ground by evening,* he thought to himself as he laid his head on his feather pillow. Still reeling from it all, he dozed off about three in the afternoon.

Sometime in the night he awoke from deep out-of-body sleep to partial consciousness. He pictured Mamie's embrace, her head nestled into his chest, the feel and smell of her hair on his cheek. It was one of the only times that he felt really nurtured. The sound of the wind and sleet on the roof just above his head along with the warmth of the wool blankets gave him a feeling of safe refuge.

Before dozing back off he remembered the windfall. *When I get up today,* he thought to himself, *I will hide most of that in a safe place. With the rest I'll buy some nice things for Mamie and Mum at Shirley's store. It's a secret that will be hard to keep. Where to put it for safe keeping and easy access?*

His mind began to ponder as he dozed again. Carl certainly never heard Pop come home last evening, only the faint murmurs of Mum's and Pop's voices while they had supper.

"I ran into Old Ford on the trail last night, Hon. He wants to meet with me tomorrow at noon to discuss business prospects. Said it was important if I'm up to the task of a new position."

"Sounds like you'll be overseeing the other lots, taking over his load so he can be home more,."

Her intuition and knowingness were accurate as usual. "You know dear, we are lucky to have the work—you and Carl both. We might be able clear the land debt next year if you both can keep steady this winter," she added. They spoke softly till bedtime so as not to wake the boy.

Pop stoked the woodstove just before turning in. "I'm taking Sadie down to the lots again in the morning; Carl can ride down with me if he wants to." Then he breathed a deep breath as he got comfortable in their bunk.

"I think he'll be rested up by then," she whispered. "He's been sleeping all afternoon. He had a long day of it yesterday. I wanted him to get his rest; we don't need him coming down with this cough, too," she said. Then she cleared her throat with her hand over her mouth to muffle the sound as she suppressed the tickle. She took a sip of water and kissed her husband goodnight, but he was already breathing heavily. She wondered if he heard her words.

The last flat stone was heavy, and Carl groaned lifting it back into place. The corner foundation stones at the lower barn stall were the best place to hide the money, he thought to himself—at least until he could explain how he came by it without breaking his word on the secret. He'd just pull out a little at a time for emergencies, 'cept this two-dollar piece. This is gonna get Mame somethin' nice. We'll head to the store soon as I get Sadie, or maybe I can use one of Ford's horses now, he reasoned.

Pop was up early and headed out, taking Sadie, the Morse family's only horse. Sometimes Carl would ride double to the wood lot with Pop and take Sadie for the day or, when his dad would stay at the job camp, he would take Sadie for two days at a time. A mild and gentle mare, Sadie always seemed to know what the routine was and where she was headed.

The walk down the trail to Hubbard's place through two inches of wet snow was arduous and took a little longer, it seemed. That was because he was so anxious to see her. He contemplated the whole way if he should confide in her about the event at Fords.

Finally, he made up his mind not to say anything for fear of it getting back to old man Ford. A rifle shot echoed through the valley, and he stopped in his tracks, trying to judge the direction from where it originated. Dismissing the thought that it came from Ford's place again, he remembered that the bucks were coming into rut. Fresh snow on the ground made prime conditions for hunting deer. "Shoulda brought the rifle," he murmured to himself.

The side trail heading southwest along the ridge had a single fresh horse track in the few inches of snow. It was most likely Pop and Sadie from when they left earlier. Ten minutes on the trail he could hear the woodlot workers, voices shouting in French, axes falling on the trees and the horse team drivers coaxing the draft sledges.

Just up over the rise he spotted Sadie tethered to the line in her usual place. Pop's silhouette was easy to spot near the shack with a clipboard in his hand.

Carl looked at his dad's stature from that distance and couldn't help but admire the strength, and the sense of integrity and authority he conveyed. Then Pop noticed Carl standing by Sadie and waved for him to come up the knoll.

With Sadie's halter line in hand, Pop asked, "You gonna be back by dusk?"

"Yup, I'm just gonna get the chestnut mare at Fords that he said I could use and take Mamie down to the valley store. Mum gave me a list of particulars she needed, too."

"He said I can keep the chestnut for a few days!" he added.

Pop cocked his head a little. "Old Ford has been generous lately, hasn't he? Wonder what's gotten into him?" He took off his hat and wiped his forehead with the cloth hanging from his back pocket. "Hokey doke, then. I'll see you here at dusk."

Mounted on Sadie, Carl rode down the snow-covered trail towards Mamie's place quite excited about the prospects and his plans for the day.

No one was at Ford's when they pulled into the barnyard. Mamie even noticed that no smoke was coming from the house chimney, which was odd for any morning, especially this cold one.

Carl figured that Mrs. Ford must have left to be with relatives or a friend, but he didn't say anything to Mame about how distraught she was. At Mamie's farm her Mom was the only one home, and she gave Mame a list of supplies to put on the credit marker sheet.

It was common practice in those days to have a grocery account for only main staple goods, a system that worked well if you were a member of the community and working or in a trade of your own. Barter of hardware was also common with the store clerk who served as a broker of sorts.

They went directly to the corral behind the barn and haltered and saddled the chestnut mare. She was a tad reluctant as the saddle went on, knowing she would be getting a workout.

Carl mounted the mare and Mame rode Sadie. They trotted the two animals out of the barnyard at a quick pace until they reached the travel road; then they walked along side by side.

Even the two horses seemed to enjoy each other's company.

Carl and Mamie made small talk along the way, giggling as they talked. Mamie was excited just to go to the store. All the while Carl felt anxious about his secret and the abundance he just received, but he kept it to himself.

As he looked at her in her wool coat and her broad rim hat and scarf, he noticed how pretty she looked. He wondered how he could get Mamie to go off with him to build their own life together.

Maybe come next summer he could make that happen. She was chit-chatting away, and he only heard her say, "Is that okay?"

He replied anyway, "Ayup. I think so," not really hearing her question. She giggled again, just happy, looking at him and smiling with content.

15 General Store

The snow dissipated rapidly as they rode downhill into the White River valley. The day was warming up quite nicely with just a whisper of the occasional cloud. They could hear and smell the activities of the small town as buildings in the valley came into view—the chugging from the one-lung engines running the lumber mill belts and the echoing saw blades slabbing through the timbers. Woodfire smoke at the bakery filled the air with wisps from each chimney.

Old Diane, the steam-fired tractor, was putting along the Puddle Dock timber yard across the main road just down from Shirley's general store. Two horses hitched to the post out front and one buckboard wagon with two draft horses were parked outside.

A couple of Frenchies were loading sacks of grain or beans, yelling at each other in French, and one was flapping his arms up over the way the other was stacking. The bowl mill whistle sounded off in the distance, signaling the noon hour. It was truly an exciting and different world for both of them compared to the upper ridge farmsteads; the hustle and bustle of the small town of Granville in the valley was an adventure.

The bell rang as Carl pushed the door open, holding it for Mamie. Mr. Shirley looked up from a Sears Roebuck catalog with his specs near the tip of his nose and a pencil in his hand. "Well, young Mr. Morse and Miss Hubbard! What brings you two off the hill this fine day? Elwin is out back stackin' grain sacks, so we won't be disturbing him just yet, if you know what I mean." As he smiled at Carl, he made the last notation in the ledger with the pencil.

"Yes, sir, we catch your meaning. When we get done looking around, I'll go back there to make sure he ain't sleeping on those sacks." Carl replied.

Mamie giggled again, then made a beeline to the hard candy jars. Carl leaned in close to her and whispered, "Get what you want, I come into some money!"

"I hope your dad and mum are feeling better," Mr. Shirley said.

"Seems so, Mr. Shirley. Pop was back at the woodlot this morning." Carl

General Store

said, eyeing the new buck knives on the shelf. He looked over at Mamie as she was going through and holding up different fabrics.

The bell on the door rang again as an older fellow came in and took off his hat. He looked around the store briefly, glancing at Mamie first, then Carl, giving a nod of acknowledgment.

"How can I help you today?" Mr. Shirley asked, again looking over the rims of his bifocals as store clerks seem to do.

In a deep voice, the man said, "Well, I been down at White River in Hancock, workin' the stream gravel just below that notch at Churchville. They said you would have some spade selections and some new pans. Seems I broke the handle off my other, but it's pretty much wore flat out, so time for a new one with a good edge on it."

"I think we have what you need over there in the corner for pans and tins," Mr. Shirley said, "and all the shovels and spades are out at the rack on the side of the store. Just pick the one you like and bring it in. Having any luck in the river?"

"Well it was a couple of good earn days with pretty good color to show for it. I'm hoping you'll accept some of what I panned for the barter?" He held up a leather pouch.

Mr. Shirley then stood up from his bench seat and took off his glasses, giving the man his full attention. "We will have to weigh it out on the scale and calculate the rate."

"That will be fine with me!" the man said, "I don't want to travel all the way to Rutland to redeem it if you're willing to barter for simple supplies right here."

It was the first time Mr. Shirley had ever handled payment in the form of raw gold. He had heard that some folks were panning and coming up with color here locally in the streams and in the White River, but those fellas were working hard with little or nothing to show for it. The diggings that he did know about were limited to only production of fines and minute flake traces. Nuggets were rare, and if someone found a vein or source, they certainly were not advertising it.

The man allowed Shirley to look in the pouch, after surveying the store again and not perceiving Carl or Mamie as any threat.

"Yes, I believe we can do business!" Mr. Shirley said, slowly putting his specs back on his nose.

"The name is Bagley. Fred Bagley," the man said, extending his hand.

If gold could be had in these hills, and apparently it could, Mr. Shirley thought, a shrewd businessman will be the only redemption outlet for miles, making a handsome profit on both ends. He gladly shook Mr. Bagley's hand.

Mamie set some cloth on the counter and found the licorice sticks. Glancing at Carl for approval, with a sparkle in her eye, she reached up for a jar of molasses.

"Get two of those," said Carl. "My Mum could use one, too. Could you pick out some fabric for her, too, something you think she would like? I'm gonna go out back to harass Elwin, so come out back when you're done."

Elwin was sweating, stacking the last sacks of oats under the shed roof when Carl came up behind him. "I'll be needin' you to carry one of those to my chestnut out front, please!" Carl announced, bragging a bit about the horse, "and the nice clerk inside said you won't be needin' a tip either!" he joked, just to rub it in a little more with his good friend.

Surprised to see him, Elwin, still sweating a little, wiped his brow with his shirt sleeve. He replied, "I'll tip you after you carry it yourself! So! What brings you down the hill? Snow too deep for your tender loins?" Then he chuckled a bit. "You really need the oats?" he asked.

"Yeah, Sadie needs a treat once in a while, too!" They both grabbed the 50-pound sack, lugging it out front past the prospector looking at the shovels in the rack.

Mamie was in her glory getting the household staples her Mom put on the list and the gifts Carl had her pick out for herself. She was excited about the new dress she could make with her roll of fabric. Just coming off the mountain was a treat and thrill. Even the horses got a small bag of the molasses-coated oats as a treat while Carl and Mamie loaded the supplies.

Carl and Elwin finalized their visit, making plans to go hunting in the next few days.

The old prospector, also loading his gear, caught Carl's attention, "Excuse me, sir," Carl said as he reined the chestnut up.

"Fine horse you got there, son," he said as he looked up from his saddle bags.

"Thanks. Is there really gold in the river?"

Mamie reined Sadie up just then, curious about the answer, too.

"Yep, there is sonny, but one must know where to look, where to dig. And one must have a god-awful lot of patience," he replied. "Don't recommend it to make a livin' or raise a family on." Then he smiled at Mamie. He went on. "Yep, if you scrape the ground in the right spots you can find it. You can find it most anywhere, but knowin' where to look is the key to the puzzle!"

As he cut off a chunk of chew and stuffed it in his cheek, Carl asked, "Is it Mr. Bagley, sir?"

"Yep, that's right" he said as he spat out the first saliva from the chew. "You been paying attention in there, haven't you?"

"Yes, sir. Well, I couldn't help it 'cause I was always curious about pannin' like they do out west. I'm Carl Morse; this is Mamie. We live up on West Hill there," he said as he pointed, "Well, I live up Texas Gap. Mamie and her folks live off West Hill. Could you show me how to pan for it sometime, Mr. Bagley?"

"Why, sure, but you got to come down to just a tad below Hancock and find my camp. It's just up by Churchville. If you ask the clerk inside, he'll tell how to get to it. I could always use a little company." With a crooked smile he spit again then went to strapping the gear on his horse. The offer was valid, and the prospector figured a day of 'instruction' would be a day of free digging labor, saving his own back.

Carl looked at Mamie, content with the thought of a new venture. As Bagley come up to rub Jenny's nose and stroked behind her ears, admiring the fine animal, Carl asked, "Do you think we could find some right here in the White River across the bowl mill yard?"

Getting right to the point, Mamie asked, "Could you show us how to work a pan some before we go back up today?"

Thinking it over for a moment, Mr. Bagley replied, "Well, I 'spose we could do just that as soon as I get everything square with that fine store clerk inside. That's the mill over yonder?" he asked, pointing towards the bowl mill. "Looks like there's a bend in the stream, so you both can meet me near that in a bit if you want, and I'll catch you all up there."

"Yes, sir!" they both said, excited, at the same time.

Mamie's eyes were lit like candles and Carl smiled, enthralled with the new adventure to share with his girl. Clicking his cheek, they both nudged the horses gently with their boot heels.

Just as they were pulling out of the general store toward the mill, Elwin came running out. "Carl! Hold up! Here's the mail sack to drop along up hill." He threw the sack up over the saddle horn. "Oh, and my Pop wanted me to ask you if you've seen Burke lately. I guess he's gone missing. One of his kin was here at the store and left a notice about it."

Carl's heart leapt into his throat. Mamie was already ahead of him with her back to him, so no one else noticed his expression and perspiration. He reined the mare in a little, turned partway to Elwin and said, "Nope, ain't seen him 'cept at Ford's three days back now, I guess."

Elwin said, "Yeah, me neither." then there was a pause for a second as Carl just looked at the ground, but it seemed like forever. Finally, Elwin said, "Hey! Catch you for huntin! That's if your wife there will let you!" Then he grinned, letting the rub set in.

Then Elwin slapped the mare's rump, turned, and walked back inside the store. Carl could hear the bell ding as he rode off to catch up with Mamie. Composing himself while trotting, he determined not to let it ruin his day. "I will think this out later when I'm alone," he whispered to himself.

Mamie's hand was warm and its feel washed his anxiety away as he held it, absorbing her soft touch. Both horses walked alongside each other for the short distance up the well-trodden mill road, as if they wanted them to be touching.

16   Pannin' Eon's Ore

Eons ago, the Green Mountains were formed from the earth's crust by immense pressure causing upheavals and seismic shifts. Molten rock coagulated deep below the cooled crust layers. A chemistry beaker full of various minerals coagulated—granites, schist, quartz, and gold, just to name a few. Vast deep earthly pressures pushed these molten mixes upward.

Granites and other hard rock cooled slightly shrinking leaving fissures in between. Molten coagulated quartz would be forced up into these fissures and sometimes up to the surface, forming vast veins that adhered to the other types of materials combining as they cooled. Veins of quartz would many times break and spew out on the surface. Gold in Vermont is 98 percent pure and is always associated with quartz due to its density. Silver, copper, and iron, being heavier metals, have different densities that allowed them to be deposited in their own fissures.

Immense pressures over millions of years pushed the semi-molten crust layers ever upward to form the jagged Green Mountain range. Multiple Ice Age cycles of glacial movement contributed to the formation and vast erosion of the jagged peaks. As great flooding torrents of water ripped down the slopes exposing the long-cooled bedrocks and deposited the smaller, loose heavier ores and tills all along the vast crevasses of granite rock and schist. This scraping of the glacial ice and forces of water exposed and broke down the ancient veins of gold-bearing quartz. Like a huge trammel machine, the chunks of mineral deposits were tumbled and gyrated for eons, further breaking down the ores, trapping them within the clutches of the subterranean bedrocks.

On the eastern slopes of the Green Mountain range, the schist was pushed up in mile-thick layers during the upheavals, outcropping them closer to the surface than the western slopes, more of harder granite and marble.

Nineteen times heavier than water and five to ten times heavier than many other minerals, this dense soft pliable commodity broke down into minüte proportions and powdery fines that lie within the crevasses and holes in streams and brooks. Trapped on the bedrock and impermeable clay layers of till deposits, placer gold, as it is referred to today, can be found in certain places within the Green Mountain range, the larger subterranean veins lie there unexposed within the fissures. Where the White River begins in Granville is known to be one of those bearing placer fines.

Carl and Mamie stood there on the embankment of the White River just at the long curve holding the horses' reins. Carl pondered the gravel bar formed by the stream's current on the outside bend. At first glance it looked like a sand bar, but as they led the horses down onto it, larger rocks and stone were locked into each other like a puzzle with fines in between creating a hard-packed gravel bar.

Just upstream almost directly across was a smaller stream feeding into the White River. The White was only about 15 feet wide on average, but a keener eye would notice the width between the higher embankments. On either side it was 40 to 50 feet across with steep gouges of over eight feet in some places where the raging spring flood waters would swell the White over those embankments.

Carl wondered if the gold was in the gravel and sand in the bar below their feet. Mamie wondered the same out loud. "It's here, I just know it!" she exclaimed with eyes starry as she looked at Carl with her beautiful smile.

The horses took water from the stream while Carl kicked at the round stones and sand. Mamie sat on one of the bigger boulders admiring the gentle flow of the two streams merging together.

"Can you imagine how much water it takes to move all of this gravel till, Mame? It must have been huge torrents to carry all this material here. Betcha' there's some gold in here somewhere!"

"I want big nuggets, honey bunch—so you can make me a necklace and a ring!" She came over to him and took his arm, pulled him to her and kissed him passionately. Just a little preoccupied with the prospects of gold, he tried to regain his focus on where it could be in the stream. She gave him a pouty look just as the gravelly voice of the old prospector came over the embankment.

"Oh, there you folks are—figured you'd be at this spot!" He led his horse packed with supplies down onto the sand bar. "Yep, I know what you're thinking, son. You're thinking you can just pan it up right in this sand, aren't you?" Mr. Bagley said.

"Yes, sir, Mr. Bagley, but I'm getting the feeling you're gonna tell me different," Carl said, smiling.

The old prospector had their full attention.

"Yeah, well, I worked plenty of these bars before and it damn straight never panned out for me! Follow me. Hope you aren't afraid of getting a little damp," he called out.

"First, I'll say to ya both that sometimes knowledge can be a good form of monetary compensation or barter, so I'm gonna teach you all a couple of simple rules. First one for today is that if we find any color, it goes straight into my pouch unless it's a big piece. Savvy?"

They both nodded with approval.

"Now then, let's try this spot over here." He said pointing just across the brook. It was a boulder on the inside curve just downstream from the side stream flowing into the White. "You see, all heavy metals including black sand is 'bout six times heavier than all other rocks or materials of the same size, and gold is nineteen times heavier than the water. You follow?

"The gold fines are like talcum powder and will stay with the black sand. It takes a lot of water to move it and gravity brings it down to the deep crevasses, holes and eddies in the stream."

"What's an 'eddie'?" Mamie asked.

"Ah, finally a smart question!" he said, laughing a little. "Eddies are these places just behind a rock, boulder or obstruction in the current of the brook. It's were the water pools around the rock and becomes still as the current flows by on each side. So, what happens in a heavy flow after a long rain or floods is that the heavy metals like gold get eroded out of the embankments up stream or up from these other streams that flow in like this one here and are moved out and downward with the force of the current. It then settles in the gravel on the downstream part of boulders like this one, or under them. It's always found on the inside curves while all the lighter gravels and sands collect on the outside curves forming those bars." He pointed to where the three horses were nibbling the oats that Mamie had put out to keep them occupied.

"If there is a source of it upstream it doesn't generally travel too far down. Larger flakes and nuggets won't go far downstream at all, but trace particles, say the size of a half grain of rice and smaller powder size, will get trapped in the crevasses of the ledges and bedrock that the stream flows over."

Carl just listened intently, absorbing and hanging on every word, his eyes focused on the hills and terrain where the White River came out of West Hill. "So, Mr. Bagley, all this erosion where the river has cut through the mountain up there," Carl started to ask, pointing up to the notch in the mountain that their road trail home meandered through, "has brought down gold for years and years?"

"That's right—another smart observation! It's more like thousands of years, though," he said lifting his hat and scratching his baldness under it.

Carl grabbed the spade and splashed out to the big rock, not caring much about getting wet. The stream was only about six inches deep at that spot.

"So, if I dig here like this and put the shovels in the pans?" Carl gestured.

"Yep, that's pretty much the basic idea, but you got to dig down under the rock as much as possible and get the finer sand. Here—let me show you."

The old guy took a couple of fist-size rocks out of the way, reached down under the water with both hands and pulled out some bigger ones, then told Carl to dig with the shovel.

"All right, Sweetie," he said, looking at Mamie. "Bring those pans over here."

The first shovelful of sand rocks and aggregate went into the 12-inch round pie pan.

The next few shovels went deeper and deeper yet. The old fellow showed Mamie how to put aside the big stones that were obviously not of value, retaining the smaller stone and sand. It was so exciting for the two youngsters that it did not seem to them like the work that the old prospector knew it really was.

He then showed them both how to jiggle and shake the pan of material just under the water in the slight current that swept the lighter fines and silt away, by swirling the sand in a round motion and jiggling it once or twice, pausing every so often to observe the contents at the bottom of the pan.

Mamie stood up abruptly as the sun glistened off a piece of stone shining in the pan about the size of her thumb nail, "I think I found one here!" She held it in her palm towards Mr. Bagley for approval.

Carl stared at the contents of the sifted out remains of the first pan. An awful lot of that was glistening in the sun, too! He held back on his excitement, to watch the old man's reaction.

Old Bagley smiled at Mamie, took her stone from her hand, hardly looking at it, and said, "Everyone gets excited when something sparkles at you. But better that you learn this right off so as not to waste time and work analyzing this stuff. What you got there is iron pyrite. It's also called 'fool's gold.' I've seen many grown men spend time collecting it thinking it was the real deal. Look here," he said, as he held the piece up to the sun. With two fingers he broke it in half and crumbled it between his fingers as it turned to a glittering powder.

"Most common mistake for beginners. It's light and it's brittle; that's the clue. Most of the time it will wash out of the pan. See here?" He took the pan she was working, dipped it in the water, and swirled the contents in a fluid motion. Almost all the sand floated or washed out, leaving only some heavier stone and some fine grains of black sand. He picked out the useless pebbles with his fingers and sifted the pan again.

"Come close here now. Look close," he said as he jiggled the water in the pan some, and sure enough, there in the crease of the pan were some dull yellow particles glimmering, just a few tiny specs really, but real gold, nonetheless.

A few trace specs derived from two shovelfuls in one pan? Carl raised his brow, and Mamie giggled. They set that pan down and began to sift the other two out the same way they were taught. Mr. Bagley carefully poured the fines into a glass container he had in his saddle bag.

"Real gold will always show up a dull yellow even if the sun isn't out, that's a sign, too! You don't get a lot in a dig like this one unless you're real close to a source vein. But see the way the mountain has eroded down to this valley here? Well, that means it's probably a lot deeper. It was carried down by storm water from upstream thousands of years ago, if it didn't get trapped up in the ledge ripples and big boulder till up stream. This little bit more 'n likely came from up land off this feeder stream 'cause of the steeper terrain just up there a few hundred yards," he calculated.

He was referring to the hill coming off Puddle Dock adjacent to the general store where the lumber company staged the logs and floated them from the man-made pond for spring flow down to Bethel. They could still hear Old Diane chugging in the distance up on the hill.

They panned out the rest of the ore and found some more trace particles in the teaspoon worth of black sand left from the full shovel. Old Bagley promptly placed it in his stash jar. He produced another small jar from his saddle bag and had them both gather around holding it up to shine in the sun. "See this here? *This* is the real deal!

"This is the accumulation of about a week's work in the right place." He said displaying the jar. The bottom of the jar was coated with gold particles and thin flakes half the size of your baby fingernail. "This is what you can get here in these Vermont streams if you know what you're doin', son!"

He then smiled that crooked smile at them, saying "I can't tell you all my secrets, but I can show you some things if you all are willing to work for it."

"Yes, sir, Mr. Bagley," Carl agreed. "I'll come down to find you soon as I get caught up with my work and chores, maybe in a couple days or so!"

"Well, you best hurry. The winter snows are movin' in here pretty quick and I'm thinking of headin' south some unless I can find a room and board. I ain't wintering in a canvas tent, that's for sure!" Mr. Bagley said. "Worst thing is I'll be back in the spring after the ice flows out. You can find me around down there in Hancock workin' my diggings there."

"Good luck to you and thanks for the teachings, Mr. Bagley!"

"Well, good luck to you, too, there, Mr. Morse and Ms. Mamie. Remember, there's gold just 'bout everywhere if one knows where and how to look, but patience is the key!" He leaned over to Carl from his saddle and in a low tone said, "Take good care of your Miss Mamie there; she's some punkin, that one."

He winked at Carl and clicked his tongue urging his horse up on over the bank with all the gear clanking as he went.

"Wow, that's the real thing, Mame! We can really find gold here!"

Mamie rolled her eyes, smiling, and jokingly said, "I think you will be working at that for a long time before I get my ring!"

Carl just eased back in his saddle and grinned. "Maybe not as long as you think." He reached for her hand, "We best get heading back up trail. We're burnin' daylight!"

As he looked up toward the mountain trail of West Hill, he could not help imagining how the White River stream wore and eroded the vast slopes on each side of the gap over thousands of years. He envisioned gold pieces the size of nickels trapped in the rivulets of the ledges all the way up and down the stream bed just waiting for someone like him to pick 'em out at his leisure in the low flow of summer's cool water. He smiled at Mamie again, feeling rich anyway.

17 Secret Rendezvous

The first small schoolhouse up on West Hill, known as District Four, was about one mile downhill from where they lived. It set off the main trail up on a little knoll adjacent to the White River. They passed it on the way down to the general store, noticing that no school was being held this day. The schoolhouses were simple one-room structures with a small wood stove and benches for the pupils with a blackboard and a table for the instructor. Never locked, these buildings also served as a mail drop and a public shelter for any traveler who might need respite from the elements or cold.

Carl sorted the mail and placed the letters for that district in the canvas sack on the door of the school. After hitching the horses to the post, Mamie opened the door.

Taking Carl by the hand with a twinkle in her eye, she drew him inside.

Smiling, she leaned in close; no words were needed for their passion to unfold. Carl with both hands held her cute face and stroked her hair letting it comb through his fingers. She pressed her body against his and their lips touched softly.

He then rubbed his nose with hers, laughing a little. She pushed back some and said, "What was that?"

"Oh, that's an Eskimo kiss! It's what the native Eskimo people in Alaska do instead of kissing on the lips."

"Well, that doesn't sound like too much fun! Why do they do that?"

Carl held her face with both hands gently and said; "cause it's so tundra cold in Alaska that if they kiss on the lips with their tongue, they can get instantly frozen and stuck together like that till spring thaw!"

She slapped his chest with both hands, laughing out loud, then snuggled back into his embrace. "Is that all they do, those Eskimos? Just rub noses?"

"Well, not exactly." Carl replied as he put both hands down under her lose wool pants and felt her soft skin on her buttocks and round hips. She purred and cooed, and pressed her breasts tightly to his chest, kissing him with her moist lips.

To young lovers, exploring each other's bodies during the throes of passion is the most exhilarating experience anyone can have. Every motion, every sensation of touch, every part of exposed skin and taboo regions is an adventure in itself.

When two lovers surrender themselves to their mate, uninhibitedly giving their energy willingly to each other, it can be only what God intended in this earth's natural rhythm, a spiritual event enabling the universal energy to create life from the pure essence of love.

And that they did there, in that little schoolhouse on a sunny afternoon alone with no interruptions. They lay there, both expired, in each other's arms. Pecking little kisses on his face, Mamie whispered, "Is this how Eskimos stay warm all winter?"

"Yep. They just stay right in their igloos made of ice blocks and lie bare under polar bear fur for six months at time! They chew whale blubber like beech gum for food, too!"

He laid back a little, thinking of the gold again. "Did you have a nice day, Mame?"

She snuggled in closer still and whispered, "I love you so much, Mr. Carl Morse."

"I love you, too, Mame. I wish we could stay like this, like Eskimos!"

She snuggled in again and kissed his neck and put her head in his shoulder and cooed some more.

The sun sunk lower through the schoolhouse window.

They stopped at Ford's, hustled out the chores of graining and watering the horses and stock in the barnyard, putting Jenny the chestnut mare in her stall with the door open so she could go into the corral in the morning.

The wood was still stacked untouched on the porch of the main house. "No smoke from the chimney," Carl noticed out loud, gesturing toward the house to get Mamie's attention.

"Mrs. Ford must have gone off the hill for a few days," she said.

"Yeah, must be." He looked over at the little carriage shed. "The buggy and one of the quarter horses are gone."

He knew that Mrs. Ford left in a hurry; whether it was under a forced ultimatum or by her own design or embarrassment no one will know for sure. Carl's intuition favored the latter. Then his stomach began to ache as he remembered what Elwin had said earlier at the store. In his mind's eye he foresaw the law badge, a sheriff and two deputized armed men trotting their horses up the mountain road towards Ford's farm.

He then regained his composure, wondering how long he had drifted off on that thought and feeling, looked a Mame and announced, "Time to get you back, girl. I don't want to get on the bad side of your Pop just yet!" With that, they double-mounted Sadie and headed up to the Hubbards' farm. The one inch of snow was still unmelted on the trail as they plodded along up the hill.

Mamie thanked Carl for the wonderful day. Not really wanting him to leave, she kissed him for a length of time longer than what he thought was comfortable in their barnyard in full view of the house. Carl thought he saw the window curtain move some from the corner of his eye.

Mame held the embrace with her body against his and told him "I love you, Mr. Morse," not wanting to let go.

Carl did not want to let go either, but summoned the willpower, saying, "I'll come 'n' see you day after tomorrow. I got to do a full day's work at Ford's all tomorrow and part of the next day, so I'll stop by when I'm done with that." He then leaned down and kissed her again, glancing at the window.

He mounted up on Sadie and touched her hand again as he reined Sadie around, nudging her with his heels. Watching him ride off, Mamie waved with that starry look in her eyes. She was smitten in love, pondering being his wife and waking in the morning next to her man.

18   Home Cookin'

Carl pulled into the timber lot where Pop was working. It was just about dusk. They both mounted Sadie and headed home for some well-deserved supper, talking of the new work positions they had with Ford and planning their next few days. Though he didn't show it, Pop was excited about the things Carl had gotten at the store, and as Carl told him about the prospector's success, the gold panning really piqued his interest.

They could smell the aroma of venison stew, potato, leaks and biscuit as they rode into the barnyard. Sadie got her water, hay, and sweet grain and went into her stall for the night.

Mother was standing in the doorway smiling as her two men came home from their long day. It was now quite dark with the stars just starting to peek out in the crisp evening sky.

Mother was ecstatic with the fabrics that Mamie had picked out for her, "How did she know I would love these patterns!"

Pop didn't seem all that enthusiastic over the cloth. He was interested in the iron pots and pans that were made down off Patterson Brook trail. They had "Deere" logo stamped in the center on the bottom of each one and a deer with antlers stamped on the handle, the trademark for the local smith shop that made them.

Pop ended up with a new pair of heavy wool trousers of a forest green and some tan suspenders. Carl got himself and Pop new pairs of deerskin gloves for winter workdays.

Dinner was delicious; this hot meal hit the spot just right for father and son. "Thanks, Mum, that was some good eatin'!" He mopped up the gravy with another piece of her fresh sweet bread. Pop's eyes were already drowsing as he settled into his chair with his pipe.

Mother began the clean-up by pouring the hot kettle water into the big oval dish bucket. "You should get to sleep early tonight for that full day tomorrow, Carl—and next you see Mamie, thank her again for me. Like me to pack you a lunch for tomorrow? I'll be putting some up for Father, anyway."

Pop sat up from his dozing, hearing his name, "What's that, dear?" he called out.

"Oh, nothin,' go back to sleep, Hon."

"Okay, Mum, I'd like that." Carl replied, then he came over to her and whispered so as not wake Pop again, "Glad you like the presents. Mame really liked hers, too!"

"You and Mamie are getting along. I mean you really like her, don't you?"

Carl looked at the floor first then at the window, feeling embarrassed. "Oh, yes, Mum, she is special to me! I told her I love her today, Mum, after she told me first. I can't get her out of my mind."

His Mom looked at him in that mothers' knowing kind of way, cocking her head with a half-smile as her intuition kicked in. Carl told his Mom about the gold-panning experience and the offer from Mr. Bagley.

She advised him not to put too much stock in that venture, "Keep it only as a hobby. Your job at Ford's will provide more security, 'specially if you plan on courting Mamie formally with her parents' approval, Carl! You not only have to win her and demonstrate that you're a good provider, but until she becomes more mature, you also must win her folks, too. When she does, she will be looking for the same security after the puppy love wears off, and it will! Enjoy it while it lasts, but it's more your job than hers to be careful about some things right now." His Mom then reflected back on her own personal experience of love when she fell for Pop.

Carl confided his innermost thoughts with his Mom because of the close trusting bond he had always had with her. They whispered about the responsibilities of men and women coming of age, and the pitfalls of young love. The Burke incident at Ford's irked him inside—a secret that he thought best not be confided to mother just yet. He knew there would be a time for him and his Mom to talk that out. He dreamed vividly that night.

19 Chestnut Mare

The note on the chalkboard at the main barn door at Ford's indicated no one was around. It read:

> stack wood inside house
> light woodstove
> tend livestock
> back in afternoon

This meant that all the normal tasks at the barn yard needed to be done and last. Restocking wood inside the main house and prepping a fire meant someone would return to a warm house later today. Carl speculated that Mrs. Ford was coming home or that both Mr. and Mrs. Ford were heading back. Either way, the house was to be occupied tonight.

He set about his tasks trying to envision what other responsibilities he was to tend to. Checking the hen house, he collected fresh eggs, milked the one cow and placed the containers in the pantry as he had seen Burke do many times. He dismissed the events of Burke's demise many times throughout the day. In early afternoon he separated two piglets into the holding pen, as they were to be picked up by the buyer in the morning.

Wiping his brow after wrestling those piglets from their mother sow, he wondered why the sweat still came even though the air was 30 degrees and he could see his breath. As he leaned against the rail taking a breather, he glanced up at the upper meadow, which was just barely visible from the barnyard. The tilled area now covered in snow gave him little comfort. The whole episode flashed in his mind, and again that pit feeling came back to his belly.

He decided to take the chestnut, Jenny, home for the night rather than waiting for Pop and doubling up on Sadie. Just as he was chalking that note on the board, he heard the trotting of horse hooves and rattling of a wagon pull into the barnyard.

"Whoa up!" the big burly man shouted at his draft horse pulling the work wagon, "Hey, there, son," he said to Carl. "Aren't you the Morse boy?"

"Yes, sir, I am." Carl replied.

"Well now, can't say I've seen you since you were just a squeaker! I know your dad, though. He's a good man! He used to deliver birch logs to us at the mill, you know," the man went on. "Well, I got a chance to break away from millin' to pick up those piglets. Ford said they'd be ready."

"Yes, sir, Mr. Whitney, I just wrestled 'em in the pen around the back there," Carl replied, thinking that he really was not wanting to fight them into that wagon. Carl grabbed some crabapples from the bin, and some feed grain, as a lure. Whitney put a plank at the tail gate of the wagon.

Even with the bait placed on the floor of the wagon, a rope around their necks, it still took a lot of coaxing, pulling and pushing to get 150 pounds of live bacon up a plank. Especially when they instinctively knew they are going to their doom! About 45 minutes later, both men wiped sweat from their brows. As big as he was, Whitney sat there puffing a little as he tied a couple more half hitches on their lines.

"Burke delivered 'em to me last year! Yup—right to my pen at the mill. This time, I had to pay the same price and do the loadin' and unloadin'!" he said, a little disgruntled.

"Well," Carl said, "I'd be happy to help you unload 'em, but it so happens I'm goin' in the other direction this fine evening." The half-smile on his face told Whitney he was being a little sarcastic.

"Heard Burke's come up missin.' You must have known him from workin' here at Ford's. Did he say where he was heading?" Mr. Whitney asked.

The pit of Carl's gut cinched up tight, and he was sure the grimace on his face would give him away. He averted his eyes to the ground and mumbled, "No, sir, I didn't know him too well—'cept for his yelling my chores out from across the way there. He wasn't around most times 'cause I'd get here after school." He glanced up at the upper meadow.

"I s'pose he'll turn up sooner or later." Whitney said as he climbed up on the buckboard. "Good to see you, son. Thanks for the help. Stop in at the mill if you get a notion; we always keep some coffee on in the control room! And give your daddy my regards!" He clicked his cheek and snapped the reins. The big draft lunged forward with no effort, as if the heavy work wagon was just a toy.

Carl composed himself again, torn between feeling good with his new responsibilities and guilty about how he came into them. "Don't know how much longer I can do this," he muttered to himself.

He mounted a saddle on Jenny and headed towards home, happy to leave before one of the Fords showed up. He did not want to feel any more conflict in his gut today! Even the mare seemed glad to be leaving, Carl sensed. Just the ease in what he could intuit from the connection with animals gave him instant freedom from negative feelings.

He talked to the horse out loud all the way home, confiding what he was feeling inside and his plans to take Mamie as his bride. They stopped so Carl could relieve himself, yellowing the snow. He readjusted the burlap sack of grain for the horses overnight, another benefit from Ford's well-stocked supply barrel. "Don't mind my callin' you Jenny from here on, do you? It's a good name for you, girl," as he put his forehead on hers with his two hands caressing behind her ears. She nuzzled her nose closer in agreement. A simple moment with any creature can form a special bond. Jenny was his favorite of all the stock at Ford's because of her smart and gentle nature.

With daylight fading, it began to snow just a light flurry. The air was silent and windless, and time stood still with the beauty of heavy flakes dancing as they fell. They both took it in for a few moments longer before moving on.

20 Deer Hollow

Late November brought heavy snow, accumulating to more than a foot and even two at the farmsteads along the upper elevations. Just like the bear, fox, bobcat, and many woodland creatures retreating to their dens, humans prepared to hunker in for the winter. Wood was stacked, goods were canned and stored in root cellars or buried in compost mounds, hay and grains were cached for the hooved domestic animals.

The snows came in squalls every other day, dropping two or three inches at a time as light fluffy powder, daytime sun warmed and partially melted the top to form overnight a frozen crust that would support the weight of a hunter's boots. The deer didn't fare that well, herding and bedding together under the heavy pine thickets at night, rooting and foraging out the crabapples from under the deep snow, and nibbling the abundant beech nuts during the mid-mornings and early evenings.

Narrow hooves break the crust at every step. Exerting too much energy in deep snow is detrimental; every creature seems to slow down, metabolism seemingly in sync with nature's winter pace. Carnivorous predators fared much better in winter. Coyote, bobcat, wolf, catamount cats—all could maneuver with advantage on the crusted snow. Yearling deer and moose with horns dropping off by January could defend only with kicking hooves.

Catamounts can leap from above out from a limb for a swift neck-breaking kill. Coyotes hunt in packs, wearing their prey down until the weaker are separated and venerable. Each carnivore has its own hunting technique.

Each word and its breath was seen evaporating in the still, 15-degree air. "Oh, boy, I think we got a big buck going here," said Elwin, pointing at the fresh tracks in the shallow, wet snow.

They were under a thick pine stand next to a small beaver pond. The hill rose gently up, giving way to the bigger timber of hardwood, beech, and another stand of white birch.

"Yup, they like hangin' under these pines feedin.' There's more than four, maybe six, and they ain't gone too far!" Carl's words were half-whispered, so the voices didn't carry.

"If you hunt the low side of the pond, I'll take the uphill side and I'll meet you upon that ridge. Something should shack out before the ridge."

"All right. Whistle out if you jump one running."

"Good enough!" Elwin used the lever-action 44-40 as a crutch to stand himself upright from the kneeling position, his dark green wool pant cuffs encrusted with snow half way to his knees.

Carl's were just wet from the swamp and stream he had crossed. The Sears Roebuck rubber-bottom boots kept the water out nicely.

Be careful not to step in anything deeper than the tops, he thought to himself. *It would not be fun getting those wool socks wet; his toes will and would surely freeze in this cold. Hate to have to make a fire to dry 'em out. Not now anyway!*

Deer Hollow was a vast expanse of terrain providing plenty of cover, water, and feed for moose and deer. The area was not yet inhabited by any homesteads or permanent camps. Men had made temporary lean-to-style camps while spending a few days hunting it.

Deer and game trails networked through the lows and the uplands, and beaver had built their dams backing up small streams in strategic areas, creating small ponds of one to two acres and balancing the ecosystem for all the wildlife. Deer Hollow truly was an enchanted place any time of year, but with the snow-covered landscape it filled the eyes with beauty that changed with every other step. Carl always had a hard time focusing on the hunting part of woodsmanship.

The old Winchester 30/30 just plain got heavy after a while, especially when trudging through a foot or more of snow. Carl switched its cradle to his left arm to better navigate his footing traversing up a small slope, the thick snow-covered scrub pine as tall as he could stand. He heard the loud snort within the thick pine knoll up from him.

The gentle almost-still wind was in his face; he stopped and shifted the rifle to the ready, "feeling" the buck or bucks in the thicket ahead. Intuition told him to kneel, and his knee absorbed the moisture in the moss under the two inches of snow.

A tuft of wetland grass was protruding through the snow next to him. He reached slowly and picked a blade of the tough grass, with both fingers he split it making a slot of two inches in its center seam. Wetting his lip and holding the grass taught, he blew air across the reed, and a barking sound or a bleat filled the still cold air. Once more should do it, he thought to himself, waited a few more seconds then blew another low tone bark.

One minute could seem like a day in this scenario, knowing deer were there but not seeing them.

Both man and beast were playing the waiting game, ever quiet and stealthy. The blade of grass still held between his closed lips, both hands ready on the rifle, the game trail he was kneeling on did not have any fresh tracks on or near it, so these deer, he surmised, were pushed out to this side of the beaver pond by Elwin.

Deer will almost always use the terrain to circle out and around predators if spooked, but in this case, they were staying close to the pond edge under the tall pines where the snow was only a few inches and the scrub pine provided an almost impermeable screen. Carl would have to walk up on them to get a line of sight—best to stay put and wait it out, he thought. This deer would most likely bound from the thicket onto this trail rather than go the other direction into the open woods where the snow was much deeper.

The high-pitched whistle from across the pond filled the dead air. It meant only one thing—Elwin had jumped the does, their flagged tails straight up heading around the pond toward him, too! The bucks always hung back from does. Only the bucks would snort.

Suddenly from the pine scrub, a deep long groan five seconds long with two short grunts echoed through the cold air. Carl instinctively came to full alert, not feeling the cold seeping into his knee and fingers.

The woods came alive. Not one but two bucks leaped onto the trail ten feet in front of Carl, then bolted 20 yards side by side, stopped abruptly as three does met them head on from out of nowhere; they must have been in the thicket the whole time just over the knoll. The more dominant buck scented one doe and, in a flash, began to mount her from behind. They were oblivious to Carl standing there not thirty feet away. He put his rifle sight on the other six-pointer.

Not many have witnessed a full rut mating ritual in these deep woods. Carl had seen the mating of domestic livestock, yes, but nothing like this with the grunting, and bleating calling each other, then only the dominant buck procreating with the in-heat doe. It was over almost as fast as it began, with the other animals standing there scenting each other and then nibbling beechnuts, mists of breath forming with each exhale.

He suddenly sensed the numbness in his fingers, then his wet knee. The bigger buck just walked to the edge of the pine scrub. Carl slowly turned and put the rifle on his neck, then in slow motion lined up front and rear sights just under the deer's ear.

It instinctively raised his head. Carl's whole body went rigid on alert. All eight points of the buck's large rack glistened in the sun. The others were in the same stance, each looking in a different direction as if they all had a mental communication.

Elwin had made his way to this side of the pond tracking the does in the snow, and his movement was noticed 60 yards distant as he stalked slowly under the larger pines.

Carl had a decision to make.

Something inside him did not want to take the deer's life, admiring the sheer beauty of the animal, and minding the basic spiritual aspect of taking any life. There are so many deer in the woods; hunting game in this way is a way of life for all creatures.

"We could use the meat, which Elwin and I will share," he rationalized. He put his lower lip on his bottom teeth, breathed in deep and let go a loud one-note whistle that echoed through the pond area. Elwin came to an abrupt stop, his attention focused in the direction of the pitched sound. The shot reported with a crack at the first split second and resolved with the lower boom in the next half second, the echo bouncing off the surrounding mountain terrain twice more over another five seconds.

Snow fell from all the pine boughs, seemingly from the sound shock itself, covering Carl's left face and shoulder. The buck leaped to the left under the large snow-laden spruce, and snow tumbled off the branches, whiting out everything where the buck had been. Carl quickly brushed the snow from his face and shoulder, regained his focus for the thirty yards. His peripheral vision saw the three other deer with white tails bolt in two directions. Two does leaped simultaneously towards the pond edge.

The other buck leaped directly into the thicket of snow-covered young spruce. The only sound now was the breaking of dried branches and the thud of hooves hitting the ground from the scattering herd. Then all went quiet, becoming somewhat unnatural and eerie.

Carl stepped quietly and slowly toward the tree of his target, all the while looking to his left for movement or a silhouette. *Damn! I missed. Should have aimed for the shoulder*, he thought as he made his way to the tree, now free of snow on its lower limbs.

Two short whistles came softly from Elwin's direction. Carl whistled two short times back in response to indicate that the deer were still around the area and to say, "I'm over here." Carl finally stood in front of the tree, no sign of the buck, the track in the snow showed him coming in next to the tree, but no track showed him jumping out. Carl stalked slowly around the tree from left to right in a 15-foot circle. He heard a snap behind him, turned, and concentrated his focus in that direction, seeing the silhouette of Elwin between the distant scrub pines. Carl whistled two shorter bursts. Elwin approached in silence.

They both continued looking out to the surrounding area for movement.

Carl stepped backward through the deep snow to get closer to where the buck was standing. When Elwin came up to him, Carl said, in a whisper, "He was right here next to this tree. I shot him through the neck, but there's no blood, no track jumping out!"

"He's big. He can't be too far." Carl, continued to step backward looking for any sign of where this buck went.

Elwin was now in a crouched posture, surveying the area under the tree limbs.

Still confused, Carl started to say "I don't know if I miss—" stumbling backward, he fell completely down on his backside while holding the rifle in both hands up protecting it from the snow. Something under the two feet of snow tripped him up. He let out a groan from the impact and then a "Damn!"

As he got up, the buck's antler was caught up in his wool pant cuff.

"Holy crap!" Elwin exclaimed.

Carl just said, "What the hell! I thought I missed him! Dropped 'im right where he stood! The snow come off the tree and covered 'im up! Damn! I walked all over here. No wonder I couldn't find any track!"

Elwin pulled the buck's head up by the antlers. "Jeeze, this is a big deer! I'm countin' eight—no, wait—its ten! Holy crap, it's a ten-pointer!" A small bit of blood trickled from the hole just under the deer's left ear.

The camaraderie between the two friends was at one of its highest peaks at this moment. There are no words to describe or none that are even needed for this kind of bond between men. It's a deep spiritual moment where the synchronicity of the whole event unfolds to a final manifested conclusion. The elation of this bond is the stuff of ancient native tribal ancestral birthright.

After making the initial incision opening the soft belly cavity up to the base of the rib cage, Elwin reached up inside. As the steam and smell of the internal parts filled their nostrils, he pulled out the still-warm heart of the animal. He held it up in his right hand towards the sky, the steam rising off it. Then Carl took the organ and held it looking up at the sky in an offering gesture.

He took a bite of the red tissue, and as blood dripped down his chin, he handed it back to Elwin, who, now standing, held it up in the same gesture and took a bite as well. "We give thanks to almighty earth spirit, and thanks to animal spirit for giving himself to us. We release this deer spirit back to the universe and earth, as we are all one."

Both Carl and Elwin were taught early on by their dads on the first hunt and first kill to release the animal's spirit in this way.

"This will insure a successful hunt for the next time you need meat to live and survive. Do this with any creature you kill, no matter how small. Birds, we save and offer the feather; rabbit, we offer a foot; deer, bear, or moose, we offer the heart. By taking an animal, you take it into your own soul."

"If it is not done in this way, you may never have any success hunting game again. "This is the way of all our ancient ancestors of the earth, and that is why the native Indians adorn themselves with feather, claw or bone. So always give thanks for your bounty in some way."

The two both looked at each other, wordlessly approved of the ritual, and went to work field-dressing the animal.

The antler rack would go with Carl, as he was the shooter; the rest of the meat would be divided evenly between the two for the shared successful hunt.

The snow began to fall more heavily as they dragged the carcass out to the trail. After dragging the 200-pound animal a half mile, their tethered horses were a welcome sight.

21 Tundra Cold

February snows in the Green Mountains were fierce and unrelenting. Accumulations could reach four to six feet annually, binding both humans and animals to their areas of domain. Cabin fever is very real when one is confined too long in a small space.

Getting through the deep snow was a hardship and drudgery. Most trail roads upland were by now narrowed down to just a footpath of packed snow that had fallen in December and January, where hooves of horses and two sled rails were previously ridden.

All metabolisms slowed during these cold extreme winter conditions. Most days were spent hunkered indoors with short trips to the woodshed and feed for the animals. Water must be boiled down from buckets of snow or multiple-pail trips to the spring pipe. The women of these times, bound to the cabin more than men were, suffered the depressions of cabin fever more often from the simple lack of sunshine.

Carl's winter routine was to trek daily down to Ford's with the chestnut mare he now called Jenny to do all the necessary chores, feeding hay and grain to all the livestock once a day, and shoveling any new heavy snow from the pathways at the woodsheds and grain bins.

This work took three to four hours per day depending on the conditions. Then he generally headed home to do the same there. Every couple of days, as planned with Mamie, he stopped down at her place to have a proper visit. As her Mom or Pop were close by, to steal a kiss they had to make up a chore to do in the barn.

On his way home, Carl would hook up the snow sledge to Jenny, plowing the road section he was traveling on up or down to his destination, dropping the sledge at the turn-off for the Texas Falls trail to his house for the next traveler to continue the community effort.

Pop would trek out to the timber lot camp every other day, laying overnight at the shack occasionally to keep the skeleton crew of Frenchies making a minimum daily sledge run of at least a couple of logs hauled out with the ox team to stage area.

Snow days and extreme cold temperatures would be the exception for working. The cold could set deep to the bone; the thick heavy woolen clothing was the best technology of the time, but still it held moisture.

Pop felt the congestion in his chest, and it interrupted his ease of breathing deep air in. When he did, he would cough profusely; sometimes it would bring him to his knees, and he knew in his core that while providing relief, lemon honey tea was not the cure. Still he hid it from everyone as best he could and worked his routines, shrugging it off as tough men were expected to do.

The bunk in the cabin at the wood lot that night was nowhere as comfortable as at home, nor was it as warm, especially without his sweet wife to snuggle in with him. The temperatures dropped significantly just after sunset that clear February night, and the small wood stove in the cabin needed feeding every couple of hours in the sub-zero temps.

The three Frenchmen fast asleep sandwiched under their layers of woolen blankets, with one on the bottom and two on the top. The bunks had only a thin straw-filled canvas mattress laid on top of the oak board frame.

Pop's bunk was too short for his tall stature and was not provisioned with the extra wool blanket on the canvas mattress. The single wool blanket had seemed adequate when he first lay down with his back on the cold canvas. The dry air made him thirsty, and all the unfrozen water was used up in the small pot of stew. No one else had bothered to melt down any more water for later that night and the Frenchies only took care of their own anyway. So, tired and thirsty, Pop just lay down, keeping to himself.

The fire went down to embers sometime in the early morning hours, and the Frenchmen's snoring got louder throughout the night. Pop could not force sleep, although he tried, so he lay in a fetal position, cramped, cold, and parched. His lungs would allow only short breaths that he could only sustain under the warmer wool blanket. Any fresh cold air in the room provoked his coughing. Out of pure exhaustion he finally dozed off at about four in the morning, but the blanket fell from his head and face, and cold air filled his lungs. Because of the natural body's unconscious need for oxygen while sleeping, Pop began to cough uncontrollably.

About 5 a.m. that morning Carl heard voices outside in the barnyard. Both he and Mother looked at each other, bewildered, as they got up and threw on some pants and boots. The voices in French were now just outside, and then the knock pounded on the solid oak door.

Mum's keen inner gift of knowingness and Carl's gift of claressence flashed them both at the same time as they looked at each other's eyes; no words were needed to question why the knock came.

Carl's dad passed on sometime in the early hours of that bitter cold February morning.

It was just a few hours after the Frenchmen brought him home and helped get him into the bed; it took all three of them and Carl to do it, as Pop was too weak. Mother prepared the bed with warm wool blankets after the Frenchmen left.

She lay alongside him using her body heat, constantly massaging with her hands, desperate to bring his core temperature back up. The long trek to Rochester to fetch Doc Merriam and the return would have taken most of the day. Mother's insights were for Carl to stay close by until she could get Pop warmer and respondent.

All Carl could do was to stoke the fires in both stoves to keep the room as warm as possible and to make honey tea.

Getting Pop to drink it was to no avail. Carl dozed off while sitting in the chair, but he woke abruptly to the sobbing, then a loud wail from his mother's tired frame; she cried for another three hours. Carl joined in her tears, glancing at his dad's motionless body a hundred times in disbelief. Leslie Karlton Morse had passed to the other side at the age of 36.

Mother suddenly stopped her sobbing, stood up, and instructed Carl to help her bring Pop outside after they wrapped him in his wool blanket. "The cold outside will keep him until we can do a proper burial." She looked at him with bloodshot, watering eyes. "I'll need you to go down to town and post the notice and get some men to help us with digging a plot."

"But Mum, I can't—I won't—leave you alone just yet. Let's get you to bed for some rest; then we'll do all that together." They both cried and hugged each other for the rest of the day and night.

Carl did not sleep. He suddenly felt alone and responsible, thinking how he should or could have taken over for Pop while he stayed home resting. Mother cried and sobbed through the night and finally fell to sleep briefly.

Carl could hear her talking to herself or in her sleep at different intervals through the night. A few times he tried to comfort her by holding her hands and hugging her, that lasted only until he himself dozed off.

A knock on the door jolted him awake. When they left the Morses' place that morning, the three Frenchmen went straight to Ford's farm with the news of Mr. Morse's condition. They then dispatched a horseman down to Shirley's general store, and the networking began.

From there runners were sent to Rochester. Doc Merriam was finally intercepted between Hancock and Rochester up on North Hollow Road that evening well after dark. He was found treating another patient, a young boy whose horse had stepped on his foot. Doc and the horseman, Bill Parish, proceeded to Shirley's general store, lying over there in one of the board rooms for the night.

At first light, Doc Merriam, Elwin, Mrs. Shirley, Mr. Beatty, and Mr. Ford himself began the trek up to the Morse's farm by way of individual horses and sleighs with some additional blankets, medical supplies, and food. Elwin diverted off to Patterson Road to notify the Farrs, they being the first establishment on that trail. Mrs. Shirley stopped at the Hubbards' farm, and Mr. Beatty headed towards Bagley's on the Finney Road.

Within a few hours the network spread the news throughout the valley and both upper ridges on the east and west sides of Granville valley.

Mrs. Shirley, Doc Merriam, and Mr. Ford were the first to arrive.

Doc first treated Mrs. Morse by giving her a sedative of aspirin and Valerian root. Mrs. Shirley went right to preparing some coffee, stew and warm bread, then sat with Carl's Mom. Doc and Ford went outside and verified and documented Pop's time of death and worked on additional preparation and securing of his body, not something close family should have to do.

Elwin got there soon thereafter and sat with Carl for a spell, then convinced him to take a walk, get some air and tend to the livestock, but more just to be with his friend.

With his arm around Carl's shoulder, Elwin said softly, "Mame and her family should be here right soon. You should be with her for a while today. Don't worry 'bout any work stuff, I'll head down to Ford's later to take care of the chores there until you're back up to it." Carl managed a half smile and a nod, appreciating his close friend and comrade more than ever.

Doc Merriam and Mr. Ford both came into the small barn where Carl and Elwin were just putting some grain out for Sadie and Jenny in their stalls.

Doc came right up to Carl, grabbing his wrist, checking his pulse and looking at his eyes, kind of performing a quick exam on him. "How are you holding up, son?" A question to which he already knew the answer.

"It's been a pretty long day for you, so I want you and your mum to get some good sleep tonight. You don't need to worry 'bout nothing like cookin' or chores; there'll be plenty folks here to help out with all that for you, and I got some aspirin and valerian inside to help you sleep."

Looking at Mr. Ford, Carl said to doc, "I'm okay, I guess, just been quite a few surprises lately. I can't figure out—why this—what's happening . . ." his voice trailed off a little as he began to tear up but managed to keep it inside again in front of the men. "Thanks, Doc, for takin' care of my Mum," he managed.

Ford then said in his gravelly voice, "I'll be takin' care of all arrangements for you and your mum, son, and the chestnut Jenny—well, I'm signing her over to you permanent. She's a good breeding mare, so you won't be needin' to worry 'bout any of that."

Both Doc and Ford could best console in their areas of expertise by not letting any further emotions arise. It's better for people they're helping to stay focused and strong in these matters. They would dig the burial plot just down the trail on a small knoll in the corner of the Morse meadow. The deep snow insulated the ground from freezing, so the task in winter only entailed clearing snow from enough area for the folks to stand at the service.

22   Out of Body

Doc Merriam was the only practicing physician in the area. His residence and office were in Rochester, ten miles or more from Granville center. He routinely cared for folks up and down the valley, paying visits during the week house to house, farm to farm.

He checked in on folks with priority—pregnancies and fevers being the most common requiring home visits. Other health issues like broken bones and such would be treated at the office if the person could get there. Doc was always welcome for overnight and meals whenever he was on the home rounds.

His buggy, sleigh, and horse were always kept in the best repair free of charge at any of the smiths' shops. Barter for goods and services was the common form of payment in these times, anyway.

A very busy fellow following in his father's practice, he was a special breed of man who used a lot of common sense in his work. He didn't use much sugar-coating when he explained the options with a patient's diagnosis, "It's best to give it to 'em straight as an arrow," he said, in that distinctive calm, no-nonsense monotone voice, believing that to be the best way to help the patients heal themselves.

Periodically, Doc Merriam would stop at the schoolhouses and the general store to teach and post written papers for folks to better prepare and store their foods, always boil the water from a spring, use garlic, honey, and apple cider vinegars to boost natural immune systems, "and flush your innards."

He taught of herbal plants, extracts, oils and roots that grew wild for use as teas, compacts, and cooking. He even made a toothbrush prototype using hog or boar's hair from an English design and horsetail hair, then had them produced in Middlebury for sale at the stores, to be used with baking soda or chalk—toothbrushes that the whole household would share by if you were fortunate enough to own one. In his teachings for oral hygiene he encouraged the use of a simple stick cut from a beach or birch tree branch to be chewed and frayed at one end then as a brush for teeth and gums. A paste made from fresh mint mixed with baking soda gave it a sweeter flavor.

Carl managed to doze off for a little while after taking some aspirin that Doc had suggested. He wondered if he could sleep at all with all the people milling around, coming inside the cabin, and the whispered murmurs of conversation. But once his head hit the goose down pillow, he went completely out of body and dreamed.

The big black catamount cat stared over him with piercing round yellow eyes that looked straight into his soul. He had just lain down in a small meadow of tall hay grass, just looking at cloud formations in the blue sky. The clouds formed faces of people close to him and others—Pop, Mum, Elwin, Mamie, then others that made him feel distant with a knot in the pit of his stomach—Ford, Burke, a Frenchman who spoke in broken English at his door, and old Bagley smiling, passing him a pan full of gold dust that he fumbled and dropped, spilling the gold dust back into the river.

The feeling was that he wasn't ready for it or didn't deserve prosperity that easy. Then Mamie's soft touch and warmth of her body next to his as they lay in the grass. Suddenly the cat came running towards him from a far distance down a straight trail with tree limbs on both sides overhead as if in a tunnel. Just a black speck at first and in a flash of fast motion like an arrow, the catamount loomed directly over him and stared, and then the cat moved his clawed paw onto his right shoulder. Yellow eyes pierced his whole being; a direct mental communication occurred from some very deep spiritual origin to his higher self, an ancient language heard not with his ears but with his soul.

It seemed to be a choice of life path, and a test of worth. The cat took him into his powerful jaws, and he became one with the cat. He found himself seeing through its eyes, climbing effortlessly up a massive straight oak tree, ten feet around or more at its base, rising like a tower high above the canopy of the earthly forest.

They settled on the top branches where he was balanced, centered and at one with the earth, the cat, and himself. He had no sensation of fear or even of any physical body; he was now viewing himself as the black cat from just above his cat body.

Then he looked upward and found his essence being drawn to the stars, leaving the view of the earth, terra, below. With no sense of any physical body, all he could see was stars, universe all around him.

A small cluster, a solar system familiar to him in the clear night sky as Pleiades, was the destination it seemed. He could go there, thus the choice. Glancing back and downward, viewing the earth and then the one tree he just left high above the forest canopy he suddenly felt out of balance, with only a thin tether like a silk thread tying him to the earth.

As fear of the engulfing stars entered his awareness he began to fall. For what seemed forever, he fell; the closer he got to the canopy the heavier his body began to feel. His heart pounded in his ears. Passing in slow motion through the single higher tree, its top limbs and straight trunk down into the branches of the forest well below.

He felt no pain as the branches scraped and tore at his being, he saw the grassy meadow fast approaching; he was sure to hit it hard. The pit of his stomach became a knot just before impact—an impact that never occurred. His whole body twitched as he felt himself sucked back into it. The lightness sensation disappeared all at once.

Mamie's face was the first thing he saw. Her soft whisper and touch of her hand on his face was his next sensation. He jolted back, letting out a verbal exhale. As his eyes came into focus in the dim light of the cabin, he was still not sure of the moment's reality.

Her eyes were tearing. Smiling at him, she whispered, "Hi. Were you dreaming? Are you all right?"

His heart was still pounding as the air refilled his lungs in one short gasp. After he collected himself, he told her of the dream.

Mamie and her mother had arrived at the Morse homestead an hour before bearing comfort food to support Carl and his Mom. Mamie wanted to be with Carl as soon as Elwin knocked on their door with the news. Mamie was going to go with Elwin, but her Mom said, "We should let Elwin make the other stops, and you and I can prepare some things to bring."

23   Cold, Cold Ground

Mamie went right out to hitch up the small sleigh. Mother collected two jars of her pickled string beans and corn, some fresh sweet bread was just cooling from her oven, so she cut it in half and wrapped it in a cloth, the wrote a note for her husband as to where they were going and left it on the table under the half loaf of bread.

Pete Hubbard had left for work down at the Farr turkey farm about daybreak and was sure to get the news soon enough. The girls would make sure his diner would be waiting for him when he got home, then they headed up to the Morse's small farm, Mamie drove the horse hard, anxious to get there.

The three women folk, Mrs. Shirley, Mrs. Hubbard, and Mamie did most of the tending to things inside making sure Mrs. Morse and Carl got some sleep and comfort the best that they could and keeping the wood stoves fired taking turns with cat naps of their own. Elwin's girlfriend Lola appeared that evening and the four women all helped with preparing and organizing foods for the men working without side chores and preparations. This would continue for a few days through the burial service, all while other folks, paying respects, would come and go.

The snow flurried lightly as the reverend preached long passages from Gideon's bible at the hand-dug grave site. A small knoll in the half-acre meadow ten yards from the tree line, just down slope from the Morses' cabin, was the appropriate place for Pop to be laid to rest. Mum was having a hard time with it all, sobbing, then with her jaw set she would try to act strong. She held Carl's arm tightly for the duration of the service and then fell to her side, sitting in the snow instead of on the chair that was placed nearby for her as they lowered the rough-made coffin into the grave. Her man was gone and all she had was her son to fill the void. Still in a state of shock, Carl held onto Mame's hand through the service with his Mom on the other arm.

A lot of folks from both sides of the Granville upper ridges and the valley were in attendance; Mr. "Les" Morse was a respected member of the community. Everybody in the area was recognized for their talent or individual ability, expertise, or trade.

Many folks spoke words at the service about how they knew Pop, or how he had helped them with a project or a problem. It seems that Pop had a special talent for calculating the board footage of a load of logs and how to load the log sledges just right so they wouldn't break lose during the horse team haul down to the mill. One fellow from Puddle Dock lumber mill said that Les Morse's loads never come apart and his measurement was always true to the tally.

There were no flowers this time of year, so a small apple tree was planted just above the headstone. Rob Ford had made the arrangements for the stone.

Mum could not handle the strain of watching the men shovel dirt over her husband. After she and Carl threw the first handful on, the women folk and the preacher brought her back to the cabin, Carl had to accompany her to the door because she would not let go of his arm.

Once she was inside, he hugged her hard and long; then, with her consent, he went back to the grave with Mamie by his side and sat and watched the men complete the burial.

The snow began to fall a little harder by then. Carl just sat there with his eyes closed and his face upward letting the snow fall on his face. He dozed off again, oblivious to his outer body, hearing only the breeze whispering through the tree limbs and the brown beech leaves still on the branches.

He stayed close to home the next few weeks, tending only to the immediate chores, mostly shoveling the deep snow, keeping clear the pathways to the barn, chicken pen, and wood pile.

Mother was missing her husband and not acclimating well to life without him, so she didn't want Carl to leave for very long. Mum's state of depression was a concern, as was her coughing.

Folks would stop by occasionally bearing some potluck dish just to check in on mum. They had been lending support and an ear since the funeral, but the winter made that hard for the women's network, and they assumed that time was the best healer. Given that a few weeks were plenty enough for mourning, the visits became less frequent.

Four times a week Carl would head to Ford's for the paid chores there. One of the Frenchmen took up the slack for him after the funeral, but the winter tasks had slowed to a crawl anyway, as they did everywhere. At everybody's homestead, cabin fever tended to set in about this time of year with the short daylight hours, but it was especially hard at home for his Mom.

One day it was relatively warm, about 35 degrees by mid-afternoon. Carl was able to coax Mum to take a walk outside. He planned on mounting her on Sadie to take a ride down to Shirley's general store in the valley or at least down to Mamie's farm.

He had wanted to see Mamie and did not want to leave Mum alone. The fresh air and visit would certainly do her some good and she was finally convinced, but by the time they rode down past the burial plot Mum reined Sadie to a halt and she just stared at the small apple tree barely poking up from the mound of deep snow covering the grave. The only sign that there was a grave at all were the colored ribbons tied to the apple tree sapling.

Mum began to sob; then she resolved herself, wiping the tears away, and said, "I think we'll just head back home. I'd like to make some honey bread."

Carl was happy just to get her outside for a change, so they headed back, and he stoked the fires for the night. Mum sobbed a little more, trying to muffle it so Carl couldn't tell, but it was to no avail in the close confines of the small space. Cabin fever had already begun to set in.

24 Jenny's Bear

The beginning of March brought warmth in the early afternoons—a bit of relief from the winter's harsh bite. As Carl was heading down to Ford's to put the paid chores to rest, at just about the rise in the trail road where he saw the catamount, Jenny came to a halt abruptly, her ears laid back, a sure sign of some pending stress that animals can sense. He spoke to her in a whisper, "What is it girl? It's all right."

Carl could in his mind's eye feel her emotion. Suddenly in a flash the moment he connected with Jenny's vibrations he saw the black bear rustling in the brush just to the left of the trailside, then walk into the trail, pause and rear up on its hind legs to sniff, staring directly at him.

The bear, a large snorting male, then bolted off in the brush, breaking the low branches of the pine boughs.

As it vacated the area on the run, Carl knew it was his human scent that had set the bear off. Jenny stood on alert for a few moments longer, and then she was ready to resume the walk.

All of this was just a vision in his mind, just a flash, but very clear and vivid. He shook his head, regaining his real eyes focus and noted it to himself, dismissing it as his imagination. He nudged Jenny's quarters with his heels, clicking his cheeks for her to move forward. Within fifty yards, as they come over a slight rise in the road, the whole scenario unfolded again—this time for real in real time, just as he had seen it a few minutes ago. Jenny's ears went back as she stopped in her tracks, alert.

The male black bear had just emerged from its den and was out on the forage. Looking thin for its size as it stood up on its hind legs, the bear just acknowledged their presence with a snort. Carl knew in his soul that there was no threat.

Jenny seemed to know it also, and she held her ground. After the bear had run off, Carl recognized that his vision was not coincidental. There was some deeper purpose and meaning to this insight.

He now had something new and refreshing to share with Mum openly about his and her gifts. He was eager to get home and looking forward to the evening's conversation, knowing it would perk Mum up from her depression.

He also made a pact and promise with himself to listen to the insights and the core feeling of them when they occurred from now on.

His inner sense of people was always confusing before today. He now recalled the way his gut would feel if a person were of good intention or not. He always could get a read on people when they came into his presence and a feel of their character or mood. He now understood why he wanted to avoid some folks and felt drawn to others.

It was why he remained quiet and timid with the older boys at school. Then his thoughts went to Mr. Ford with his intimidating nature and how he saw and felt Ford's fear in the upper meadow that evening when they buried Burke.

He recalled how he knew something was drastically wrong when Mrs. Ford had stood in the doorway trying to hide her tears and emotions. Now Carl understood the colors he saw surrounding a person's body—colors he saw all the time, not knowing that others could not see them. For him it was second nature and a natural thing, and he had ignored it up till now, a gift that he was just beginning to understand.

With most folks he could see or feel their essence, good folks in good health would give off a fine white light just immediately and all around their body, and he could sense their emotions. He now recalled how if someone became angry their light would change color to an orange or red tinge. If they were in fear or stressed or ill, the light would become darker in hue. His intuition could tell him clearly the demeanor of the person, their health, and true spirit.

All this became suddenly very clear as he pondered this bear event and the late-night whispers with his Mum about his Great Grandpa and his healing gift. He then thought of the catamount and his out-of-body dream. He could not wait to get home to his mother to share his new insights. Mamie would not comprehend any of this, but mother would. He pondered if he should tell her his secret about Ford and Burke.

They sat up half the night, talking of the seer gifts and visions, sipping tea well after midnight. Supper was the honey bread and venison stew. Carl started the conversation with a very direct statement, "Mum, I had a vision today that became real within ten minutes!"

Mother's eyes lit up, her slumped posture straightened, and she focused in anticipation for the details with her elbows on the table and a slight smile. Carl knew immediately that this night of discussion was going to revive her from the depression. He could not believe he was talking out loud; it felt strange not to have to whisper anymore.

The Burke experience, he decided, could stay put for a while longer.

25 Trai-'teurs

His mother, Deanna, was a southern girl with a Cajun Louisiana heritage. After her grandpa passed, her ma and pa came north seeking a better life with dreams to have a small potato farm and to raise a few hogs. The climate change with four seasons of New England's clean crisp air was more enticing than the nine months of stifling humidity of any Louisiana town.

The "great panic," one of the first economic recessions the country had known, was taking its toll on folks, and the word of land grants in a new northern state of Vermont had somehow reached her dad. While other folks headed west seeking fortune, they headed north where the security of land grant titles seemed more realistic.

On that journey north she met Pop, a young French-Canadian on his own quest. As many folks did, they traveled together, working small jobs on small farms along the way, bartering for food, shelter, and supplies wherever they could—until her dad was kicked by a horse while attempting to re-shoe it. He lingered for a few days, then died in the small town of Lyme along the old Boston Post road in Connecticut. The young people had already fallen for each other and their lovers' secret no longer mattered.

Carl's Pop, Leslie Carlton Morse or "Les" as folks called him, found himself supporting her Mom and younger brother. After a month her Mom took up residence at a dairy farm in Connecticut and signed on as a kitchen cook with board in one of the outbuildings for her and her son. Mum and Pop married and made plans to continue the quest to Vermont, sharing her Pop's dream. They would send for her Mom and brother after they settled a homestead. It was never to be.

Her mother lived just another two years and died quietly. Her brother left at age 15 for the West and was never heard from again.

His mother could never bring herself to open to her gifts due to some inborn fear most of her life. She could see the auras of people, and sense the emotions of folks, but occasionally she would get flash visions of events regarding others, and it always came on when she was centered or relaxed. These flashes would always take her by surprise and throw her into an uncomfortable state.

Once she heard and saw an apparition of a spirit standing next to a friend at school in Louisiana and it scared her out of her wits, so from then on, she never would allow herself to relax or stay centered. She remained always on edge. But as she recalled now, it was just another person trying to communicate through her from another dimension, a message for her school friend.

Grandfather explained that she had the power and could turn it on or off as she chose, and that people from the "other side" would sometimes know her ability of openness and try to talk to her to relay messages to loved ones. He added, "But they need your permission, so you can choose." Now, she thought to herself, maybe I could be a healer, and a seer to help people. Then her fear welled up again of what others would think, or if she were too old, and how she would be accepted. That fear canceled her openness to using her gift.

Mum fell to coughing and Carl held her in a hug, "It's late, Mum; let's get some sleep."

She took both of his hands and with tears flooding up. "Do not fear your visions; use the gifts for only good and know that you are a *trai'-teur*. You can choose to turn it on or off; you can decide to talk to folks from the other side; it's all your choice, but they will always come. My Grandpa is always with you if you need guidance with it. Just ask him out loud and he'll come to you."

Carl looked at her, cocking his head in question.

"Oh, you will know."

Carl was not so sure what mother meant, but he knew it was from her deeper self and experience. He squeezed her closer in a hug and tucked the blankets on her like a child, as she so many nights had done for him.

Mum fell straight to sleep, He looked at her thin frame lying there and in a flash in his mind's eye he saw only her young and pretty girlish essence, just like the way he saw Mamie, innocent, smiling, and free of inhibitions. In another flash her Grandfather, his Great Grandpa, was next to her, both were sitting on a bench. She was about ten or twelve, and they both were smiling at him.

26 Puddle Dock Logs

Mid-March brought snow melts much faster in the valley, and mud. All the roadways and beaten trails were rutted where horse and oxen trod, and the wagons they pulled left deep ruts in the thoroughfares. Up higher it was just plain wet everywhere. Snow that fell at night quickly turned to rain at sun-up. Draft animals labored hard pulling log loads up and out of the lots and winter stockpiles, but this was a busy season in Granville, its being primarily a timber town. Carl could hear the steam engine and the whistle of Old Diane chugging up the hill to skid another sledge of logs down to the stage area at Puddle Dock. He had just finished morning chores at Ford's and was grateful Old Man Ford himself was not around this day, being off at one of the timber lots, Carl supposed. Mother was at home feeling better about herself, but her cough was constant, and after his work he would trek to the store to pick up household supplies and some remedy for her. She had wanted to stay home and do some sewing on patches for a quilt at an upcoming sewing bee.

Surprised and excited by his visit, Mamie saddled up her horse and rode beside him to get their own needed supplies. She didn't need much convincing. Neither did her Mom, who wanted to go, too, but decided to stay and finish her own patches for the same women's event.

Sewing bees were great social events, breaking the cabin fever and allowing the ladies to catch up, gossips and folklore and a support system where they planned out events and helped each other with a wholesome, strong network. The patches were sewn together into quilts and then donated to the needy families or to new mothers in the community.

It was always exiting to go to the general store with all the hustle and bustle of folks and the goings on of things, but it was especially exciting to see the opening up of the levy at Puddle Dock where the lumber company released the staged logs from the platform into the large pond and with the huge surges of water from the levy, usually twice a day, they floated them out into the White river. Each log had its own "end mark" stamped on the end to identify the lumber company it came from when it got down river for sawing into boards.

107

The French lumberjacks, or log drivers, a special breed of men, wearing caulk boots, rode the logs and guided them all the way to Bethel, some 40 miles downstream. The water in the river was high and dangerous at this time of year, with snow melt levels that sometimes flooded over its embankments.

These experienced nimble men were made up of a few specialized crews. The Jam Crew were the front-line men working with peaveys and dynamite, preventing jams from happening. They were also called the *beat crew*. The *rear crew* collected the straggler logs and wash-ups stuck on the banks or hang-ups caught in the rocks or river obstructions. To free them, they used pike poles, peaveys, ropes, and horses on either side of the banks. Last of these special men were the Bateaux men and the men who worked the wannigan. The Bateaux men ferried the rear crew men back and forth as needed; the wannigan was a floating kitchen supplied with everything from tents, blankets, and dry clothes that served up four meals a day.

Pay for these men was high; it was the only incentive for such a dangerous job. Many novice men lost their lives getting crushed or maimed by heavy logs in the frigid waters. Here in Granville, mostly all these men were of French-Canadian origin, lured by the quick money. Many of them endured only one spring season. Only the well experienced could work two or three seasons, teaching the apprentices the tricks and protocols of the trade.

This profession consisted of a special team and a brotherhood of Frenchmen, highly valued by the logging companies of the era.

Carl and Mamie got down to Shirley's general store just in time for the first mid-morning levy surge. Puddle Dock pond was just next door, and it was an awesome sight to see that much water and men working the flotilla of logs.

Most everybody nearby stopped their work to witness the first flow of the short spring season. Quite a few folks gathered. They were already assembled along the White River's embankments where Thatcher Brook, a small tributary, first flowed into Puddle Dock pond and then married into the White River. The flotilla of logs now on their way represented prosperity for most everyone in this Vermont timber community.

"Now that was the cat's meow!" Elwin shouted, as he walked up to Carl and Mamie, still mounted on their horses. Some folks were clapping, and others were heading to the bowl mill side of the river to watch the Frenchmen work the logs farther downstream. Some of the other men were already preparing heavier hardwood logs for the next run in a couple of days. "You should try to make it down again in a couple days to see the next run go out! Bet there'll be a lot more people," said Elwin. "I'll post it on the bulletin board at the store today after I talk to the Yard Boss."

Logging crew taking a break

The first run was mostly pine and hemlock to be used as ship masts and jibs. The lighter pine logs floated higher in the water, with much less chance of catching up in any jams. The beat crews removed any natural obstacles with the lighter logs on the first run, clearing the way for the next run of heavier timber that would float a lot lower in the water in a few days' time.

As the excitement settled down, folks meandered over to the store just to warm up near the wood stove, a rather large pot belly in the center of the large room, and to have some of the hot coffee always brewing. Here they could pick up the mail, browse the Sears Roebuck and Montgomery Ward catalogs, place the orders, and later pick them up, as the store was the only station for shipping and receiving.

Most local folks had credit at the store whereby they could acquire their main staple supplies and barter or pay by coin over time by signing the ledger, a large book depicting purchases, amount owed, and the name and address or road of the farm or business. Reasonable time was allotted for payment.

No one would ever think of not paying a store debt. Even if someone fell on hard times, they could always barter off a debt with goods or labor. If a person became disabled, another family member or a friend could redeem the debt for them. It was not uncommon for another farmer to redeem a grocery debt for bartered services.

If a family were in dire straits, the town had a special fund derived from taxes —a welfare fund for the poor and needy, those who needed main staple food and clothing. Elwin Shirley's dad, the town clerk, had initiated this program. All the town's business meetings and functions were administered at the general store by the Select Board, a group of five men with high standards.

The inside of the store was abuzz with folks as Mame and Carl came in. They made a beeline to the "belly" to warm up a little from the brisk morning air. Outside, they could still see the mist of their breath exhaling as the morning mist rose to a higher elevation.

Carl poured coffee into one of the tin cups and added some sugar from the bowl. He figured to himself that he would try the luxury of it. He tried to act like some of the other men, as if it were a regular thing for him. After a few sips of the steaming brew he handed the cup to Mamie. She cocked her head a little, took a sip, and crinkled her nose, disliking the bitter flavor.

She shook her head, indicating a No. Smiling, she said, "I'll stick with my tea; thank you much," and gratefully handed the cup back to Carl.

Elwin, his Dad, and his Mom were quite busy with all the folks in the store, placing orders and loading supplies for them from the storage shed.

After squaring up at the counter, Carl and Mamie went out to load their own food stuffs and supplies. They could catch up with Elwin while loading their sacks and then head out back up hill. As they went out the front door neither of them noticed the "MISSING" poster hanging on the door for Frank Burke.

Loaded with the supplies for both households, and the mail sack, it would be a long afternoon till Carl got back home to tend to his ailing Mom. Foremost on his mind was the twinkle in Mamie's eye and the soft smile she always wore. How much he had missed and longed for the quiet moments alone with her since Pop died!

The two horses seemed to simultaneously stop at the closed schoolhouse without even reining them in. Carl built a small fire in the wood stove, Mamie latched the wooden closer on the door from the inside, and the new woolen blankets came carefully out of their brown paper wrappers.

An extra hour of long-awaited passion relieved a lot of anxiety for Carl. He fell deeper in love with her that afternoon, and he told her then of the money he had saved, and his dream of the future. He came short of asking for her hand, thinking to himself, No, not yet. I'll save that for another occasion very soon.

27   Dream Visit

The rutted road home became frozen on the surface again as the late-afternoon temperatures dropped rapidly and the sun was blotted out by cloud cover. As Carl approached his cabin, he knew something was wrong. There was no smoke from the chimney! His heart throbbed in his chest, imagining the worst.

His gut wrenched in the pit of his stomach, a feeling he knew well. He barely got the bridle off the mare and dropped it over the coral rail. He ran into the already-dark house to find just the dimly lit lantern and mother bundled in her bed sound asleep.

He shook her gently and she wearily opened her eyes. She whispered to him that he had grown to be a good man, that she loved him and she wanted him to listen to his intuitions.

"Remember what we spoke. Try to be a *trai'-teurs* healer for goodness like your great-grandpa was."

A few hours earlier she had just started to prepare the evening meal, chopping some hard vegetables for the pot of broth, when she began to cough uncontrollably, driving her to her knees. Her lungs suddenly felt full of thick fluid, and she could not breathe deeply.

The violent cough reflex after a couple minutes finally dislodged a wad from somewhere deep within her chest. She gladly was able to spit it out onto the floor. The episode took almost all her energy. She could breathe only in short, slow breaths, and remnants of the fluid still wheezed with her exhales. She crawled to the water basin, sipped the cold liquid, and managed to get herself to the bed and pull some blankets over herself.

As she teared her fears out, careful not to inhale too fast or deep, sleep finally came, with her last conscious thoughts the warmth of the wool blankets and that she might not awake to this side of physical life. She welcomed the slumber, feeling centered and at one with it all.

She awoke from someplace out of body to Carl's gentle nudges and touches on her shoulder and his words, "Mum, Mum, are you all right? Wake up, Mum!"

She wasn't sure at first if it were real or in the other dimension. In her dream state she was sitting on the bench as a little girl with her Grandpa.

She had no sense of her current physical body. Even as she opened her eyes and looked at Carl in the dim light, she had no memory of the few hours before or even awareness of where she was. Her body felt light and floating.

He got some hot tea and broth in her and laid her back into her bed for the night. The wood fire finally caught and drove the cold air out. Exhausted, Carl finally dozed off in his bunk, planning to wake after a short nap to check on Mum. She hid her coughing episodes well these last few days and her weakening condition was kept behind her gentle half-smile.

The rooster in the coop was the next sound Carl heard, jolting him into consciousness. He felt a kind of peace in the morning air as he lay there getting his bearings, as if everything was as it should be. His sixth sense and higher self told him that the quiet peace he felt was not his own; it was Mum's. Mother never heard the rooster that morning.

All alone, Carl prepped her body in some nice linen and brought her outside into the cold air. He fed and watered the animals from the spring that ran all year round, staring at the trickling water and appreciating its life-giving force and refreshing consistency.

He thought to himself that it seemed every time he had a loving or fun experience, or if he got too close or shared his personal feelings, something negative soon followed. He began to think that it was a payback of some sort—that any form of companionship or love in this world came with a price.

Why is it that every time something good happens to me some strange negative event occurs just after it, deflating my happiness? Am I a jinx?

Still taken with the simplicity of the flowing water and the spring buds forming on the trees, he dismissed this guilt feeling. Breathing in deeply and slowly filling his lungs with the cool air, he stood and accepted his situation—of being alone with new and unknown responsibilities from this day forward.

The cold clear water seemed to cleanse his inner soul as he sipped it from his cupped hands. It seemed to enter every space and crevice, refreshing the inside of his body.

The saddle fell onto Sadie's back, and she knew to head straight down to the Hubbards' farm. Once there, Carl just sat in their barnyard on Sadie's back, not knowing what to say or if he should even go to the door. Mamie's dad noticed him from the window, put on his boots, and came out.

"What is it, son?" he asked as he pulled on his jacket. "It's my Mum, Mr. Hubbard, sir. She is gone now, too—I'm real tired—I don't know where to go." His voice faded off to a whisper as he lost the thread, and the tears welled up and rolled down his face.

Mr. Hubbard made him come down off the horse, taking the reins and tethering Sadie into a stall with a bucket of grain. "You best come inside and get warmed up. We'll settle you in for the night here. Then tomorrow is a new day." With his arm around his shoulder he took him inside their home.

Carl tried to compose himself before they went in, but the signs of fatigue were on his face. Mamie held him openly till he fell asleep.

The burial took place on a warm spring day with the sun shining. All the same folks attended, and Carl accepted all the attention and promises from folks offering help with anything he needed; all he had to do was to ask. He smiled and nodded his head, hugging the ladies and shaking the men's hands as they departed. He could hear the whispers as some of them departed: "Oh, that poor boy." Mother, Deanna Valarie Morse, was laid to rest next to Pop with a new apple tree just above her headstone.

By the end of that day all he wanted was to be alone and go to sleep. Mamie's Mom and Dad were the only ones who stayed that night. Then, after tidying up and helping with light chores, they prepared to head home the next mid-morning. Mamie choose to stay longer through the afternoon, promising to be home by dark.

They invited him to stay at their farm for as long as he wanted, knowing that he wouldn't. Mamie's Mom really didn't want her to stay with Carl unchaperoned, but under the circumstances her father told mother, "Let them be this time; they know what they're doing."

Carl held and whispered with Mamie till he fell asleep in her arms. He never heard her leave, and when he awoke, he wished she could have stayed the night. The note he found on the table in the morning said for him to come by later for dinner.

Carl contemplated this forced solitude. The dew dripping off the trees and the water gurgling from the spring nearby all sounded louder that morning.

He didn't leave the cabin for another three days, sleeping most of the time except for using the latrine and feeding the animals. Feeding the fire for the cool evenings and drinking only cool spring water was the beginning of his deep depression.

On the third morning in which he had no concept of time, he stood out on the small cabin porch. His body felt light and floating; his head felt as if he was outside his body with all senses sharp and highlighted as he looked at his barnyard. It all seemed surreal, like he was standing there inside a painting.

In the garden area a misty movement caught his eye, an inner knowing, really, like another type of seeing in the core of his mind. As his attention focused, he saw it was Mother, a younger version of her, like when he was five or six years old.

Her tall thin frame as he remembered her then was there, now clear and vivid, working happily in her spring garden. Then she stood straight up and smiled her pretty smile directly at him. Both Sadie and Jenny were in the coral alert with ears forward, looking at her as well.

As her form faded, the last glance was of her smiling at him, and he heard her voice softly say, "I love you, my darling son. Follow your heart, talk to me when you need to. I will be listening." Then he was suddenly back in his heavier physical body.

With a renewed energy, after a long contemplation at mum's garden, he surveyed the farmstead, turned on his heel and went directly in his cabin. After he washed and shaved for the first time in days, he headed straight to the Hubbards' farm, riding Jenny, who for five days had not been out of the coral.

Mother's gold ring bounced against his chest each time Jenny came into a trot. He reached down and fastened the top two buttons on his heavy Sears Roebuck woolen shirt, insuring that it not bounce out.

28 Tejas

The Morse farm was one of the last 'steads on the Granville and Hancock town boundary. It was located up the ridge on the "Old Texas" road that headed west toward Texas Falls. Texas Brook was another tributary of the west branch of the White River, which hosts a beautiful gorge at the falls. Early settlers called the falls "Devil's Kettles" because of its worn ledges in the form of massive round kettle shapes from eons of time-worn waters and whirlpools.

Originally *Tejas* from the Hasani Indians, who were native to the region prior to European settlement, the word meant "friend." Folklore has it that the Indian culture placed high value on the crystal-clear cold water and the spiritual energy surrounding the beautiful falls and the smooth rock forms in the gorge.

During the summer, Texas Falls was a favorite destination for young folks as a swimming hole. The smooth rock in the main trough of the brook served as a natural slide, cascading down into the 25-foot-deep whirlpool at the base of the falls. Known for being the coldest all year round, the water in this brook takes your breath away even in 90- or 100-degree July heat.

The sheriff coming from Middlebury reined his horse in at the falls to take in the natural scene of the gorge. Stretching his legs from the long ride through Ripton, he watered his horse in Texas Brook, rested, and relieved himself before continuing his afternoon journey to reach Granville general store by dusk. Texas Road was the shortest route between Hancock and Granville.

According to the request letter he had received from one of Frank Burke's relations, his job was to investigate the hearsay that Frank Burke might not be missing after all. In the French workers' community, word had spread from the two men who were hired to dig a grave in Ford's upper meadow. It seemed the hole was too small for a horse—and their normal foreman, Burke, who abruptly went missing, also didn't hide his affections with Mrs. Ford very well when they were working near the barnyards.

They even joked a bit about it when Burke would disappear into her house for far longer than it takes to restock kitchen wood.

The Frenchmen's murmurs had filtered through the workers' community just after Ford terminated their employment for no apparent reason. Murmurs and hearsay were as far as it went, as the French workers' creed did not allow interference with their employer's business affairs for fear of being terminated. The French would keep to themselves and take care of their own in these types of matters; they were there only to perform the jobs they were hired on for and tend to their tight-knit community.

Sheriff Trunske would reluctantly start his investigation at the general store. Granville was on the outskirts of his jurisdiction, but his jurisdiction none the less. He looked forward to the room for the overnight stay to rest his oversized bones after his all-day travel.

Mrs. Mabel Ford was not a mentally frail woman, but she barely retained her sanity after the event in her barnyard. She had suffered a form of controller's abuse by her husband over the years of her arranged marriage. Old Mr. Ford was a hard, demanding man bent on his own daily agendas. Marital life for her was one of daily routine, lacking any compassion or tenderness. She had to become an obedient, subservient wife, presenting an image of happiness when in public. For years she hid her unhappiness well, but she often thought of leaving him during one of his vacancies at the timber lots.

It was then when Frank Burke began to stay longer at dinner time on her porch instead of retreating to the workers' bunk house. She began to welcome his conversations and openness. Over time she looked at him as a friend, and he knew he could take advantage of her trust.

He eventually hoped that she would leave Ford (along with some of his wealth) and run off with himself. He had genuine feelings for her, but he knew deep down the risk he was taking could put them both in jeopardy.

She reluctantly allowed the affair to evolve, getting caught up only in the passion and frenzy of the heated moments—something she needed but never had with her husband.

Within a week and a half of that fateful early evening, she traveled to Rutland by buggy, a two-day trip with an escort, one of Mr. Ford's hired Frenchmen. She was sent there by her husband because of her now-unstable state of mind.

She was sworn to secrecy about the shooting of Burke, not only out of fear of what Mr. Ford was capable of doing to her, but also because of her own shame of the taboo affair. Her status and her family's status in the community were in jeopardy.

Her depression, fear, and low self-esteem became severe. She had tendencies toward suicide, or so he thought. Mr. Ford arranged to send her off to a nursing home outside of the local town to give her time away from the farm and from him—time to rest and contemplate her situation. A one-month sabbatical, in the care of some nurses, conditional upon her return to resume her role as head of the household and never to speak of Burke again.

The Fords' marriage was to remain a façade, a condition in which she had no voice. It was nothing less than an ultimatum posed to her by her controlling husband. Folks were to be told she was going to be visiting her relations. And she was in no position to argue.

With her bags packed and loaded, she climbed into the buggy. Looking back at her home as they departed out the barnyard, her thoughts were that she would never return to it or to him.

She hated him for what he did—the years of controlling abuse, starting the argument that ended up in the shooting of the only man who ever brought her companionship and pleasure, and worse yet, forcing her to live a lie.

He took all that she had, including her right to divorce him. She would not return; her mind was set on that. As her tears welled up, his dark silhouette standing in the yard faded from her peripheral vision.

She felt a sense of release as the buggy rounded the first corner and her home was no longer in view, and as she turned her head looking ahead at the road, a slight lightness took her, free at last of all the negative energy now behind her.

"Please, let's stop at the general store!" she said to the Frenchman, "I need to post a letter." Mabel Ford had relations out in Illinois, and she had no plan to return to Granville.

29 Lawman

Sheriff Trunske was a special breed of man. There was no ego or control drama in his personality; he liked people in general, always finding the best quality in them at his first introduction. He would focus on persons facial and physical features and find some appeal in each. When he spoke, he always had a sparkle in his eye, making his own personality likable and magnetic.

People were never intimidated even if the star he wore at the first introduction caused it, but any discomfort soon wore off once the conversation began. He wielded his authority with a gentle sternness, in a manner much as a grade schoolteacher would with the young students.

This quality always put people at ease and caused them to subconsciously open to him. It helped him in his job as sheriff in many ways because folks who knew him would seek him out with a dispute or problem in advance of its becoming a legal matter, and he had a way of suggesting the perfect compromise or solution, pointing out the consequences in their own scenarios.

Sheriff Trunske favored this type of law enforcement, and he enjoyed being a keeper of the peace. These next few days would take him to Granville, a town he had not been through in over a year, on a task slightly different from the domestic or monetary disputes.

The town had grown since he was here last; his thought was that it might be time to appoint a constable who could cover the district, a "hands-on" man of strong conviction.

It was only through a monthly correspondence from the town clerk who happened to be Mr. Shirley, Elwin's dad, who ran the Post and the general store that informed his office with updates. The regular monthly report depicted a summary of important goings on, such as business disputes, accidents, debt disputes, and any resolutions of the like. The last monthly report was only one paragraph, with a vague mention of Burke's disappearance. "Presumably left town" was the last notation. Not much information accounted for the growth the town had seen in the last few years.

"Yup," he said to himself as he rode into town, and surveyed the bustle of a growing community, "time to interview some potential deputies."

The simple dinner Mrs. Shirley had prepared set well with him, as did the light conversation with the Shirleys. He retired, nestled into the bunk in the ten-by ten-foot room for board, and turned down the lamp. He had made an appointment at dinner to discuss his investigation with Mr. Shirley for eight o'clock in the morning over coffee and to get his input as to who could be good candidates for constable.

Sheriff Trunske had a deep respect for Mr. Shirley and his wife performing the duties of town clerk and postmaster along with operating the only store the town had known. Knowing the character of almost all the residents, he was sure Shirley's candidates would be of staunch mind and stature for the position. "That itself," he said to himself, "should be the first order of business at the meeting in the morning."

Then he would move to the Burke business. "I shall retrieve Shirley's take on the matter first and the names of folks he was closest associated with."

That would be the sequence of the morning meeting. *Maybe I can put this business to bed by tomorrow afternoon*, he thought. It was his last conscious thought as the soft bunk sucked his large frame into its clutch.

The Shirleys were normally up and about quite early to prep the store for the day. Restoking the large pot belly stove was first on the agenda on a cool morn, then sorting the mail, placing it in its proper slots and canvas bags for distribution.

The Missus would prepare a simple breakfast of sourdough biscuits, eggs, and coffee for the boarded tenants. For themselves and Elwin, she would add a side of bacon, venison or sausage depending on her stock.

The rest of the day would consist of restocking shelves and waiting on customers and placing the mail orders with Sears Roebuck or Montgomery Ward for the clients. That morning they both were eager to meet with Sheriff Trunske, curious as to what would bring him all this distance.

They both pondered the question just before retiring the night before, and at the dinner table that evening discussions were kept to pleasantries and personal welfare and generalities, as was the custom.

Elwin, a little late getting up, smelled the breakfast, threw on his pants and plaid shirt, and ran to the privy barefoot, feeling the cool ground on his feet to wake himself up. Then he hit the washbowl and went out to the store were the aromas were coming from.

His dad gave him the "look" because he had had to stoke the stove himself, a chore that was always Elwin's responsibility.

"You know son, early birds always get the worms," he said as Elwin sat at their separate table. "Here's your list of chores for this morning before you run off for the day," he said, and handed him a list of five restock chores all out in the back barn area, including placing the wheelbarrows and shovel items at the store front for display.

Instead of shoveling his food down and barely tasting it as he normally would, Elwin sat and ate very slowly, hoping to get in on the meeting with the sheriff.

It didn't go unnoticed, and finally mother said, "You know, father, maybe it's time for El to start learning more about the bookkeeping and management."

Pop now gave mother the "look," staring at her over the spectacles pushed down low on his nose. Then, rolling his eyes, he said, 'Well, I suppose—if the sheriff don't mind him at the meeting—but it's right to the chores afterwards!"

Elwin smiled and ate a little faster in his excitement. "I'll set the displays out now and do the cleanup inside first before he comes in," he said, wiping his chin with his sleeve in the process.

"Slow down and chew your food," Mother told him. "The first thing you will do is brush your teeth with baking powder, young man, and put on a better shirt!" It was his favorite plaid wool shirt, so favorite that the holes in the elbows were worn through to put your fist in and frays were hanging at least two or three inches. It kept him warm in the mornings and evenings; when it warmed up at mid-day, he would roll the sleeves up.

Being a part of the high business affairs in the store was intriguing; it made Elwin feel a little important with the family business that would soon be his.

Adrian Trunske could smell the biscuits right off the feather pillow. He hoped he had not overslept. The arduous ride from Middlebury had taken its toll on his large frame, and he felt he could sleep for the rest of the day.

"Top of the morning," he pronounced as he entered the store, closing the door behind him so as not to let the heat out. "I do believe there's a much larger version of your son Elwin, just outside working the hardware display?"

Mrs. Shirley smiled, "Yes. Has it been that long since your last visit, sheriff?"

"Well, maybe some of this coffee will jog my memory!"

"Help yourself to the biscuits, they're hot out of the oven, and there's some melted butter and hot oatmeal in the pot on the stove. I'll get Elwin Senior; he's just in the back room.

"Oh, sheriff," she added, stopping and turning, still smiling, "Would it be all right if young Elwin sits in at the meeting? We would like to begin to let him experience other workings of the business and the community."

With the ladle in one hand and the wooden bowl in the other, he looked up and pondered the question, then cocked his head a little, "I suppose that would be just fine."

As they all settled at the longer thick oak table, Sheriff Trunske, still munching one of the biscuits, thanked them all for meeting with him at short notice and providing a fine breakfast and bed over last night. "Boy, that mattress was entirely a pleasure after that day's ride! Oh, and thanks much for graining and watering my horse, Elwin!" It was a way of acknowledging Elwin's status at the table.

"I suppose we should get to it. It seems we should be looking to appoint a qualified person here in Granville to serve as a constable who would be deputized through my office.

"I would like to interview some three or four candidates who would bear staunch bipartisan qualities with genuine common sense for fairness.

"We look for men of sound character, moral integrity and physical capability. His territory would be all of Granville and northern parts of Hancock until we can set up a constable in their town as well.

"I will be honestly appreciative if you could provide a list of your personal suggested candidates. I do believe your selection would be of the best references, Mr. Shirley." His eyes met Elwin's dad's and then moved to his mom's and then his, indicating that this selection process was to be by agreement of the three of them.

"I will be in town for the rest of the day today to try to conclude some other matters, then more than likely another overnight here, if that room can be reserved for these weary bones!" he said, smiling, looking forward to Mrs. Shirley's home cooking at supper again.

She knew what he meant because he was staring directly at her when he said it.

"So, if it's not too much to ask, maybe your candidates list can be submitted before I leave in the morning."

Mr. Shirley pushed his specs back up higher on his nose after making his notes and gave the sheriff a nod of acknowledgment.

"The position will be part time for the start" said the sheriff, "and paid monthly from our main office until we can set the funding up directly from the state.

"I would like to leave it up to you through mail or personal direct to contact your candidates for their agreement letter. I can interview them here at my next visit to town, possibly within sixty days."

That was very acceptable by Mr. and Mrs. Shirley. Elwin's dad made some notes on his pad for all that info, while his Mom refreshed the coffee cups and hot water for her tea.

After some more pleasantries were exchanged, Elwin spoke up first. "Sir, what are the other matters of law that you have to tend to in town today?"

Sheriff Trunske looked directly at him, then he spoke to Mom and Pop. "This young man does not miss any details, does he! Thanks for asking, Mr. Elwin. It's a good question and one with which I may need your personal help." He now had the whole family's attention.

"It seems there is a missing person here in Granville. I received some correspondence a few weeks ago from a relative of a Mr. Frank Burke, who believes some hearsay that Mr. Burke did not just move out of town or go missing hunting in the woods. So, because of the request letter I am in Granville to clarify and gather more information from folks who knew him, his demeanor, and character. I can then determine whether to start an investigation or verify some closure on the case."

Mrs. Shirley's body language was noticed by the sheriff and Elwin, as she thought of the rumors that the ladies of the town were circulating about Burke and Mrs. Ford—rumors she would never voice, and certainly not something of which Mr. Shirley, being a staunch businessman, was even aware. Elwin, however, had a concern at that moment because he knew Mr. Burke from working at Ford's farm, and he had heard the same rumors through the wives' tales and his good friend Carl.

Most folks in town knew Mrs. Ford had departed with little or no explanation. But Elwin's mind was racing with the excitement of being part of the lawman's work and all.

He decided he would relay some of that to Sheriff Trunske later.

Elwin just about jumped up from the table, then sat back down, remembering that the meeting was not quite over.

"Sir, I can go get the horses saddled if you don't need me here anymore."

"That will be fine, son," said the sheriff. "But I'll need just few more minutes to conclude this meeting, so sit tight. Now have you had any responses from the notices and postings about Frank Burke?"

Mr. Shirley responded in his businesslike manner, "Well, Adrian, nothing concrete, other than the first reports that he went up hunting into Bear Wallow, which is an area northwest of Ford's farm where he worked as the ranch foreman. He was supposed to have gone up in there alone, not something a seasoned hunter would normally do by anyone's opinion.

"No one has made any other offerings here since the notices have been posted to the contrary. Now I'm just a clerk, and not much of a woodsman, like my son here. The real woodsmen that come through say a man can get lost in there easily, so I'm told, and men have in past years."

"Most folks of the 'got lost' stories seemed to occur up over the Braintree Mountain ridge on the eastern side here," he said, pointing behind him, "east of North Hollow trail and Puddle Dock trail; that's why they call that area Lost

122

Nation. They say even a compass will not work up there. Compasses just spin around, and men's tales speak of sudden confusion, disorientation, and light headedness. Some folks have reported similar effects up in Bear Wallow. I know it's all folklore, but that's what I'm hearing over coffee around the wood-stove."

"You should know also that a fella was up there hunting some years ago, one of the Frenchmen, who slipped and broke his leg, was unable to get out or find shelter from a snowstorm. They found his scattered remains the following spring, flesh eaten off by some carnivore. He was identified by his rifle and his possibles bag. His people reported that he had frozen to death first. But there were big cat tracks all about."

"How much stock do you put in these stories?" the sheriff asked.

"Well, Adrian, I've heard these tales from quite a few sources over the years, and to tell the truth, with conviction from the teller I'd put stock in it. One of these days I'd like to join in on a hunting camp and get up there to see for myself—if mother here can watch the store for a few days!"

Rising from the table, the sheriff looked at Elwin. "I could use your help today in interviewing folks that Burke last worked with or associated with."

Mr. Shirley rose up from the table to stretch his legs and mentioned that Elwin could and should be the one to work with the sheriff by taking him up to West Hill and introducing him to some of those folks. "That's if the displays are all set out front," he added. Elwin's dad thought it would be a good experience for his son to learn about law and investigative work.

"Adrian, that's if Elwin can be of assistance to you for that job. He did know Mr. Burke some when he worked at Ford's farm. I got nothing else for him here; maybe he can gain some experience with you today in your field of expertise."

"Yes, sir, and I know all the shortcuts too!," Edwin said, not wanting to sound too enthusiastic. Adrian Trunske knew he had the right direction now for this investigation, which in his mind had already begun. As he rose from the table, concluding the meeting, he sensed there was much more to this Burke story.

"We should start at the Ford farm as soon as possible, young Mr. Elwin!"

Father had written on his note pad three names—E. J. Briggs, J. E. Blair, and L. K. Webb. He handed the list to his wife for approval for first constable candidates. As the sheriff and Elwin headed out the door, she looked at the list, nodded with approval, then took the pencil and added E. R. Hermenway. Then she circled one name—it was her own first choice of the four.

One of the first stops on the way up West Hill was the Farr Farm just off Patterson Brook Trail. Sheriff Trunske wanted to interview some local businessmen who might have had interactions with Burke. The Farrs were well noted for their large turkey operation, selling poults, eggs, feathers, and plump birds for the broil.

After a brief interview the sheriff was satisfied with the vague amount of information, being only general hearsay from the two Farr brothers that Elwin knew from school and their father. Adrian Trunske and Elwin headed out on a cross trail head that would take them to Ford's place without doubling back.

Along that trail was the Hubbard farmstead. As they passed by the entrance the sheriff asked, "Whose place is this?"

"Oh, that's the Hubbards' place. My friend Carl, who works for old man Ford, is really sweet on Mamie Hubbard, and I don't blame him for it at all!"

The sheriff smiled, knowing he meant that she was pretty.

"Can you tell me a little more about your own experience with helping out at the Ford farm and your friends?"

"Do you mean 'bout Mr. Ford or Mr. Burke?"

"Well, I suppose a little of both, and in your own words what you think your friends thought of them, too."

After a short dialogue on that subject there on the trailside, Adrian Trunske reined his horse around and said, "Let's go see if the Hubbards are about today!" His sixth sense was to talk to young Miss Mamie. Young folks had innocence with revealing truths with words and body language that one could depend on.

They went through the bar way on up to the Hubbard's barnyard. Mr. and Mrs. Hubbard were tending the chickens and greeted them with a smile, recognizing Elwin right off.

Short as it was, the interview with the Hubbards revealed no additional hard facts about Burke's disappearance, except that Mrs. Hubbard's expression was similar to Mrs. Shirley's when they approached the topic of Mrs. Ford and Burke and how often Mr. Ford was out in the wood lots. It was no secret that Mrs. Ford had left town and had not yet returned.

With this slight information and the ladies' reactions, Adrian Trunske's keen mind began to formulate a familiar scenario that could lead to a reason for Burke to leave town or be in a conflict.

As they departed out of the bar way, Elwin said, "Just up the trail here a ways is Ford's. Unless you want to go farther up towards Texas Falls trail, we could talk to some of the other farm folks first, or we can go up to the timber lot and talk to some of the Frenchmen."

The sheriff asked Elwin if he thought Mr. Ford would be at the ranch today.

"Hard to say, sheriff. It's on the way just up here a short stretch. We could stop there first, and you might catch Rob Ford there unannounced."

"I agree wholeheartedly with that logic, Mr. Shirley."

Sheriff Trunske thought to himself that Elwin would make a fine candidate for the constable position if he were just a little older and seasoned. They reined the horses into the Ford Farm bar way. The air seemed slightly heavier as they approached the barnyard, even if it was an unconscious sensation.

The large cabin home came into view perched just up on a knoll. The five-foot girth of the 100-year-old sugar maples lining both sides of the trail way indicated a certain style and affluence.

The heavy horseshoe knocker echoed through the thick oak door of the house. It hung upside down to catch the luck.

It knocked plenty loud for anyone inside to hear, or even anyone at the barn-yard, for that matter.

After a long-enough wait and one more rhythm of knocks the sheriff stepped back off the porch. He glanced up to the chimney to verify the lack of smoke he noticed as they rode in.

Elwin stayed mounted on his horse waiting for the response at the door and to be invited in. It was then that they heard an axe on wood out behind the large barn. They rode around the barn. Ten feet from his back, Elwin's horse exhaled loudly, revealing their presence. Startled, the Frenchman whirled.

30   On Wounded Knee

As Sadie trotted past Ford's trail head, Carl glanced up at the entrance and got that inner pit knot in his gut again, sensing something amiss. He had no way of knowing that Elwin and the sheriff were there at that moment interviewing the French farm helpers hired by Mr. Ford. But he knew something wasn't right.

Carl dismissed the feeling, resolved to get to Mamie's to reveal his affection for her and ask her dad for her hand. If all went well he would do his chores at Ford's later, on the way back or just come down in the morning to catch up.

He needed to secure his new position at Ford's anyway as lead farm boss, the foreman position offered to him. He felt he was ready now, with Mom and Pop buried, and he could start his life fresh over with Mamie by his side.

He wanted to get started on his new responsibilities and commitments. For the first time in over three months, he felt excited about his dreams, being in love, and the prospect of building a family.

Inheriting the homestead and the money he had stashed away flashed through his mind. His horses and livestock along with the foreman position gave him a status equal to any man twice his age. All of that would make a good dowry for Mamie's family to consider.

Feeling his self-esteem return for the first time in many weeks, he thought, *It's the right time for me to make this step.*

He pictured Mamie tearing up with joy, and her Pop shaking his hand and the warm embrace of her Mom welcoming him into their family.

They would be his family now. He would take care of them all as they got older, and he would teach his son how to hunt and fish and care for animals and respect the forest and nature's ways.

He would not scold or act cold toward his children like his dad did; he would teach them about the ways of the world and the *trai-teurs* in them and not to fear it if they had the gift. They would be respected in the community and have prosperity and he would acquire more land to farm for his family estate.

As much as he found Rob Ford distasteful, he admired and hoped to mirror Ford's entrepreneurial nature.

At Mamie's bar way entrance, Carl brought Sadie to a halt, dismounted, and walked out in front of her staring up the narrow trailhead to the farmstead. He then turned, faced Sadie, and caressed her muzzle as she pushed her nose into his arm and chest a little.

"Well, Sadie, old girl, I guess this is it. I 'spose the worst that can happen is she can say no, or her Pop will make us wait." At that he took a deep breath, felt and squeezed the ring dangling from his neck, looked at Sadie, kissed her nose, and climbed back into the saddle. Sadie didn't need any nudging to proceed; she knew where they were going, and Carl felt that Sadie knew why they were going there today.

The Hubbards were all inside when Carl knocked on the door; they were surprised and delighted to see him finally out and about. After some pleasantries, Mrs. Hubbard mentioned how today seemed to be full of surprise visitors. "Why just a spell ago Elwin Shirley and a Sheriff Trunske from Middlebury just left. Did you encounter them on your way down here?"

"No, ma'am, I did not," he said, as the pit in his belly started up again.

"Oh, they must have been at Ford's farm when you passed through. They said they were going to stop there."

Some insights just flashed into Carl's mind at that moment as to why he felt his pang in his belly at Ford's entrance and now here. The mention of the sheriff could only mean one thing. Carl broke into a bit of a cold sweat. His nervous tension was noticeable but not in the way that he thought. Mame's Mom and Pop just put it off to his recent let-downs and the grieving time he had endured.

They invited him in for some soup and tea. "So, what brings you by on this fine day?" her father asked with a half-smile. Mamie's eyes met his for a moment and calmed him, during the long pause.

"Well, sir, I was hoping to talk with you privately." He stammered a bit trying to ignore his previous thoughts about the sheriff and the knots in his belly. "It's about some man-to-man questions I have, sir."

Mr. Hubbard looked at his wife, then back at Carl, and rose from his chair.

Slightly smiling with a bit of question on his face, he said "Well, all right, then, I'll just get some tobacco in the pipe and we can go out and fetch some water at the spring. Will that do you?"

He thought that the boy just needed a little fatherly advice about running the farm and all the new responsibilities he now faced. After all, they did tell him he could come to them if he needed anything. He felt flattered that Carl chose him as a peer.

Carl looked lovingly at Mamie and managed a smile. "I guess we will be right back in shortly," he murmured. "Take you up on that soup and tea when we get back, ma'am?"

"Of course, Carl. Maybe we girls will put a few honey cakes in the oven while you fellows are out back," she said, smiling at him and then at Mamie.

Carl backed his way out through the door so darned nervous, he actually took his hat off again, held it to his chest and stammered again, "That will be just fa—fine," then he could not believe it either even as he did it, but he half-bowed going backwards halfway out the doorway and stumbling onto the porch. He murmured to himself, "Oh, you damn fool, get a grip on yourself now!"

Wiping the sweat from his brow, he stood and looked up at the sky and stared at the only lenticular cloud in the blue background and remembered why he was here. Centering himself, he rehearsed how he would ask Mr. Hubbard for Mamie's hand.

After running a few scenarios through his head, he finally settled on describing his estate inheritance and his assets first, then telling him how he is in love with his daughter, and that he thought he could provide her a good life here in Granville.

The rest would be up to Mamie's acceptance, if her Pop gave him his blessing and permission. Looking at Sadie, he said, "I hope this all comes out right."

Mr. Hubbard emerged through the doorway pulling his suspenders over his shoulder. "Well, now son, let's go up to the spring. We should walk and talk, you think? You sure seem a little dispatched, and I know you been through some rough changes lately. So let's start off by letting me tell you to relax a little. There's nothing in life that time can't patch up."

Mr. Hubbard was trying to act as just a friend, even though he had a few years on Carl. He tried to think of areas where they shared a few things in common.

He thought it would be best if they sat on the old stone bench next to the spring for a spell.

"So, what's on your mind today, Mr. Morse?" He cleaned and packed his pipe with tobacco, offering some to Carl for his cheek. Carl waved his hand in decline, and stared at the ground water bubbling from the spring.

"Well, sir, I mean Mr. Hubbard, sir," he stammered as he stood up from the bench. "I have been through a pile of changes, that's true, and I just came to realize these last few days while I was home collecting myself that now with being the sole proprietor of our farm and the stock and the paid job and all—" he paused a bit. "Well, I just got bent set to thinking about my future. What I mean to say, sir, is that I can manage all the chores well enough, but I think I could use some guidance in a few matters."

Mr. Hubbard was somewhat flattered, as he puffed his pipe and started to respond by asking, "Do you need some help with the paperwork and such? I think it's just a matter of filing a letter with the town clerk to file a change of the deed and a couple of things of the like that we can help you with. I am certain Mr. Shirley will walk you through that down at the store.

"Any will and testaments that your dad and Mom may have had should be presented, but if they don't have any paper of that sort, it shouldn't be a problem if you have someone to vouch, like me and the Missus."

Carl was surprised at his assumption, as that topic was least on his mind, so he thanked him for the info and the offer and began to pace a little, trying to get his mind back on track.

"Mr. Hubbard, sir, I came to talk to you this day about another matter."

Mr. Hubbard sat upright on the bench and felt a little the fool for rambling on so much on his assumptions.

At that moment, Carl flashed in his mind's eye the catamount staring deep into his soul; it helped him summon his courage, so he centered himself and dismissed all fear that caused his nervous stammering.

When he noticed he now had Pete Hubbard's full attention, he took a deep breath and spoke very slowly and clearly, looking him right in the eye.

"Mr. Hubbard, I am here today to ask you directly and man-to-man for Mamie's hand, sir. I believe I can provide her a good home and living with all of my assets and adequate money saved." He pulled the ring from his pocket and held it out to show his serious intent. "With your blessing and permission, sir, I would like to ask her later today, when the time is just right."

Mr. Hubbard was stunned. He did not see this coming. He slumped back onto the stone bench a bit, then stood up, stretching his suspenders some as his way of fidgeting.

Now it was Mamie's Pop who was stammering. Caught by surprise, he could only say, "Oh, Lordy. I apologize to you, Carl. I thought you were needing some advice with your home matters. Give me a moment here to collect myself, son." He sat back down on the bench and pondered the question some more.

After a long awkward moment he stood up and asked Carl to sit in his place. He looked at the boy and suddenly saw a man, saw him as his equal. Carl obliged him by sitting quietly and waiting for the response. For a long while the bubbling spring water trickling out over the sill was the only sound.

Mr. Hubbard finally spoke. "You know my Mamie is quite young; she's still my little girl. I've seen you two having affections for each other, and honestly a while ago I wanted to have you slow all that down some, but her mother told me to butt out and let the women handle their affairs. In the same breath I noticed that you have become quite the responsible young man lately, Carl, and I have grown to like you—I will give you that.

"Her Mom and I have had different plans for Mamie, hoping that she would choose to go Rutland for continued schooling. I'd like to see her get out of Granville to experience a little of the outside world before she settles down. With that said, even her goin' off scares the bejesus out me, too! What with her being way out of town growing into a woman out there somewhere, I mean to say, what if she needed us for guidance or help?

"Now I can't think of a better person for her to do that with—settle down, I mean," he said, looking straight at Carl and then extending his hand to him.

"Who am I to stand in the way of love? But from my say in it, I'd like you both to take this slow and easy. I mean, don't rush right into it, son. Make sure it's what you both want after the puppy love wears off.

"Trust me on this, 'cause it's a big responsibility that you can't take back or discard." Then he thought that he was getting too controlling, so he quickly stammered out, "What I'm trying to say is, just go slow." After a long pause, with the bubbling spring again as the only sound, he continued.

"If you promise to me that you will extend the engagement for say, six months or so or even a year after, and if she accepts your proposal, I would be happy to give you my blessing."

It was the longest handshake Carl ever experienced, and then it evolved into a man hug. They both felt a sense of relief and stood back from each other, neither knowing what to say next.

Mr. Hubbard broke the silent moment. "Maybe we should fill these two pails and head back to the kitchen. I'm betting the ladies have something sweet waiting for us. You should plan on staying for dinner, son. In fact, I think I will insist!"

Dipping the pails in the spring while on one knee, Carl replied, "Yes, sir. I 'spose I should." Hesitating a little before he handed the pail to him, Carl looked up and said, "Thank you, Mr. Hubbard. It wasn't easy for me to come down to ask you this today. I hope I did it right."

Mr. Hubbard remembered when he proposed to his wife, and how her Pop chased him off the property, forcing them to run off without her parents' blessing. That's how they ended up in Vermont staking out their own land claim. He remembered his own stress and panic over their choice to rush into the huge commitment. Looking back, he wished he'd taken it slower. Mamie had arrived in the world two years later.

"Son, you did it right," he murmured. He looked at Carl and nodded his head. "You did it right."

Supper that evening was cordial with light conversation of how Carl was making out with the new responsibilities and transformation, and the paper-work that he would need to file with the clerk's office as a matter of probate.

Mamie just smiled a lot with that sparkle in her eye, fidgeting some due to the excitement of spending some alone time with Carl out in the barnyard after supper was cleared off. She played some footsies under the table with him during dinner, purposely trying to interrupt the seriousness of the conversation. She had no idea of what Carl had in mind; she only wanted to be alone with him outside, out of sight and earshot of her Mom and Pop.

The ten days of Carl's Mom passing, and his own regrouping from that, caused her to miss him even more. Her puppy love bubbled out her. She was giggling and laughing as they strolled out behind the barn and down toward the bar way. The embraces and kissing ensued just as they were out of view of the house.

The ring in his shirt pocket felt heavy pressing into his chest as her breasts pressed against his, only then remembering it was there. He held her face cupped in his hands, "I missed you these last days, Mame."

She cooed and just looked at him with her starry blue eyes.

"I talked with your dad at the spring." He fumbled for the ring in his shirt pocket, and after an awkward moment pulled it out and put it in her hand. She first thought he was giving her a trinket, a little surprise gift because they had been apart so long. Carl would always give her a little present for fun, picking her a single flower, or a pine cone, as they walked along. One time he just reached down and handed her a single ball of moose dropping, calling it a tasty moose berry!

As she looked at it closer the significance of his gesture finally sunk in. Her mouth dropped open as he began to stutter out some words, "Will you come live with me? Could ya—I—I—mean—Wo—d'ya—then he took her hands in both of his, and taking a deep breath to recompose himself, he clearly sounded the words, "I'm lovin' you a lot, Mame. Will you be my wife forever?"

He felt a huge sense of relief as soon as the words came out. It was if he were outside of himself as he spoke, as if he were a third person standing above himself. It felt perfect. Now he was finally relaxed as he had not been for weeks.

Stunned and trembling, her hand involuntarily shaking, she stepped back from the embrace, her mouth still wide open. It was all she could do to look at the ring now in her hand, she held it out and looked at it, then she looked back at Carl's eyes. Stepping back again one more step, she held the ring to her bosom with both hands, her eyes filled and dripped tears down her cheeks, a half-smile on her lips.

Mamie could not speak, so she smiled again, then starred at the ring for a longer awkward moment. Many thoughts flashed through her mind, some of excitement and some of fear or uncertainty.

As Carl stood there with his head cocked a little and a half smile on his mouth, she gazed up some more then looked at the ground briefly, her eyes bright with tears. The only words she could utter she whispered, "I'm really scared. This is a surprise to me. I do love you! I was not expecting this—I'm just feeling this is very big and scary."

She returned his embrace moving back in closer to him, holding the ring in one hand against her breast and her other reaching up to his face.

"I need to sit with mother. Please, let me talk with mother on this; it's scary for me." Then she leaned in and they kissed and held on tightly for a long time.

Both of their minds raced during the embrace. As fear gave way to emotions of love, Mamie whispered, "I want to do this with you, my love. Please just hold me now. I'm just a little scared." She clutched the ring to her bosom.

31 Deputized

Elwin and the sheriff were heading back down the trail towards the store coming from Ford's farm. When they stopped at the trailhead leading to the Hubbards' place, they both noticed the fresh horse tracks in the soft mud heading in from upland; they were not there two hours before. Elwin said, "Betcha' that's Carl Morse stopping in on Mamie!"

The interview with the French fellow in his broken English at Ford's place could only reveal that two of his comrades were sent back to Quebec after working at Ford's farmyard for a short while. That information piqued the sheriff's interest. Then the name "Burke" came out as a question from the sheriff with his hands gesturing the questioning in limited French to inquire if the man had known Burke.

Elwin could not tell if it was Burke's name being uttered or if it was the sheriff's star just under the lapel of his coat that caused it, but that is when the Frenchman became suddenly silent and unresponsive to trying to continue the limited dialog.

Elwin noticed Adrian Trunske's sharp intuition in talking to the Frenchie. The sheriff's jaw set firm, then with a slight nod of affirmation, he turned and mounted his horse.

Reining his horse to head out of Ford's barnyard, Mr. Trunske spoke to Elwin. "That's enough here for one day. The Frenchmen know more than they let on. Time we headed back to the store,. I think I'll be needin' to speak to your friend Mr. Morse to finalize this visit before I leave. You say his place is up on Texas Gap road?"

"Yes, sir," Elwin replied, "It is. He usually comes down to do paid chores at Ford's about this time of day. Sometimes I come up here and help so we can go huntin' later, but Carl's been stayin' at home lately mournin' over his Mum."

"Fine—then that should work out in our favor," the sheriff commented, squinting his eyes a bit. "I think I'll just visit him on my way back to Middlebury on the morning trail."

"I been meanin' to get up and see him," Elwin continued. "You know, to try to get him movin again, get him back out in the woods and such. Maybe I'll come with you in the morning and then drag his bones out of that cabin after you're done with your talkin', if you don't mind?

"I should've done that sooner 'cause he's been holed up at home for over a week now. Probably needs a friend. And he should get down to see Mamie Hubbard, too! That would do him some good!"

Sheriff Trunske acknowledged the morning plan by looking straight at Elwin and nodding. He wanted to interview Mamie Hubbard again, too.

The fresh horse prints may just provide the chance to speak to the both of them at one final stop if they burn a little more daylight, he thought to himself.

"Let's pay young Miss Mamie Hubbard one more visit before we get to your mother's fine cooking. What say you, Mr. Elwin?" They reined the horses up the Hubbards' trailhead.

The daylight remained noticeably longer now—the afternoon sun was just about ready to give way to the evening moon. It seemed to be resting just above the highest peak in the western skyline.

Lenticular wisps of clouds hovered low just at the mountaintops, with their pink and purple and blue pastels painted over the multiple shades of forest green throughout the mountain ridge.

Brightly illuminated greens stand out brilliantly in on the eastern slopes where the sun casts its last radiance as if to say good evening to the faint moon rising across the valley peaks.

This is what Carl was looking at as he held Miami's embrace, the perfect setting for what he thought was the happiest day of his life. His dreams finally felt like a manifestation to reality. He felt revived, strong, and centered for the first time in months. This day's simple sunset seemed like it was put there just for him and Mamie, just for this occasion. He quietly decided to view each sunset at the end of every day from now on.

"Hey Mame!" He whispered in her ear. "Look at what God has painted in the sky! I think it's a gift just for us."

The silhouette of two men on horseback came up over the rise of the Hubbards' farm trailhead just 100 yards up from the bar way. Both Mamie and Carl turned, startled, as one of the horses snorted mildly; the horses first noticed the two standing there. Then Elwin saw the two of them holding hands.

Feeling proud to be guiding the sheriff all day and helping him with the investigation, Elwin was eager to show off a bit with his friends and happy that they found the two of them together before the end of the day.

"That," he said with a slight hesitation, "would be my friend Mr. Morse and Miss Mamie Hubbard, as I expected, Mr. Trunske."

Carl was startled to see Elwin ride up. As his mouth went agape, the pit of his gut acted up as he focused on the stranger riding alongside Elwin. He couldn't believe the tender moments he had just shared with Mamie were being shattered.

Carl by now had learned to listen to his gut and went immediately on alert. He instinctively put his arm around Mamie and brought her to his side and slightly behind himself, as he intuited something negative was about to occur.

"Hey Carl!" exclaimed Elwin, all proud of himself. "I was thinking you were out and about! We just come from Ford's place; this here is Sheriff Trunske out of Middlebury. I been helping him out with interviewing some folks up here on West Hill. He's looking into what happened to old Burke."

Carl stared in disbelief, totally off guard.

Before he could speak, Adrian Trunske dismounted. "Evening, Mr. Morse. I beg your pardon for the inconvenience." He tipped his hat at Mamie. "Evening again, Miss Mamie. Sorry to intrude on you again. I was hoping to speak to both of you before I conclude my day."

The big man was somewhat intimidating, especially to Carl, for what he represented, and why he came. Carl calmed his emotions as his power animal flashed in his mind's eye. The catamount for some reason kept him centered. Shaking Elwin's hand, he said, "We are now engaged."

The interview took place just behind the Hubbards' barn. Mamie and Carl sat on the old wood bench while the sheriff stood, jotting notes with his pencil and pad.

At first Carl felt lightheaded and his mouth parched. The vision of Burke's body rolling out from the manure shot through his mind. He recalled his words to Ford and giving Burke some last words at his grave site. Soon he was able to calm himself and get better centered. He knew he did the right thing for Burke.

Neither Mamie nor Elwin noticed his discomfort, and as the sheriff did not know him at all, Carl concluded his nervousness was all in his own mind.

Mamie was still innocently smiling from her exciting day. She still clutched his hand and he noticed she had put the ring on her first finger where it fit the best.

After offering congratulations, some man hugs, and then apologies for interrupting their special moment, Elwin was beaming from ear to ear. First, he was glad to see his good friend finally out of his depression with mourning for his Mum. At the same time, he was surprised at the news of their engagement to each other, and last he was just fool proud to be working with the sheriff.

"I understand that you work at Ford's performing barn chores. Young Mr. Shirley here has filled me in some with your background, and I am very sorry for your recent loss."

"Yes, sir, just after schoolin' and every day or so for the past summer, except when my Ma and Pop went to the other side."

Carl then summoned some gumption from down deep, stood up still holding Mamie's hand, and said, "Excuse me, Mr. Trunske, sir, but Mamie and I had just concluded our engagement vows and we were ready to go back up to the house to celebrate with her folks. That was exactly as you rode up on us, sir."

As he spoke the fear lifted completely and he felt himself getting irritated over the intrusion at what he thought to be the most personal day of his life.

The sheriff was caught off his guard. He set his jaw a bit, then after a brief moment looked at Elwin and put his note pad in the upper jacket pocket. "Well, now, it has been a long day for us after all," he said. "My apologies to you two. We shall depart your company for this evening and let you all get back to your joy and celebration."

He added, "I would still request an interview with you. Perhaps tomorrow afternoon on my way back through, after my other rounds? Or on my way back to Middlebury? It seems I'll be passing along Texas Falls trail past your place as Elwin here has described. Do you expect to be there later in the day?"

Insensitivity is not how to win cooperation in this business, thought the sheriff, especially with what Carl Morse had just been through. He could afford to spend the day tomorrow catching up with Mr. Ford, anyway. Spending yet another night at the Shirleys' beat sleeping on the trail, certainly. He could stand some more of Elwin's Mom's cooking and the soft mattress. There was something in Carl that he liked—bold but respectful manners. He could sense why he and Elwin were friends.

Carl could clearly sense the sheriff's aura and demeanor. He knew deep down that he was a fair and righteous man, powerful in stature and nature.

"Yes, sir, I should be back at my own place in the afternoon to tend to my stock, but I'll be staying over here tonight till about mid-morn."

"Fair enough, then. I look forward to our discussion. Again, I beg your pardon for the intrusion."

"Wow!" Elwin exclaimed, "I had no idea you two were planning this out! Now Lola's gonna be pressuring me when she hears this news! Thanks very much!"

They all laughed a little. Elwin and Carl shook hands and man hugged again. As he hugged Mame, Elwin said, "I'll catch you up on everything."

The two rode off down the trail. Darkness was looming in fast. Carl and Mame walked slowly back up toward the cabin. Carl pondered revealing his secret to Mame or Elwin. As they walked hand in hand, Mame said, "Boy, there must be something going on with that Burke fellow."

"Yup, there sure is," said Carl, dismissing the event to get back on track. "But let's go talk with your folks a bit about just us."

She nestled in even closer, and they walked a little slower.

Mother was eagerly looking down the trail for them to appear.

32 Dowries

"Had an interesting talk with Carl, honey bunch! I believe I do like that young man!" Pete said to his wife just after supper as Mrs. Hubbard was cleaning up the dishes.

"Oh, why is that, dear?" she asked.

Pete Hubbard looked out the window, squinting to make sure Mame and Carl were not within hearing distance. The two had just left the house for their evening stroll after graining and watering the stock. Pop saw them walking down toward the bar way through the window. He spun around and came up to his wife from behind at her dry sink. Holding her waist, he kissed her on the neck. "Do you remember when we ran off together and got hitched?"

"Remember the passion and the excitement? And the fear?" she injected. "I was crazy scared to death, but we still did it!" She exclaimed, with a half-smile and her head cocked a little.

"Yup, we did. I thought your Dad was gonna shoot me dead!" he said as he spun her around from the sink. Taking the dish towel from her wet hand he pulled her to a closer embrace. "Well, we turned out not half bad after the adventure of it all, don't you agree?"

"All right, do you want to tell me what you're buttering me up for now?"

"Well, let me get right on down to it then! I think in due time we may have ourselves a new son!" Mother went rigid for a moment; then with both hands she pushed him back from the embrace.

"What exactly do you mean, husband of mine?"

"I mean just that, dearest. Up on the hill at the spring, our very own Carl Morse stood on his hind legs and for about an hour, very convincingly asked me for our Mame's hand!"

Mother lightly slapped his chest with both hands and then clasped her own face on both sides with her mouth dropped open. "And what exactly did you tell the young man? Wait—I'm not sure I want to know! You know she is just too young and innocent!"

Holding her by the shoulders, he said, "Now, Mother! Hold your horses and calm yourself. We know they've both got the grip of puppy fever. Remember when we were like them?"

"Now that young man has some substantial assets behind him; he's got some coin salted, and the livestock—a lot more than some men twice his age! He's a damn hard worker, trying to do and plan it all out proper and right, and nervous about it to boot."

"After our near hour of discussion up at that spring, I feel I know him better now than I did yesterday! So, yes, I gave him my blessing—only under certain conditions, including constraint of time, and the total acceptance by all of us—most important, and especially, our Mame."

Mother set her jaw at her husband, frustrated the she hadn't been able to get her input in before the men did up at the spring. At the same time, she was excited about the affair in its entirety. Now it was her turn to inject her motherly views and advice on Carl and have a long women's talk with Mamie.

Eager to do so, she pulled the curtain aside from the window, peering out into the twilight dusk to see if the young couple was on the way in.

"Oh, husband of mine, I do hope those two have not conjured up a plan to go runnin' off to Timbuktu!" She peered out the curtains again. Turning back to her husband, she hugged on to him. "Tell me they won't do that, please."

"Now, woman, you must have some faith in those two. If they were planning that, then why would he go through all the trouble to talk it out with me with all that man's business? Besides, the only place they would run off to would be his own Timbuktu just uphill from here!" He smiled as he pointed in the direction of Carl's cabin.

"Oh, you're right. I'm just nervous about it all, dear, just not sure if he's right for our Mame. I mean, she's just too young yet for matrimony. Look at us. I was too young, and we ran off and it scared me wondering how we were going to manage. My Daddy was right trying to stop us, and it wasn't easy, God knows!"

She peered out the curtain again, "Well, honey bunch, we sure didn't have it easy, and we sure didn't have Mum and Pop livin' just up or down the trail to help out or to show us the way into raisin' a family. But they do!"

The latch on the door slid up, and holding hands, the young couple stepped inside. No one said a word for a long awkward moment. They all just stood there—the older couple still in their embrace, and the younger, arm in arm.

33 Morning Plans

The oil lamp flickered at the long trestle table. Sheriff Trunske finished the last few bites of chicken pot pie, sopping up the gravy residue with a thick slice of sourdough bread. "That was delightfully delicious, my dear Mrs. Shirley! I am certainly not looking forward to leaving your hospitality tomorrow!"

Elwin's mother smiled at the sheriff as she cleared away the tin eatery ware, satisfied that the meal was well received. She did not know they would be having any guests again this night. Had she known she would have used the better china.

Elwin and the sheriff returned just after sunset. Supper conversation was limited to the interview plans for the next day with Mr. Ford and Carl Morse, only after Mr. Shirley had asked how their day had gone.

Elwin managed to spill the news of Carl and Miami's engagement as well, which raised an eyebrow with his Mom. "I should think that Miss Mame is slightly young for her folks' approval!"

"Well, Mum," Elwin said, "I suppose something been talked out, 'cause they had a ring and everything at Hubbard's Farm."

The sheriff lit his pipe and unstrapped his suspenders from his shoulders.

"Have you been able to come to a conclusion with the Burke affair today?" asked Mr. Shirley, lighting his own pipe.

"Well, let's just say, I should be getting some stronger answers by mid-day tomorrow, once I set down with Mr. Ford and one or two younger folks who may help shed some light about Mr. Burke. I will say that I don't think he has left town voluntarily or perhaps even at all.

"I will share with you my hypothesis—Mr. Burke is truly a missing person. I say that because no one with a good paid position in these times would just up and vacate without some notification. I believe he may have fallen to some form of ill fate or... an accident, of his own demise.

"With that said," he continued, "by most accounts today I surmise he was not well liked." The sheriff rubbed his chin with one hand while holding his pipe with the other, as if he were thinking out loud to himself.

Elwin was surprised at that assumption. He then remembered some of the subtle reactions of certain folk's interviews. Elwin was now thoroughly intrigued with this work.

"Lookin forward to takin' you up through Texas Gap Road tomorrow, Mr. Trunske. I'm pretty sure I know where Ford's active timber lot is if he's not back at the ranch."

The French worker community was already buzzing about the sheriff's appearance at Ford's yesterday afternoon. Word could spread fast in this small valley and hills, and it already had been received by Mr. Ford himself. It seems his loyal French foreman who interacted on his behalf and was compensated well for his liaisons with all the French workers had briefed him of the sheriff's inquiries.

Ford decided to cut short his stay at the timber camp and return back to the farm, tend to the animals and to take care of any business that would no doubt be presented by the lawman. He departed the log camp just at sunup.

Meanwhile, the morning chores at Hubbards' were tended by Mr. Hubbard and Carl. Breakfast was prepared by the ladies. Carl's bones ached from the hard floor on which he attempted to sleep in front of their hearth.

The evening conversation was fitted with Mother's elation of their engagement and advice from a woman's point of view. A long engagement, or more like a trial period, was the focus on which the men had no choice but to agree.

Finally, after Mother was caught repeating herself a few times, Mr. Hubbard spoke up, tamping the spent tobacco from his pipe, "It's been a long day, dear, mornin' will be upon us soon enough. I suggest we all get some sleep! I bid you all good night." And with that, he put out some blankets for Carl and closed the door to his small bunk room just off the kitchen.

Mother tried to think of something to add to her spiel but remained quiet. With a simple smile, she bid good night and followed her husband into the room. Her last words as she turned in the doorway were, "Oh, Carl, the hearth floor stone should keep you warm tonight—and Mame, you should say good night now and head to your loft."

Mother was worried that they might attempt to sleep together, something that she could not condone. She felt the need to make her subtle point, if only to get her last word in.

Carl and Mame sat whispering for another half hour kissed and hugged as quietly as possible. Then Mame climbed up to her loft bunk. Sleep eluded everyone except Mr. Hubbard.

Morning comes as early as the rooster crows for most folks, and the crisp spring air on the way to the privy is enough to get anyone's blood moving. A view of the valley usually shows the wood smoke pillars from the restoking of the cook stoves coming up through the treetop canopy marking where the cabins are. This morning was of a clear blue sky with just a few wisps of morning condensation hanging low in the dells of the mountainsides.

Mamie rubbed her eyes as she emerged from the loft clad in her ankle long night gown. Carl and her Pop had just headed out to fetch firewood and some eggs from the coop, giving the women some time to gather themselves. Mother began to prep some breakfast of potatoes, salt pork, and the eggs. Mamie brewed up some tea on the stove top in their cast iron pot.

After breakfast, Carl bid the senior Hubbards a good day and proceeded out with Mamie to grain and water the livestock and turn the horses out to the pasture, making some plans with her for their next rendezvous, this time at his place. After a long embrace out of sight of Mother and Father, he departed back to his own cabin to tend to his stock. Mamie, after milking the cow, headed in to sit with her mother for the long talk that was brewing in Mom like that pot of tea.

Adrian Trunske awoke again to the smell of biscuits and hot coffee brewing. His large bones ached back into motion from his deep sleep on that comfortable bunk, his frame remembered the long day of riding the day before.

Elwin had already accomplished the morning main staple chores, anticipating another day in the field with the sheriff.

After some brief discussion at the breakfast table, Mr. Shirley submitted his list of constable candidates, which would be refined to one after the interviews.

Elwin now wanted to be a candidate. This he verbalized at the table, finding the job to be interesting after being part of the discussions and the interviews yesterday.

Appreciating his enthusiasm, the sheriff agreed that "in a few years and a few more miles of living" he could apply for the position. It was a nice way of saying he was still a little too young.

The plan for the day was to head up to find Mr. Ford at either the log camp or the farm, and then to Carl Morse on his way back through to Ripton for the night. He would then trek back to his base office in Middlebury.

All of the other business with the clerk of Granville, Mr. Shirley, would be done through correspondence.

"And yes, young Mr. Elwin, you may accompany me for the interviews up to Mr. Morse's—but only if your folks here can spare you two days in a row. I could ask him to guide me to that timber lot after all."

Elwin's folks nodded with approval.

After saddling the horses and packing a lunch bag that he strapped over the saddle horn, the sheriff bid the senior Shirleys farewell. They headed back up the West Hill trail. Elwin felt very important to be part of this work, and he also wanted to reconnect with his friend Carl. He had some catching up to do with him anyway, and even Elwin recognized that he should be there in case his timid friend got intimidated by the sheriff's inquiries. He knew how Carl could get distracted sometimes.

He wondered if Carl knew any more about Burke's disappearance from working at Ford's more than he did. The sheriff's observations the night before concerned him, especially because he was pressing the interviews with Carl and Mamie separately.

"Mr. Trunske sir?" Elwin asked as they rounded the first bend in the trail, "What makes you think Mr. Burke is still here in town? I mean to say from the interviews so far, that is?"

"Well, Elwin, call it a hunch or a gut feeling, but when you do this work, you have to look at the body language of the people you are talking to. Body language can reveal a whole different truth other from what some people verbalize. Then you also have to follow your instinct. Most times your first gut feeling turns out to be the right one in the end. It comes to you in this business over time and experience. Call it an art if you will, but that's why we need to choose our deputy candidates with care.

"Now all of those ladies," he continued, "seemed to look at the ground or at the sky and some of them set their jaws as if they knew of some hearsay or gossip that should not be repeated. Women do gossip you know! In confidence they will love to repeat the hearsay. It's most folks' favorite pastime in any town.

"Now why do you think Mrs. Ford has left town at the exact time Burke went missing? Also that Frenchman at Ford's yesterday—well, let's just say I think he understood more English than he let on. If he was working there or others from his camp were for a while under Burke's supervision, well, he just appeared to be evasive and even a little fearful of my badge. I ask myself why he would be intimidated. It's the body language, very revealing!"

Elwin was just plain awestruck, "So it takes a special breed of man to do this work?"

"Oh, yeah, Elwin, but also a fair-minded and physically strong, staunch personality, who can sense trouble a-brewin' and nip it in the bud, especially with domestic disputes and petty arguments. I guess, son, if you can cultivate those particular traits and remain bipartisan, in a couple years you could make a good candidate for a deputy position." Trunske was now looking at Elwin with one eyebrow up a little and a slight squint in his eye. He was definitely sizing Elwin up some, checking his reaction.

They pulled into Ford's first timber lot after a quarter-mile of side trail. Most of the Frenchmen, still a skeleton crew, were milling about the makeshift cabin. One sledge was loaded with hardwood logs, and three men with wool beanie caps and heavy wool sweaters were hitching a two-horse draft team preparing the haul down to the Puddle Dock staging area next door to the general store.

The only English-speaking foreman waved them over, "Ailo, frien', how I can help you all?" He was the same Frenchman who informed Mr. Ford of the sheriff's visit at the farmstead yesterday.

Sheriff Trunske made sure his badge on the lapel of his canvas coat was visible, "good day to you sir! We are lookin ta speak with Mr. Ford, understanding that he was here at this log camp?"

"Ahh, yeah, Mr. Boss no here now, he go back up trail to beige house. He leaves at first light these morns."

Adrian Trunske and Elwin headed up trail out of the timber lot just as the last cloud of morning mist burned off.

34 Women Folk

The hot tea and honey tasted good as Mamie and her Mom sat at the small table out on the porch.

Not that he needed to, but Pop figured it be best he if headed down to Farr's farm to barter some turkey eggs, or so he said when he shouted his intentions from the barn, wanting to leave the ladies to their business. He knew full well there was no stopping his wife on trying to control this event, anyway.

It was quite the long heartfelt and enlightening conversation, one of the first that Mamie had ever experienced. An hour and a half of her mother's views on the topic of being a woman and rearing children and then the complications and responsibilities. It very much melted away some of the enchantment of her fairyland perspective of her girlish views and dreams of things, especially romance.

They both encountered deep emotions during their chat, anxiety at first, in just approaching the whole topic. That gave way to some laughter about men in general and their simplicity.

Then the joys of motherhood along with the fears of child rearing starting at the complications of giving birth, then there was the crying and holding each other out of the life changes involved in marriage and love. Mother cried just from the fear of losing her baby girl.

Mamie was now just a little more confused with her decisions, forgetting that she had time on her side, and she did not have to rush into leaving her girlhood.

In the same breath she still missed Carl's embraces and could not wait to spend some alone time with him up at his cabin. She imagined staying there overnight to explore or pretend to be married.

After talking with her Mom, she contemplated it all deeply as she went to the barnyard to be alone and with her own thoughts. She began to think of an excuse that could allow her to stay with Carl for a few days without her Mom's interference.

It wasn't that her Mom's views were not common sense; it was more the presentation that caused Mamie to want to rebel. The excitement of their secret rendezvous could now go to another level. Mamie Hubbard always had a sassy nature; this day it brought out the rebel in her even more.

35 Quiet Days

Carl made a beeline for home as soon as he left the Hubbards. His priority was to tend to his livestock, and then to catch a mid-morning nap in the comfort of his own familiar bunk.

It was such a nice day he almost felt a little guilty about stealing a snooze in broad daylight, but that hard floor and the thought of Mamie under the same roof just a few feet from him was enough to cause any red-blooded American boy some stress. Mame's Mum and Pop being in the next room with the paper-thin partition was awkward enough, not to mention the circumstances of the whole evening.

It was the first time that he had slept in another family's home. Not to say that he had not camped out under the stars on hunting trips or even nodded off in the solitude of the woods occasionally. He realized this day that he enjoyed his solitude.

Then the sheriff showing up at that exact moment! He exclaimed aloud to himself, "Holy crap! Just when I let my guard down to feel something profoundly deep and good! They show up out of the blue! Jeeze! What did I do to deserve that?"

He laughed out loud a little. "Damn! Every time something good comes my way it gets immediately canceled out by something negative. What the hell is that?"

Ahh, maybe I'm just tired,"he thought. *Maybe I should just tell somebody about Ford and Burke and let it play out as it is meant to be. The only thing I did wrong maybe was vowing silence to old man Ford and taking that deal he pushed on me.*

A lot of things weighed on Carl's mind. As Sadie plodded along, he felt his head getting heavy from lack of sleep, and his eyes closed a few times; then the sound of Sadie's hooves stumbling on the rocks jolted him alert again.

During one of his dozing spells the catamount appeared in his mind's eye, walking alongside Sadie to his barnyard. As Sadie stumbled, he was jolted awake with eyes wide open and a moment to focus. The big cat was not there!

It was very strange. At the same time, he welcomed the power and wholeness he felt whenever the big sleek black cat came into his presence.

Sadie knew the way home instinctively, and her neighing and twitching her front shoulders was her way of telling him they were home. Still asleep in the saddle, he awoke to find he was at his own barnyard. It was a good half mile of deep "out-of-body" kind of sleep.

He actually felt reenergized once he got on his feet and moving around tending to the "critters," as he called them. First, he uncinched the saddle, then grained Jenny's and Sadie's wooden trough and threw a wedge of hay on the ground just inside the coral near the lean-to stall. Next, he threw out some feed, casting it about the small barnyard for the free-ranging chickens to peck and argue over. In the coop he found seven eggs that he carefully placed in a cloth-lined basket.

Finally, Oscar the piglet had his own trough and dog-house style sty just off the side of the lean-to, and he tossed in some fermented apples out of the barrel of table scraps from a couple of days ago. Nothing much went to waste on any farm or homestead those days.

And Oscar was not so much a piglet anymore. "Live it up Oscar!" cried Carl. "Another six or eight weeks! Boy, then you'll be wishin' you weren't so fat!"

Carl always talked to the critters out loud, but sometimes he had their attention just with his thoughts. They always seemed to come right over to him and be near him. Especially the horses—they always knew where they were going or could even feel his emotions by nuzzling his arm or chest as if to offer condolence or support.

Carl headed into the cabin after giving all the creatures his attention. He re-lit the wood stove and stoked it up good, tidied up the kitchenette and replenished the water pail from his spring for Mom's dry sink that Pop had gotten for her through the Sears Roebuck catalog at the general store.

Wanting to provide a bit of impression should Mamie or anybody else stop in for a visit, mostly he wanted to impress Mamie, visualizing her staying with him overnight even though it was not socially acceptable. "But we can still dream," he said out loud.

He lay his head down on the bunk, thinking of Mum and Pop and how he missed them. He could hear his Mum's soft voice with their evening talks and Pop's deeper tones at dinnertime discussing plans and chores. Dozing off again, he pictured Mamie smiling in her way, walking into the barnyard and then the cabin, looking to wake him up.

How long he was asleep? He woke with the sound of horses braying, and he remembered that the sheriff was supposed to stop for the interview. He heard his heart pound in his ears. As he started to scramble up, the sensation was as if he was falling back into bodily form from some astral place.

36   Truths Be Known

Elwin barged right into the cabin. "you're like an old man—nappin' in the middle of the day!" Catching Carl rolling out of the bunk just off the dry sink sitting on the edge trying to put his socks on, with his hair all sticking up and uncombed.

"Yeah, well it's been a long day and night" he responded, combing his fingers through his head as he headed to the water pail. "Is the sheriff out there waitin?" Carl asked as he splashed water from his cupped hands onto his face.

"Nope. He's down at Ford's Farm. He told me I was dismissed from service! We parted company at Ford's gate. He wanted to interview him one on one. I decided to come up here and catch you up as to what he's lookin' into. Said he was gonna stop here in on you on his way through to Middlebury. I'd guess another hour or two till he gets here."

"So! Mr. and Mrs. Morse, is it? Wow! You have been busy these last few days! I guess congratulations are next in order, right?"

Carl filled the tea pot and placed it on the wood stove. "Well, my friend, not just yet. Got her Pop's blessin' and her Mom seems to be 'good with it if we wait, and I think Mame is scared, after the surprise set in, so we'll be waiting a while to hitch the horse to the post, but she's got the ring around her neck!! Carl smiled, thinking that that in itself was an acceptance.

"Whoa, well you surprised the snot outa me!" Elwin exclaimed. "I wouldn't have brought the sheriff over there if I knew what you were up to. Sorry 'bout that, but that's why I wanted to come here this morning, plus you need your cage rattled anyway, sonny boy!"

They sat down at the little table. Carl pulled on his boots while Elwin got out two mugs from the cupboard. He filled the steeper and hung it on the inside edge of the pot now starting steam to a boil.

Carl was glad Elwin had stopped. He hadn't seen him in a long while to hang out with, but the pit of his stomach began to churn with what the conversation might reveal. He held it in and braced for the news.

"Sheriff Trunske is his name—Adrian Trunske. He is looking into what became of Burke. I been guiding him around the hill up here so he can interview folks who might have some factual knowledge. But I got to tell you what he thinks so far from all his talking. Thought you should know from me first.

"He wants to talk to you about Old Man Ford 'cause he thinks Burke is still here somewhere and maybe not exactly vertical. And cause you were workin' chores there the couple days before Burke went missin, he's thinkin you might have seen somethin'! Well, least that's what the sheriff told me so far.

"I didn't' want him to come up here and get you all discombobulated, cause I know how you can get flustered sometimes, and then you getting all quiet and moody on me! With all that happened lately with you and your family I thought I should be here with ya when Sheriff Trunske comes up today."

Elwin had a direct way of just blurting out the truth, knowing his good friend well enough that Carl would understand him as protecting his friend. That's why Carl liked and trusted Elwin so much. Next to Mamie, Elwin was the only person he could confide in.

With his hand on Carl's shoulder and a question in his eye, Elwin asked, "What do you think Carl? You think Ford did somethin' to Burke? I mean I worked there too! I never saw nothin 'cept Burke hound doggin' round Mrs. Ford's cabin all the time."

"Yeah," Carl said as he looked down at the floor. "He sure did spend a lot of time up there."

Carl contemplated telling Elwin his deep secret. He pondered if Elwin's confidence could be trusted. Then he flashed the big cat in his mind's eye. It calmed him and removed the anxiety that he was feeling.

Elwin was still talking about some of Burke's strange occasional behavior events, but Carl briefly tuned him out. He regained his composure and said, "Hey, El, let's go outside. I need to breathe in some fresh air. Bring the mugs out."

They set on the simple wooden benches near the barn looking over Mother's little garden.

"Yup," Elwin said, hesitating a little. "Guess the whole valley is buzzin' about the sheriff and Burke 'bout now. S'pose he and Mrs. Ford ran off together? Well, no matter—that Sheriff Trunske is real smart; he'll get to the bottom of it soon enough." Elwin just kept talking.

Carl looked at him, feeling somewhat scared and intimidated of the sheriff. The urge to let his friend in on the secret grew.

"Elwin, can I trust you to keep somethin' in confidence between you and me?"

Elwin was still talking almost to himself, only half hearing what Carl just said, "Yeah, he's pretty savvy figurin' stuff out. What?"

He paused his monologue and looked at Carl. "Say that again?"

Carl cleared his throat some more. "I need to trust you here on somethin'. It's real important to me." Then he started to talk soft, almost in a whisper.

Elwin knew well enough that his friend Carl was about to get deep.

Carl knew he could trust him just by looking in his eyes. At that moment as he looked at Elwin, he could see a faint light of pinks and blues around Elwin's being. The colors wafted around his body and the energy flowed out towards him and connected with his own.

That was the first time Carl understood the insights with people and colors of the energy fields that he could sense and see. At that moment he decided it was all right to open up with Elwin.

"Burke is dead, Elwin. I don't know exactly, but I think old man Ford did him in. You can't tell anyone on this, and I mean ever!"

"Say what?" Elwin exclaimed. "How do you know?"

"Cause I got bamboozled by Ford to help bury his carcass like he was a horse."

Carl's voice got softer and began to quiver. "I showed up there to do the chores and found Ford to be the only one there, with a wagon load of manure that he wanted to spread way up in the upper field." You know how he is with his directives. "We get up there and there's a hole dug by the Frenchies, and out pops Burke all stiff and eyes wide open from under the manure. I almost puked up. Had it out with Ford pretty good and started to run out. He smooth-talked me real good about helping my dad with better pay and me and gave me the chestnut mare if I help him keep the secret."

"Holy moly, Carl!" Elwin exclaimed, "Wow, that's fucked up! Why did he, I mean, how did Ford do it?"

Carl took a deep breath then explained, "Ford must've caught Burke messin' with his wife, caught him red-handed. He says they argued an' wrestled at the barnyard with a shotgun in the mix somehow, and Burke ends up dead on the spot.

"Don't know for sure, I wasn't there for that, but I had the bad luck showin' up to work the chores and the next thing I know I'm shanghaied by Ford and giving Burke last rights. Then I made a deal with the damn devil himself!"

"Ford talks awful smooth ya know, made it soun' like self-defense or sumpthin'. He also said it will go real bad for me and my family if I speak of it to anyone. Trapped in a bear cave is how I felt. So I told him it was on his soul, not mine. Then I took his pay. God knows we needed it. I thought it was the only way out, Elwin!" Carl started to tear up some but chocked it back trying to hold up his manliness. "That's when everything started comin' unglued. Pop took sick and went under, then Mum. What's next?"

151

Having no idea, Elwin just stared into the air with his mouth open.

"Now I'm way more than scared than I was that night," Carl continued, "All I want is some peace. Why is all this shit happening? I'm needin' somethin' good to happen for once." At that, he hung his head down on his chest and just breathed in deep.

After a few moments of silence, and Elwin with his mouth still agape, Carl looked up at the sky and said, "All I got now is Mamie and this piece of land to look forward to. She don't know nothing of this. Now the law might just hang me up along with Ford! And I didn't do anything wrong!"

Elwin tried to console him by saying, "You got shanghaied and bamboozled into it, Carl. Trunske will see it as truth and fact in the matter."

"Seems like every time somethin' good happens, I get kicked in the teeth by somethin' else the very next day!"

Elwin put his hand on his shoulder, "Now your imagination is runnin' away with you there, my friend! You didn't do nothing wrong! Shit, it could've been me who showed up that day at Ford's, who knows? You got Mame and the farm and me to stand on firm."

"When the sheriff shows up here in a while you maybe should tell him what it is, just like you told me now—straight out truth. At the long day's end it's all gonna boil down to what happened between Burke and Ford!

"Messin' with another man's wife is taboo around here and everywhere. Ford was probably within his rights how that went down. Maybe Burke drew a pistol up on him first or something—either way it's between them two, and you weren't there for that; you just got shanghaied! Sheriff don't know nothin' yet anyway."

Carl calmed down a little, took a couple of deep breaths, and said, "What if the sheriff pulls me into it?"

Elwin put his hand on his shoulder, "He can't. I got you covered. I got your back. The sheriff will listen to me. It's all gonna turn out for the best; I just know it. Hell, nothing may come of it at all! There's always that."

Carl looked him in the eye. "Guess I'll decide when he gets here, then. Yup, that's what we should do—just see what Sheriff Trunske says or knows for now."

37   Apple Jack

Sheriff Trunske pulled into Ford's farm, hitched his horse reins to the post at the barn and gazed up at the front porch of the house sitting just on the knoll.

Smoke was coming out the stone chimney, an indication that someone was home or about. He had no way of knowing that he was standing in the exact spot where Burke took the shot into his chest and fell dead!

The bell on the porch echoed through the barnyard as it rang out; he heard footsteps on the floorboards as someone responded toward the closed door.

The door swung open with no one standing immediately on the other side as he expected, instead a gravel voice said, "Show yourself in, friend." He saw the backside silhouette of a man in a hat standing slightly off to one side at a bookshelf.

"What can I do for ya?" Ford said as he turned around. The sheriff keenly sensed that Ford knew full well that he was with the law, however the star on his jacket lapel may have given that away as he walked to the porch.

"Well, I am Sheriff Trunske out of Middlebury, and I'm here to speak with Mr. Ford, if that would be you sir?"

Ford looked at the sheriff straight in the eyes with just the hint of a smile or smirk, displaying no fear or surprise.

"Yes, Mr. Trunske," he said, as he nodded his head. "I heard that you were in town looking into some matters. Why don't we go out and set at the bench near the barn porch and catch sun a little, and we'll see if I can accommodate you."

Trunske felt as though he needed to formulate his questioning carefully as he sat on the bench gladly relieving his bulk from his frame. Ford again turned his back and headed straight to the barrels side by side just up on wooden stands against the barn wall. He put two tin cups on one finger that were hanging under a shelf and held them out, "Care to indulge and join me in a little cider, Sheriff?"

Hard cider was usually a common commodity at most social events and friendly visitations, and in this case the offering was a gesture to break ground with any acquaintance of men discussing business or politics.

The sheriff's nod was received by Ford that he was glad to partake.

"So what brings you to speak to me this noon, sheriff?" Ford asked as he drew cider from the wooden spigot, filling one of the cups to the brim.

"It so happens, Mr. Ford, that I'm here to try to unravel some loose ends about the disappearance of a Mr. Frank Burke." He hesitated slightly, then continued, "It's my understanding that Mr. Burke was here at the farm under your employ, was he not?"

Ford handed full cup of cider to the sheriff, as he did so he said, "We put this up late last December, bubbled it out with brown sugar maple syrup and molasses, just racked it off three weeks ago. Should set quite nicely on a sunny afternoon if I don't say so myself!"

Trunske took a sip and was joyed at the flavor. "Much obliged," he replied, sipping it again just to keep it from spilling over when he set it down on the bench.

"Yes, Sir," Ford said, as he turned back to the barrels, with a slight bit of sarcasm in his tone. "Yup, Burke worked here for me for better than a year or so as my main horse and stock breeder. He tended to the foals and all of the meat stock for resale and the basic barnyard chores, he would stay here in the bunk house for a few days a week, then go off to family down in Hancock on and off."

Ford went to the barrel to the right of the one he just filled the sheriff's cup from and spigoted some cider into his own cup. The sheriff, relishing the flavor and the smoothness as it passed his gullet warming his innards going down, didn't notice the draw from the other barrel.

"Yup, Burke was good at what he did for the last breeding season, but he wasn't so savvy on some of the other chores. He liked to pass the chores on to the French hands and the younger helpers. Started to disappear from the bunk house more often without communicating, ya know!" Ford then raised his cup to the sheriff's and clinked it to his. They both took another pull.

"Did Burke go off hunting during his stays here?" The sheriff asked, "I mean to say, what did he do for recreation during his time off, if you know?"

Ford looked at Trunske with an intensity for a very brief moment, then smiled his crooked smile. His response was evasive from the sheriff's point of view but far from what Ford was really thinking.

"Oh, I suppose his hobbies or pastimes were the same as any other man living in these hills, but I never did much socializing with the man. I tend to keep work and play separate around here and on the timber lots as you may know.

"With that said, Mr. Trunske, I noticed him gone out huntin with a rifle once or twice. Said he was headin up to Bear Wallow one time then another time he was heading to Deer Hollow. About last spring a year ago, a catamount took a calf down at Farr's, and Burke said he heard it screechin' just up here in my upper meadow, so he was gonna out after it before it got into any of our young stock."

Trunske said, "I thought catamounts were creatures of folklore. No one has yet documented their existence."

"Oh," Ford replied, looking at the sheriff with his eyes shifted, formulating in his mind. "No, you heard wrong. They exist, that's for sure, big as waist high on a man, paw prints round as any small bear, black all the way through, with a long S tail. They can take down a yearling deer and stash its carcass in a tree. Folks have seen that sight.

"In the spring, hungry enough, they can take a man out hunting easy. One fella had one pounce on him from a tree above, like to tear him up with the claws, he was lucky to fend it off with his knife. No, they exist and are fairly dangerous and they are here in the hills, don't let anyone tell you different! More cider, sheriff?"

Trunske was beginning to feel the effects of the cider, his comfort level put him somewhat off guard with his purpose of the interview, the catamount story had him mesmerized and the flavor and texture of the cider was outstanding. He gladly held the cup for Ford to refill.

"Well, Mr. Burke has been reported missing, Mr. Ford. Do you, as his employer, have any notion of his whereabouts?" It was not the question he wanted to ask because he did not want to ask any questions he did not know the answer to already, but it just slipped out and there was no taking it back.

Ford handed the refilled cup he tapped from the barrel on the left rack filled to the brim again and handed it to the sheriff. "Mr. Trunske I am a very busy man; I spend four to five days a week out at the timber lots tending to the French crews and the skidding down to the Puddle Dock stage area where I tend to my affairs for payment."

He sipped from his own cup while the sheriff gulped from his. "All of my foremen are expected to perform their tasks and coordinations on my behalf. In my absence, that is what we pay them well for.

"Mr. Burke," Ford continued, "would venture off pursuing his pastimes on his own accord from time to time. When I returned from my off-site business last fall I found things in quite a state of disarray here on that last occasion. The tasks and chores were incomplete and needed to be delegated to a few Frenchmen and the younger part-timers who turned out to be more dependable than all of 'em put together, being sons of year-round local folks.

"If you wish Mr. Trunske, you can feel free to guess as to the whereabouts of Mr. Burke." He said it with sarcasm and as a challenge to match wits with the sheriff. He then tapped his cup up against the sheriff's cup and gulped down his sweet cider; the sheriff out of habit gulped his down, too, and held the empty cup out for another refill. Ford formed a crooked half-smile and stood up and refilled the sheriff's cup for a third time from the barrel on the left.

Sheriff Trunske had formed a respect for Mr. Ford in the short discussion at the barnyard bench. He was clearly a sharp entrepreneur, well respected and depended upon throughout much of the community. The farmhouse alone was larger than most of the neighbors' steads and maintained in good repair.

Ford held himself in a strong stature with his business-minded demeanor. He was clearly not one to be intimidated by any other authority. The sheriff's original tactics were not panning out this day. His faint thought was that this Burke business was a huge waste of time. His head was just starting to swim some as he tried to compose himself.

Adrian Trunske now found himself out of character. He took the full cup of cider from his host and slurped down another swallow. He then unendingly asked his suspect questions that would possibly relieve himself from the whole investigation. It was safe to say that he had asked out of and due to the admiration of Ford's savvy.

"Mr. Ford, sir, do you think that Mr. Burke may have left town to pursue a new position or chose not to endure another hard winter in these mountains? Or might he have met with some accident in the woods or have gotten lost up there?"

Ford formed another half-smile knowing he had tailored the interview to his gain. "Well, Sheriff, he left no word of migration. Burke did mention he was goin' hunting after that catamount! He might not have been good at hunting. Folks say they could hear that cat screeching nearby in early morns. Hunter may have become hunted.

"Burke could have met with that cat up there, maybe near its den; they are carnivorous and wise. Some folk say they heard a shot a while after he left to head up there. There's many ways a fool can meet his demise in these back hills." He paused. "Guess we will never know until someone finds his carcass."

38   Stupors

Hard cider is made by squeezing the juice from ripe apples, adding sugar or high-sugar-content products or other fruits. In that day, brown sugar was available as well as molasses, and certainly maple syrup and honey. In this time the three latter ingredients would have not been affordable for most folks.

Still the cider would be placed in a barrel and bunged tight to the air with a form of air lock to allow the fermentation gasses to release but fresh air to be locked out. This was done through a vent tube rigged from the bung into a jug or mason jar of water. The barrel was kept in a root cellar where the temperature was a constant 45 to 50 degrees.

After the fermentation stopped or slowed, within a couple of months, the cider was allowed to settle and was then "racked off" by siphoning the clear cider from the top, leaving the dredges at the bottom of the barrel. The barrel was then rinsed out and the cider stored in the same barrel airtight or a different barrel with a spigot for drawing off as needed. Depending on the amount of sugar during fermentation, the alcohol content could vary from four to eight percent with this process, much the same as any wine.

After fermentation, when the same cider was allowed to freeze, say for a week's cold spell in below-zero temperatures in February, and that barrel was turned up to drain, what did not freeze and passed through the bung hole into a pail over a half hour was that cider which, maintaining its flavor of apple and sugars, had a smooth texture on the palette.

What did not freeze was the higher-alcohol liquid. Its smooth texture and sweet flavor could deceive the consumer and delay the effects of the intoxication, so the consumer of the beverage would not feel its effect until an hour later. Intoxication crept up on one, erasing any memory of foolish behavior or unintelligible dialog. Too much of that cider consumed in short order could cause one to lose track of a full day or two, awakening to severe pounding of the head and malfunction of limbs and or muscle control for another 12 to 24 hours.

We refer to that type of cider beverage as Apple Jack. When served at various functions and or gatherings it was usually served in very small quantities just as a taste tester, hardly ever more than half a wine glass full and certainly with a verbal warning of its after-effects.

In the barn at Ford's farm two large barrels of cider were in cradles against the wall just inside the porch overhang where most of the social functions took place. The barrel on the right was labeled "Sweet Hard Cider" with only one X. The barrel on the left was labeled as "Apple Jack" with three XXXs. Why the keen eye of the sheriff, who prided himself on noticing even the smallest details and clues in any investigation, missed the markings on those barrels is unknown.

It could be that he was concentrating on sizing Ford's demeanor and mannerisms or simply that sitting on that bench, facing the opposite direction, Ford blocked his view of the barrels, filling the mugs with his back to the sheriff.

Even with Adrian Trunske's large frame, three full large mugs of Apple Jack were by measure equal to approximately a full quart—well over his quota. Each mugful was by baker's measure approximately two cups worth and well over the recommended amount at any normal social function. For a man of the sheriff's stature, one mug should have been his limit.

When the sheriff stood up from that bench, onto his hind legs, his frame buckled as his equilibrium was compromised. Not realizing the full reality of his condition, he merely felt embarrassed at his stumble and hastily bid farewell to Mr. Ford. "Well, Mr. Ford, I plan on returning to Middlebury this day. Need to burn some daylight," he muttered, as, with difficulty, he mounted his horse.

Mr. Ford nodded his head, smiling in full delight.

Adrian's head was swimming as he tried to reason what just took place. He still was not in full comprehension how he would summarize the interview. As he passed the bar way to Ford's farm, he could not remember whether to head towards Middlebury or back to Shirley's general store.

It was his horse who made the choice for him, as Mr. Adrian Trunske was stone drunk inebriated in the saddle, barely able to maintain a sitting position. In his stupor, he decided he wanted to go home, unconscious that it was a day and a half ride. "Let's go home," he slurred to his horse.

The ride would take him up over Texas Gap trail, and the horse seemed to know instinctively to head towards home, taking them just past Carl's homestead. His horse knew Elwin's gelding from scent and stopped directly in front of Carl's. With his head bobbing, Trunske was all but passed out in the saddle. This day his horse bore all the common sense.

All three horses stopped nibbling the hay feed together, raised their heads to full alert, ears perked straight up and focus ed intensely at the trail. Jenny, Sadie, and Elwin's horse all trotted to the rail in the small corral as if to welcome the sheriff's horse, now standing there on the trail. The sheriff was slumped in the saddle.

Carl and Elwin couldn't help noticing the horses' sudden excitement; from their bench they both saw the sheriff and his horse just standing there, having appeared out of nowhere. It was the oddest thing, and they both cocked their heads and just laughed at the sight for a moment with eyebrows raised, then they both looked at each other questioningly, then back to the sheriff, still slumped.

Elwin stood up, taking a few steps toward him, and exclaimed, "Sheriff Trunske?"

With no response, Elwin looked back at Carl, "What the hell?"

They both walked up to the sheriff's horse. Carl took the reins in hand while Elwin shook Mr. Trunske by his arm. "Are you all right, sir?"

Elwin looked at Carl, "We better get him off this horse. Somethin's pretty wrong here."

They walked the horse up to the corral gate, and Carl wrapped the reins twice around the rail.

"Let's get him off," Carl said, so they both pulled the big man down, one on either side, expecting the man to exert some weight on his left stirrup. That did not happen, and the full weight of Adrian Trunske came square on to both young men.

Strong as they each were, all three tumbled in slow motion to the ground as the sheriff's heavy frame buckled out the youngers' legs.

"Argh," they both moaned, rolling out from under the sheriff.

"Wow! What the hell's wrong with him?" Carl exclaimed.

"How in hell do I know!" Elwin said, after wiping himself off, as he went over and gently slapped the big man's face. "You hurt, sheriff?" He quickly checked for blood or a sign of injury.

After another face slap the sheriff opened his eyes, then smiled and slurred out "Hey, there, young Mr. Shirley! Just be needin' a nap for these ol' bones of mine." He then rolled his eyes back in his head, still smiling, as some drool came of the corner of his mouth.

"Holy crap, Carl. I think he is drunk as a skunk sittin' on his ass!"

"Yeah, El, I think you are dead right on that!"

Adrian curled up into a fetal position and farted, still half-smiling.

"I've seen guys drunk like this down at the store. A couple times Pop had to toss 'em out so their stumbling around didn't break anythin'. Yup, he's drunk stupid for sure, Carl. Maybe we should get some coffee into 'im—that's if you got some."

159

Carl loosened the saddle on the sheriff's horse and turned him into the coral with his and Elwin's. Then they put a blanket over the sheriff and let him sleep while Carl mustered up the last of his coffee from mother's cupboard.

"Well, so much for the interview!" Elwin laughed.

"When's he gonna wake up? I mean how long does this drunk thing last?" Carl asked.

"Not so sure, my friend. He looks pretty fucked up, though! He may be here for the night by the looks of it!"

They roused the sheriff and sat him up. Most of the coffee from the first mug drooled down his chin with maybe half of it swallowed; the second mugful managed to get gulped in between some unintelligible dialog. The third and last half cup found its way in as well, with some assistance by the recipient who seemed to be coming a little more alert.

Carl could not quite comprehend this event. An hour ago, he was anxious, expecting the highest authority in the area to come and create a turning point in his life. Now he was looking at the same authority with vomit stains on his shirt and badge, incapacitated, and sitting on the ground against his barn. This was hardly the same man Carl had met at Hubbards' the day before. There was no sense of intimidation left.

Elwin felt embarrassment as well, as he was prepared to intervene with the sheriff on Carl's behalf by using his new status. Now he wondered if and how the investigation would pan out, or if it would even be pursued. He looked at Carl as they tended to the man, both kneeling next to him.

"Carl, if we can get the sheriff here straightened out and onto his feet, I'm thinking he's gonna appreciate our help, and that will go a long way in your favor. He might not even remember what he came here for!"

At that moment they both heard a trickle, as urine piddled from the man's pant cuff after flowing all the way down the inside of his canvas trousers. He let out a sigh of relief as the same time as the wet spot formed at his crotch.

They both jumped up at the same time. "Jeez! I don't believe this! He just pissed himself. *Sheeit!*" Carl just stood back a bit with his mouth agape.

Neither wanted to clean him up, so they just let the big man doze off sitting up against the barn, putting around him his bedding that they took off the saddle still mounted to his horse. They grained and watered the horse and retreated into the cabin.

"Best to let him sleep it off. We'll deal with him in the morning, and I'll just stay here tonight if that's okay with you."

Carl nodded with approval, "Yup, I think I could use someone to talk with 'bout all this anyway."

Mamie totted up to the gate at that moment. Seeing all the horses, she figured they were all inside and felt disappointed, expecting only Carl so she could have some private time with him. Mother had given her permission to go up for the rest of the afternoon; she was to be back for late evening dinner. She wanted to surprise him and snuggle and talk out their plans.

Her curiosity was now piqued, so she let out a "Yoo hoo!" as she tied the reins to the rail, announcing her arrival. After a long pause she let out another. That's when the door opened, and only then, Carl smiled and waved her inside.

After some tea and describing the details of Trunske's condition, they all went out to the back side of the barn to check him again. Mamie had never seen a drunk person before. She could only exclaim, "Oh, my!" over and over, her hand covering her mouth, then bursting out with short giggles in between.

"Yeah, so what do ya think, Mame?" Elwin said. "Now you know how we kinda feel!"

"Pretty strange day so far! Don't see this every day, that's for sure," Carl muttered. "Guess we'll have to see how he is in the morning, that's all. We might as well go cook up some supper! Hope you'll be staying, Mame."

She smiled approvingly. "I s'pose I can head home a tad later and stay here with you fellers," smiling as she contemplated the overnight stay scenario.

Roosters crow early enough as dawn begins to break. Mamie jumped awake, rubbing her eyes and looking around to get her bearings. Suddenly she remembered that she was supposed to go home last evening.

Carl sat up next to her, relishing the first real feeling of being with his lover without sneaking around or having to rush. Then he remembered the sheriff and Elwin, who was still snoozing on the bunk that used to be his Mum's in the adjacent room.

Elwin did not disclose Carl's secret to Mamie about Burke, keeping the confidence. They only discussed what the sheriff's investigation was about and how he had been at Ford's before appearing in Carl's barnyard.

They all organized themselves as folks do in the early morning mountains, taking turns using the outhouse and such. Mamie kissed Carl goodbye and rushed out to go back home and try to sneak in before Mother noticed she was not home.

She went to look at the sheriff behind the barn one last time before leaving. As she mounted her horse, Carl stepped out on the stoop, stretching and yawning.

"Gonna check on Mr. Trunske?"

"Oh, he's gone," Mamie said.

"What? What do you mean he's gone?"

"I don't know—he's just gone! And his horse is gone, too! I gotta get home. I'll try to stop by later. I love you," she said smiling as she nudged her heels into her horse's sides.

Carl went to the side of the barn. The only sign of the sheriff was his blanket bed roll that they had draped over him the evening before, which now lay with some wet blotches in a crumpled heap and the empty tin coffee cup lying on its side.

He went to the corral. Only Sadie and Jenny and Elwin's horse were there, eager for their morning grain. Steam came from their nostrils as they exhaled in the cool morning air.

"Hey, Elwin!" he yelled out. Elwin emerged on the stoop, yawning. "You do anything with the sheriff while I was snuggled with Mame last night?"

"Nope, I was out cold. Went to bed right after you guys did. I checked him again when I went to the privy. He was snoring away like a saw in some wood. Why?"

"Well, our guest seems to have departed our company and hospitality!"

Elwin came around the barn to see for himself, looked around, and scratched his head in wonder. "Well I'll be!" he said to himself. Then he walked to the bar way and saw the hoof tracks that Mamie left heading down hill to the left, and another set heading to the right. "Well, now, I guess the sheriff departed toward Middlebury some hours ago. Maybe the coffee we fed him finally kicked in!"

"I should maybe try to catch him up to see if he's okay. He could be lyin' on the trail just up a way or somethin'. A person would expec' the man to come to the door and say somethin', don't you think?"

"Yeah, maybe so, Carl, but he didn't have his head screwed on too straight, you know," Elwin threw the saddle on his mount and cinched it up.

Carl came into the coral. "Hold up! I'm comin' with you." And he put the saddle on Jenny.

"I figure he can't have more than a mile or so on us. If he's fit to ride over that distance, he must be back up to snuff!"

They both headed over Texas Gap trail toward Hancock and Ripton at a trot, hoping to catch the sheriff up and get to the bottom of this bizarre event.

After about two miles they rounded a rocky bend to find a riderless horse nibbling the fresh green grass along the trail edge.

"Hold up! Whoa, whoa!" Reining in the horses, they dismounted and tied them off to an overhanging branch, Carl went and took the stray horse by the halter. Elwin walked up to Mr. Trunske, who was sitting cross-legged in the grass holding his head.

"You all right, sheriff? You hurt or broken?" Adrian Trunske looked up at Elwin and set his jaw and tightened his lips flat across his face.

"No, son, I'm not hurt, and I'm not broken." He paused for a while. "I'm also not all right. I seemed to have lost a day somewhere along the line. Can't remember much 'cept somebody putting coffee to me, not sure what happened or where I was. I just needed to take some rest here in the grass for a spell."

He started to get up and fell back onto his backside.

Carl walked up at that moment. "Sir, you didn't seem to be navigatin' too well last evening. Feeling a bit better this morn?"

The sheriff just looked down and tightened his lips without reply.

"Sheriff, this here is Carl Morse," Elwin cut in. "You can thank him for the coffee last evening and the blankets and grainin' your horse."

From his sitting position the big man looked up at Carl and nodded in appreciation, trying not to show his embarrassment.

"We was expectin' you in for breakfast this morn at Carl's place—well, after you cleaned up some—and then we found you was gone!" Elwin continued. "S'pose a trailside fire right here and some of that cool stream water should take care of your morning business."

The jerky tasted good while the sheriff pieced together the catalyst leading to his embarrassment. His only recollection was sipping cider from the tin cup at Ford's place; everything after that eluded him, up until he awoke with a blanket around him lying against a horse stall in somebody's barnyard.

For the next hour the three of them sat at the fireside, each piecing together the previous evening's events. Carl and Elwin were careful not to display any disrespect toward the sheriff and his current state.

After hearing their explanation of how and when he had arrived at Carl's, the sheriff did have a vague recollection of the coffee and being at Ford's. He then explained that because he had no idea where he was or how he had got there, he had felt he should not linger in case of an unwelcome reception by the owner occupants.

With the light of dawn and the rooster crowing right next to him, jolting him awake, he was barely able to position himself upright. By holding himself against the boards on the building and with his horse still saddled, he managed to climb one foot into the stirrup. Just that little effort made him woozy enough to slump forward in the saddle over the horn.

He thought he was sick or coming down with some illness or maybe he struck his head, causing memory loss. Lord knows it was pounding now! Holding his head with both hands, the big man thanked the two young men for their assistance over the last 24 hours. Regarding the investigation, he would not pursue any more questioning here in Granville.

"I thought you wanted to speak to me, sir," Carl said, with a side glance at Elwin.

Clearing his throat and shaking his head, the still-sitting sheriff stated that it was clear now that the hard cider at Ford's had caused his current incapacitation. Talking out loud to himself, he mumbled that he would summarize his report back in Middlebury in the comfort of his small office, and mail it out to the Burke family, something about a missing hunter.

For now, his focus was only bent on one thing. "I have had about enough of Granville, Mr. Morse. I just need to get back home." He nodded his head in approval to himself.

Elwin just looked at Carl and shrugged without saying anything. The two read each other's minds, interpreting the sheriff's slurred comments. The case might be coming to a close. No need to fuel the fire now! By the look of the current situation the hung-over sheriff was about to have a head-pounding journey home—and he was hell bent to get there.

They spent another hour at the trailside fire, helped the big man mount his horse and bid him farewell. Just as Mr. Trunske departed, he managed to turn looking back from the saddle to say, "Thanks for your help, boys! I do appreciate it kindly!" Then he disappeared around the bend.

Holy crap!" Elwin exclaimed, half-laughing. "Now that was a sight! I wonder if we should tell anyone else about this. I mean the whole episode from yesterday afternoon up to now was a little out of the ordinary!"

"Sure was." Carl agreed after contemplating the whole event himself. "The whole valley probably knows by now, what with Mamie gettin' grilled by her folks for sleeping over. I'm pretty sure she must have told em 'bout the sheriff stumbling around and passed out like that, and how we all needed to take care of him!"

"Yeah. S'pose it's out by now. Hard to keep somethin' like that quiet around here, even though it's only been a couple hours. Sure bet that by noon most of the valley will know. Don't think you need to worry 'bout the investigation anymore—looks like he ain't comin' back to town none too soon on that matter."

Carl now was the one to set his jaw. "Well, Elwin, I was all set to spew out the whole story 'bout Burke and Ford to him last eve. Now whatever gossip mill starts up and gets all twisted around could even be worse.

"I just want to take Mamie home and start up new again, y' know? Just want to move on toward makin' a family or somethin'." He had a flash vision of himself and Mamie sitting on the porch of his cabin and a toddler playing in the grass.

He shook his head to clear the thoughts. "Mi'se well get ourselves back."

39 Sneakin' In

Mamie got back home early. She tried to be as quiet as could be, turning her horse out into the corral and then sneaking into the cabin pretending to have been out at the privy.

She went as far as to remove her boots down to bare foot and stripped the skirt down to her under nighty. She messed out her hair with both hands to look like she just got up from sleep and grabbed some short wood for the cook stove off the pile on the back porch.

As she reached for the door latch, she decided not to be so quiet. *Just open it regular like any other morn*, she thought to herself. Sneaking around now could only raise suspicion.

Standing in the room for a bit revealed that Mum and Pop were in fact still asleep. She sighed with some relief and putting the armload of wood at the kitchen cook stove, she decided to pretend that she was up for the day.

Her precautions and pretenses failed. There was an awkward hour or so of silence from the time her Mum and Pop arose up through the honey toast breakfast.

Not able to stand it any longer, Mother broke the silence, even though Pop recommended that she leave it be. At the previous midnight hour it was only natural that Mother noticed Mamie was not yet home. She stewed for a few hours, paced the cabin, lit a lantern for Mame to see on the front porch, and peered out the window into the dark until her husband demanded that she come to bed.

"Now woman, you need to stop with your imagination. Ain't nothing you can do 'bout those two folks bein' in love. Now you get yourself in this here bed and get some sleep or you can go out on the porch rocker with a quilt and stare out into the night. I assure you none of that will bring her home tonight."

Reluctantly Mother crawled into bed and finally dozed off.

It was Pop who heard Mamie when she clacked the corral gate out in the barnyard. "See? Told ya she'd be back safe and sound, honey," as he nudged his wife from slumber. They lay there quiet-like, pretending to be asleep.

Up until the breakfast there was a lot of pretending going on in the Hubbard cabin. The breakfast discussion was only about the condition of Sheriff Trunske from Mamie's perspective, leading up to where she had been all night and why she stayed at Carl's with only Elwin as a chaperone. Surprised with that tale, Mother lost track of her original concerns about her daughter's stay over.

40 Mountain Buzz

Down in the valley at Shirley's general store, word spread rapidly about the sheriff's appearance from Middlebury. The rumor mill was steamed up to full revolution within the circle of women folk. With each piece and tidbit of gossip passing from one housewife to the next, innuendos were added and passed on to the next with the flair of everyone's personal imagination masked as insight as to what, why, who, and when about the Burke disappearance.

The French timbermen, loggers and caulkers alike, who would ordinarily keep to themselves, were also abuzz at their evening woodstove fires. They took umbridge over two of their own being dismissed by Ford from their positions and sent out of town for no apparent reason just after digging the shallow grave in that upper meadow. The Frenchmen were very close and mostly all related by blood, and the fact remained that they were directed to perform the task by the senior boss man.

Within the several timber-lot camps, the local French-speaking foremen could not help but notice some dissension amongst the men, and one of them overheard the rumblings in their evening quarters. This talk, of course, got back to the housewives when their men came home from the long stints at the timber lots. In confidence they bore their troubles of their long work week to seek comfort and compassion from their wives.

Upon the visit from Sherriff Trunske and Elwin a couple days before, one of these ladies let her opinion take precedent just after the short inquiry about Burke's disappearance. Mrs. Bagley, who lived off West Hill in Bagleyville, a large family of farms just down slope a bit from the Farr's turkey farm, was the first to question the integrity of some of the people associated with the Ford farm.

Just after her husband consoled with her, and while bartering with Mrs. Farr for some turkey eggs, her interpretation of this event created the perfect opportunity to participate in the American female's favorite pastime. Talking about other people behind their backs seems to be an inherent trait. This included Mrs. Ford and her sudden trip out of town, and that very strange Morse boy who worked there! Finally, the mysterious Burke himself, lurking around the Ford farm while the husband was off at his business enterprise.

And so it began, a pastime for women that would alter Carl Morse's life.

41 Turkey Skills

Carl completed all the chores at his farmstead just after Elwin departed toward home—graining the animals, turning out Sadie and Bart, then stocking in some more wood for the cookstove.

As he sat in contemplation with a cup of coffee, he reflected first on his bit of solitude now enjoyed in the quiet of his own home. He began to reflect on the unbelievable events of the last couple days.

The immense joy and passion of finally having a full adult night with Mamie, like they were already married. Sheriff Adrian Trunske performing investigations that drew him into the eye of the law, then the total sense of release, what with the sheriff's drunken stupor.

The new bond with the sheriff that he and Elwin had formed by helping Mr. Trunske to get recovered and safely on the trail way home should be taken into account and go a long way with the sheriff's perspective of how Ford could manipulate and use people as he perceived they like to be used.

As he departed their company, vowing never to return to Granville, Trunske's final trailside words provided the final sense of relief from the whole Burke affair.

Elwin, the only person in the world in whom he was able to confide, had offered sound advice should Carl need to come clean with the truth of what he witnessed that day at Ford's. "The truth is always the best road to take," said Elwin. That alone was a great burden off his back. Now that Mum and Pop were gone, he had no one else to bare his soul to.

His head jerked up as he came back to consciousness, his eyes reopened from the nap he'd apparently slumbered into. As he sipped his now-cold coffee, his thoughts went from remembering his head bobbing up and down, then succumbing to needed sleep. The events of the last few days overwhelmingly had caught him up.

He muttered to himself, "Damn that son of a bitch, that old slick bastard Ford!" He felt his anger rise and noticed the sensation and his dislike of it. Out loud, he said, "I ain't thinkin' on that crap no more!" Grabbing his denim jacket and the octagon-barrel 44-40, he said, "I'm gonna call me in a Tom."

Wild turkeys were abundant in the natural habitat of the Green Mountains. Now with the small meadows and clearings that farmsteads etched out of the forest, even more varieties of seed, grains, and forage were available to the birds.

Flocks of more than 70 birds could congregate on any fall day, particularly in the mid-morning hours and again later in the afternoon. They would hug the edges of these clearings, getting ready for the evening tree roost.

The native Hasani Indians enjoyed hunting and used the wild turkey as a main staple. Hunting parties out for five days at a time would take turkeys, both toms and hens, as a reliable way to sustain their remote encampments of eight or ten men, generally five or more miles from the main village.

Sitting around the evening fire, they would chip and shape arrow heads, points and shafts from quartz and birch sapling branches. The birds were usually roasted over a wood fire on a wooden spit. None of the bird was wasted. Feathers were used on the arrow shafts or as adornments decorating their prized hunting implements. Marrow of the bone was a source of protein; breaking the bone and sucking the gelatin marrow out created a hollow tube that could then serve as a whistle or sewing punch.

Once relieved of the marrow, the wing bone sections of the wild turkey could be configured whereby the narrow end of the horn-shaped piece slipped easily into the straight three-inch midsection bone, and that again fit nicely into the last narrower-yet four-inch curved piece of bone.

Using pine sap or beeswax they could seal each joint and adorn some feathers with a strip of hide or sinew as a strap. At the narrow end of the horn, and by making a sucking or kissing motion, it would sound exactly and imitate the deep seductive chirps progressing to the rapid cackle of the mature hen announcing her availability and willingness to be mated.

The hen's calls echoed into the nearby hollows near their early morning decent out of roost. Toms up to a half mile away responded by ever-louder gobbles, announcing their presence nearby. Competing toms also made their way to the hens. These call-and-answer rituals continued sometimes for hours until the toms could finally get to a close enough to display their full inflated puffed chests and tail feather fans.

Carl sat comfortably at the edge of the tree line overlooking the small open meadow. It was one of his favorite places to sit in quiet contemplation and enjoy the warm morning sun. Since he was about eight he would come to this little clearing just a few hundred yards down trail from the cabin home and lie on his back in the middle of it with the tall grass looming two feet over him, hiding him from the world.

Daydreaming and napping, he would pick forms and shapes from the clouds that looked like horses or bears and silhouettes of men as they wisped and moved in the sky.

With his wing-bone turkey call he kissed the narrow tube several times, the horn-shaped end emitting the sound of the hen turkey. On the second try, finally remembering the correct intervals of about two seconds apart with the chirping imitation, a loud tom's gobble echoed out of the woods across from the far end of the meadow. Elated at the quick response, he began the intense call-and-answer ritual.

Time and again he chirped slowly with intervals of deep throaty purrs, then the more rapid chirps with an abrupt end to an echo off to silence. It drove the Tom into a frenzy, sending out rapidly his loud gobble, now from slightly closer to the imitated hen's location.

With each gobble response, Carl waited ten to twenty seconds before resuming the hen's seduction. When the Tom gobbled two or three times between his hen chirps, it confirmed the big boy was on his way, desperate to enjoy the lone hen's affections.

It took just one more round, then a moment of premeditated silence. Across the clearing the huge tom emerged at the edge of the tree line in a full strut. He gobbled again, loudly straining his whole body with his neck fully stretched, then inflating his breast out with a spread of tail feathers into the full fan display.

Carl purred a deep long chirp on his wing bone call, marveling at the spectacle. The tom moved to the center of the meadow only thirty feet away.

The gun's report echoed off the ridges and hills, sounding like five shots instead of one. This tom turkey had to weigh close to 35 pounds. "Not a bad morning!" said Carl aloud to himself. After surveying around the meadow, he began to field-dress the bird.

On the trail heading back to his place, he stopped to take a little rest. Carrying the rifle, his possibles bag, and the 35-pound turkey had started to take its toll.

The rifle itself weighed a good 18 pounds or so, made by Whitney Arms Company in Whitneyville, Connecticut. It boasted a 24-inch-long octagon smooth-bore barrel. Constructed under a new revolutionary design, the lever action repeater hosted a magazine that efficiently held up to six brass cartridges in addition to the chambered round.

The heavy cartridges contained 80 to 90 grains of black powder, with another revolutionary centerfire cap that the firing pin would strike upon the hammer's impact, accurately propelling the lead 40-caliber bullet down the long barrel to its target.

Upon discharge the unspent black powder particles would continue to ignite upon infusion with oxygen as they billowed out of the barrel's end in a large grey cloud of pungent smoke. If fired in the evening hours or just about twilight, one would witness the ball of flame and multitudes of spark and burning gasses mushrooming out from the end of the barrel. Not so visible during the sunny daytime it was very impressive nonetheless with its billowing cloud of smoke. The shooter would have to wait a few moments after discharge for the air to clear to regain focus of the intended target.

Resting his bones, Carl reflected on the day Pop ordered the rifle from the Sears Roebuck catalog at Shirley's general store. It was a very exciting event the day it arrived, packed in its colorful western motif wooden box along with the three dado-jointed wooden boxes of treasured cartridges. Its easy slide-open lid allowed convenient access to the 50 rounds inside.

42   Wise Advisement

Elwin caught up with the store chores that he got behind on, not so much that he was behind in his own mind but impelled by the stern look on his Dad's face. There were many daily routine things Elwin was responsible for, such as placing and locking the outside display implements in the shed for the night and graining the livestock and chickens out in the back pens.

These chores Mom and Pop had to do themselves much later than usual because they still expected his return. He was supposed to return home the previous evening whether after dark or not—not only to inform his Mum and Pop on the updates from Sherriff Trunske's interviews and safe departure back to Middlebury, but also to just keep Mother from worry and concern.

The standing agreement was that if he were going to stay up at Carl's or work at Ford's, he was to send word down with anybody heading that way, as the general store was the main communication hub and stayed open till about seven o'clock in the evening except on Sunday. Somebody from up the hill could always come in and relay messages.

Naturally Mother was concerned. The dinner she prepared went cold waiting for his arrival and Pop was a little miffed that he had to break his own routine doing all of Elwin's chores as well as tending to his own as store clerk.

When the family finally settled in at an earlier supper this evening, Elwin wasn't sure where to begin with his tale of the sheriff and how he ended up staying at Carl's. All he knew was that the pending circumstances that seemed important at the time were his best alibi. "Well, let me tell you this, I could not get back here if'in I wanted to last night, and you may not want to believe it at first, but I had me a most interesting night to say the least!"

Now that he had their attention, he began to fill them in on the interviews with the sheriff and how Mr. Trunske sent him ahead to Carl's while he interviewed Old Man Ford. Receiving another stern look from Pop, he corrected himself, "I mean Mr. Ford," he said, stuffing another fresh roll in his mouth. He contemplated about what Carl had confided in him regarding Burke, but then remembered he had vowed to his friend to keep it in confidence.

Elwin wanted to seek Pop's advice on Carl's behalf, Pop being better versed in this type of matter. He held his tongue on that part of the story, figuring the drunken sheriff and his obligation to help him would be ample enough lore. Mom and Pop just sat with their mouths agape at Elwin's conclusion.

Elwin very much wanted to confide in his Mom and Pop about the demise of Mr. Frank Burke at the hands of Mr. Ford in the very barnyard where he also worked for paid chores.

He was desperate to explain the mistreatment of his best friend Carl Morse by Ford, who had taken complete advantage of his slow and sensitive friend. He needed to find a way to protect Carl and redeem him from any consequences of the matter.

He was also very aware of how the rumor mill could twist all truth beyond any validation for his friend or the credibility of the sheriff if word got out of his drunken condition that evening.

Knowing his dad was a wise and prominent man in the community the best way to achieve his goals was to seek some confidential advice. Elwin dwelled on the matter after dinner for quite a while in his mind, while Mother took to knitting and Pop reviewed his daily ledgers.

Just before retiring to his bunk room for the night, he made a final assessment that Ford's actions and manipulations should be revealed and that they would take precedence. His dad would make advisements for Carl and to protect Ford's credibility, as he was the most prominent figure in town.

Most likely Pop would analyze the story deeper and determine that Ford was within his rights to do what he did to Burke, or maybe acted out of self-defense.

Pop might also decide to just "let sleeping dogs lie," as the saying goes, or he might end up meeting privately with Ford. Any way it went, Elwin decided it would best be brought out in his dad's confidence.

He murmured "good night" as he headed to his room.

Pop looked up in response with his reading specs halfway on his nose.

Elwin said, "I have more information I'll be needing to speak with you about in the morning, sir."

Raising an eyebrow over his spectacles he nodded approvingly as if he already knew it was to be private, saying, "We will speak on that in the morning then, son."

Elwin nodded in response and proceeded to his room.

43   Cackling Hens

Mrs. Emily Hubbard finally ventured down to the Farr farm on Patterson Trail just near Bagleyville to barter for some turkey eggs. She loaded two pans of her cornbread in the carriage along with two mason jars of apple cider vinegar pressed from the apple trees in the barnyard last fall and poured into the vinegar barrel with the "mother" that rapidly ferments into the stable vinegar state.

It was common practice to swap these kind of food staples at places like Farr's where the housewives could barter, congregate, and, of course, catch up on the current gossip. They also made deals with each other for other seasonal things like piglets, beef, venison, seeds, vegetables, yarns, knitting, and leather goods.

Places like Farr's could be described as a community hub for women folk, a farmer's market, if you will, where the majority of folk reside on the upper ridges of Granville's Green Mountains.

It also saved time and money not having to trek each week down trail to the general store two or more miles into the valley. In the wintertime that trip could become an all-day event.

Farr's also provided the best place for these women to learn the latest gossip and inject their own interpretations or input into the frenzy of hearsay. Most of these conversations began with, "So, did you hear the latest?"

Mrs. Hubbard could not help but notice that Mrs. Farr and Sophie Sargent's conversation reduced to whispers just as she was about to join the circle. Mrs. Farr recomposed herself and began to change the subject they were on. The current buzz was, of course, about the sheriff, Burke, Mrs. Ford's sudden departure, Mr. Ford, and now the strange behavior of the Morse boy "who works at Ford's farm." Sophie was all too eager to add the new bit of innuendo by leaning into Mrs. Hubbard in a gesture of confidence placing her open hand alongside her face as if it were another deep secret. What she didn't know and was not briefed yet was that Mrs. Hubbard's daughter Mamie was being courted by and just now was engaged to Carl Morse.

After taking one look at Mrs. Farr's body language and facial expression, Emily knew exactly that Sophie had just blurted something that the other women were already buzzing about behind her back.

The latest gossip circle was soon to include herself and her own daughter as topics for criticism. Even worse, her own integrity would now be scrutinized by these relentless women because she had allowed her daughter to be in a relationship with Carl Morse.

She became flushed and her complexion went two shades of red when her eyes met Mrs. Farr's. In that instant she knew it was too late, as Mrs. Farr's eyes shot straight to the ground. Then came the false smile again, trying to change the subject as Sophie innocently repeated the question, "So do you think he could have fed Mr. Burke to the pigs?"

She composed herself as best she could. Knowing Carl firsthand, she said, "I don't believe the Morse boy is capable of doing anything like that. He has always seemed very nice, with a quiet reserve in his manner, well behaved, cordial, and polite."

She looked straight and firmly at Mrs. Farr. It was her way of setting the record straight before the innuendos could damage her position in the women's social circle. But she immediately realized that her defensive stance would not do any good. Deep inside she knew it might be too late by the way Sophie was repeating the hearsay with enthusiasm.

Sophie's version was the latest update, as news of Mamie's engagement to Carl had been shared throughout the circle of women. In such small communities news of this import spreads rapidly.

The art and politics of match-making were still generally carried out by the parents, either very subtly or directly forced, mostly dependent on the dowries.

Guessing a young man's or woman's value, character, and integrity was always a welcome form of gossip and innuendo.

Emily Hubbard gathered her eggs and abruptly bid the ladies farewell. Snapping the whip on the horse's rump she rapidly headed home, bent on breaking the engagement—her selfish act to save face with her peers. With no regard for Mamie or her feelings, Emily would impose an irrational sense of entitlement.

Pete Hubbard came into the house from the back door with an armload of short wood for Mother's cookstove. He had been out attending to some afternoon errands after completing his tasks tallying the board footage of timber down at Puddle Dock for the lumber company. He was known as the "tally man" by all the timber lot owners who skidded their loads off the mountain for compensation. Pete would also verify the quality of the timbered logs and make the necessary adjustments to the fees to be paid out.

Mamie lunged half running and clung onto his waist as soon as he got through the door, crying in uncontrollable sobs emotionally shouting with gasps of breath between her words barely audible mixed with the sobs, "Daddy, daddy, oh, she can't make me go! Oh, Daddy, tell her not to do it! We didn't do anything bad! I don't deserve—" Her words reverted to uncontrollable sobs.

Still holding the armload of wood, Pete Hubbard was caught completely off guard. He knew immediately that his wife had just played out one of her control dramas. He knew how she could get caught up in her imagined fear-based scenarios. He placed his free hand on Mamie's head to provide some quick form of comfort.

Emily could get something in her head and not let go of it until it drew all the energy out of anybody within earshot, always an inconvenient ambush. Most of the time that person was himself. He had witnessed her playing these out many times over the simplest of things, like if a chicken would not go back in the coop at night or if one of the barnyard cats got hurt or if coyotes came around at night.

She could get very obsessive or even hysterical trying to control a situation that was generally a figment of her imagination. But the sleepless nights, with her pacing and or demanding that he should get out there and do something about it, were taking its toll on him. Lately his dear wife would play out her control dramas on her daughter instead of the barnyard creatures. Subtle as they were and under the guise of teaching, Pete often had to intervene before they got too extreme.

With Mamie still clinging to his waist for protection, he took one glance at his wife. Her jaw was set firm with a wild look in her eye, so he knew this issue was extreme. "Emily," he said sternly, "What have you done now?"

Once things in the household settled down some, Pete Hubbard sat down with cups of tea for the three of them and began a rational inquiry. "What in hell is going on here? My beloved ladies, I'll have you know that I had myself had a very long and uneventful day, only to come home to this type of upside-down apple cart!"

He put his arm around Mamie, favoring her innocence over his wife's demeanor, looked at Emily, and asked her to explain. Again with her jaw set and thin lips straight across, she proceeded to repeat the entire gossip collection of innuendo and hearsay pertaining to Carl Morse, the sheriff, Ford, Burke, and her own unravelling status among the social circle. She then began a rant on how in her perspective, contrary to their previous discussions, concluding, "Our daughter should not be associated with the likes of the secretive Morse boy. I will not tolerate my daughter staying at that place or meeting with him unchaperoned. She is too young to be carrying on like a hussy!"

Pete noticed that she was working herself into another hysterical fit.

Offended at the belittling remark, Mamie screamed out at her mother, then went silent, feeling totally betrayed.

Pete interrupted and scolded his wife, stating that her language was hurtful and uncalled for. He pointed his finger, "Do not do that again or you will have a consequence of your own!" He was angry that he had to come out of character. Worse still, he found himself being a father figure to his own wife. Having even to voice the reprimand was repulsive to him.

Staunch in her convictions, Emily recomposed herself. Still on the offensive, she announced that Mamie should go off to private finishing school in Middlebury. She reached for the cigar box, pulled out the family's savings, and held the money up in the air, insistent on getting her way at any emotional or monetary cost.

"So that's how it is with you, Em?" said Pete. "You would send your own daughter away from here, her life, my life, and our harmony disrupted all over some crazed hearsay and gossip from those harpies you call friends? Do you not consider Mamie's feelings? How about her trust in us as her nurturers and her guides? You tend to forget how you and I came to this place with you running off with me down south!

"Your imagination may have just severed your bond with our only daughter. If she desires the schooling, I, for one, would leave that decision to her." With that statement he hugged Mamie a lot tighter and raised his teacup as if in a toast.

It was a restless night in the Hubbard house, as tensions were very high. Supper was overlooked and forgotten. Emotionally drained and exhausted, they each retired to their beds, except Emily, who remained pacing and murmuring to herself in her corner of the cabin, then finally walking outside for a while.

To avoid an awkward moment with his wife as to the normal sleeping arrangements and truly not wanting to be next to her anyway, Pete went to his separate cot after kissing Mamie good night, "Honey, we will talk together more in the morning, just you and me. It will all turn out all right—you'll see."

Mamie got situated in her bunk, her mind still reeling from her mother's outlandish behavior and betrayal of bond that she thought she had. She'd never seen this side of her Mom before this night.

She reflected on earlier in the afternoon when her mother charged into the barnyard with the buggy. The horse was all lathered from the pace. Mamie thought there was some emergency of sorts. Then she stormed into the house, threw the canvas grocery sack on the table, grabbed Mamie by the hand, yanking her like when she was little to get a scolding for bad behavior. She pulled Mamie out to the porch and pushed her into the chair.

"I think you should cut your hair! You will never get a man with good morals or integrity with long hair down to your waist like that!" she said, pacing back and forth with her hands on her hips.

Mamie just stared at her in surprise. "What do you mean? What's the matter, Mom?"

"Do you have any idea why the sheriff came here all the way from Middlebury? Folks are saying that your Carl Morse is involved with the Burke affair! I've found out that he is strange and very queer. I believe he is leading you down a slippery slope, and it's in our best interest to avoid contact with him."

Mamie retorted in defense, "You mean only in *your* best interest!"

Her Mom began pointing her finger and escalating her volume to a shrill decibel. The dialog declined to no sign of compromise.

Her energy drained, Mamie reached a breaking point, feeling totally betrayed. Her intent now was to escape. Lying there in her bunk, sobbing, her morning plan now was to see Carl, permitted or not.

44   Confidential Consultation

The vivid colored poster depicting an army cavalry officer charging into the fray of a battle line with the Spanish soldiers' mouths agape and faces of fear in full retreat was nailed up on the bulletin board at the general store. The recruiting officer left the enlistment forms inside with Mr. Shirley for any young volunteers willing to join the Green Mountain Men regiment of the United States Army Cavalry Division.

The conflict known as the Spanish-American War was just about over. It began with the explosion of the *U.S.S. Maine*, killing 250 American sailors. The charge up San Juan Hill by Teddy Roosevelt headlined most of the newspapers, and inflated publications glorified the U.S. Army's quick and thorough victory.

The economic depression of 1893, in which 500 banks failed, was only barely offset by the Klondike gold rush. A new predicament known as the Great Panic of 1907 was caused by the failure of stressed brokerage firms, and a vast earthquake in San Francisco drained gold reserves from the country's financial centers. Most American families and just plain folk endured having only known the hardships of harsh economic times, never feeling any recovery at all.

The lure of excitement, adventure, camaraderie, and prestige of the army uniform was enchanting to many young men, who envisioned a career in the army with a steady monthly paycheck that could provide for their future advancement. Most of the volunteers were young men who could shoot well and were skilled in horsemanship. They had visions of glory where they could utilize their skills and be part of something bigger than themselves, unlike the few opportunities in most small towns. These young men yearned for some adventure and a way to escape the humdrum lifestyle of farm chores. They did not have an urge to eke a living out of the earth as their parents had. Some rebelled at the farming lifestyle; others just wanted to see the world and other parts of the country. Many in Vermont didn't care to endure another long harsh winter.

The army's recruiting office knew its strategy well. The U.S.A was already engaged in a European conflict, and the Great War was just on the horizon.

Elwin Shirley completed his morning chores, putting the display implements out in front of the store and graining the animals. Mother made some hot oatmeal and coffee for breakfast, and Mr. Shirley began to organize the newly arrived mail.

Mother was getting ready to head down street toward Hancock to meet with the owners of the newly constructed hotel. She brought the most current Montgomery Ward and Sears Roebuck catalogs for them to choose the fancy linens they would be needing for the bunks and tables to be let out for room and board.

It was a large project that required her visit on site, offering her interior decoration input as well as taking the measurements and design suggestions for other wall hangings. She also helped with the utensil supplies for the dining room and kitchen, which would be ordered, or custom made locally by the various blacksmiths and crafters.

"Elwin! Would you please hook up Marley, and make ready my buggy?"

She kissed her husband on the top of his bald head as she was ready to depart for most of the day. "You boys may be fending for yourselves for lunch and dinner. The pot of stew and cornbread is left over in the ice box. Please don't forget to save me a portion," she added, insinuating that her husband would eat it all. Smiling broadly, she headed out the store front door, content with the prospects of performing this facet of store business and the feeling of overseeing such a large and important order. With the satchel in hand she was excited just to break the monotony of being confined to the store.

Elwin led Marley in her harness with the buggy in tow up to the store front and helped see mother off. As he came on to the porch of their store, a new colored poster pinned on the bulletin board caught his eye. Reading the army's notice and admiring the detail of the battle scene, he was enchanted by its promise of adventure.

"Well, looks like Mother is off for the day!" he exclaimed, coming through the front door. One of the customers turned and acknowledged him while his Pop bagged the patron's goods in a sack.

At the customer's departure, his dad closed the ledger and looked up at Elwin. "Shall we have that discussion now, son?"

"Yep, now would be good," said Elwin, setting down the box of soaps he was carrying to the display. "It's been weighing heavy on my mind, Pop. I really need your advisement on this one, you know. I got some real concerns for Carl Morse, Pop. He's got himself in a predicament and it's not of his choosing."

Elwin proceeded to explain that the information he was about to reveal was something that he had promised and given his word to keep in the strictest of confidence between him and Carl.

Mr. Shirley sat back in his chair. "If that is so, El, why then do you feel the need to bring it to me?"

"Well, Dad, I think Carl could be in trouble with the law or worse, but it's all because of Mr. Ford. It's real serious and I'm afraid for Carl, being how slow he is and how Ford kind of took advantage of him a few months back just before his Mom and Pop passed on.

"I gave Carl my word on this, dad, so now you must honor my word with yours that this will not go out of this room. Carl ain't got nobody, and I mean nobody, to help him or anybody to talk to 'cept me and it was all he could do to get the courage to tell me about it. So, I need your word. I need it held true before we can talk."

His father recognized the urgency of Elwin's demeanor and extended his hand to his son. "So be it, Elwin Shirley. I'm always here to help you. We will help Carl, too. You have my word on that as your father and friend in any advisory."

That being satisfactory for Elwin, he revealed the Burke story, clarifying that it was as relayed to him by Carl. He began with the sheriff's expectation of interviewing Carl just because Carl also worked at Ford's and knew a little about Burke. It was to be Trunske's last stop before departing for Middlebury.

"So, when I got to Carl's place ahead of Mr. Trunske, who was down interviewing Ford alone, Carl broke down and finally confided to me what Ford made him do by burying Burke up in the upper meadow somewhere. Carl started gettin' real sick like and almost barfed up right then and there when he found out the sheriff was talkin' to Ford.

"He told me how Ford had the Frenchies dig a hole and how when he showed up to do his chores Burke was not there— just Ford, all by himself. Dad, Ford is never there to do chores alone! Never! Then he made Carl hook Bart to the manure wagon that was already loaded! Then they took it way up to the second meadow instead of the lower one that was already receivin' manure! Carl couldn't figure why everything was off kilter!

"When Burke's carcass fell out from under the manure, Carl said he almost ran, but Ford threatened him and extorted him and his dad. Then Ford smooth-talked him, offered to pay real money by takin' care of him and his dad, increasing their wages with a raise of higher pay. He even gave Carl money for his own, a lot of money, and a horse in return for his silence about Burke being dead. Carl took it, Dad! Hell, I s'pose I would've, too!

"Carl said all the last rights for Burke 'cause Ford wouldn't. We think Ford shot Burke, Dad! Shot him dead in the barnyard 'cause he was caught with Mrs. Ford up in the house. It coulda' been a tussle with the gun, but it don't matter now. Then he goes and drags Carl into the mess and really messed him up, Dad!"

Elwin started getting more upset, feeling helpless to protect the honor of his friend. His dad put his hand on his shoulder to provide some comfort.

"I don't think Sheriff Trunske is gonna ever come back to Granville on this Burke business, Dad, at least that's what he told us on the trail after we got him sobered. Ford really got him screwed up over there. I should've stayed with the sheriff. I had Carl all ready to tell the sheriff the truth about Ford and Burke when he got there. Even before he went to Ford's, Trunske told me a lot of the interviews were pretty much useless and 'unsubstantiated hearsay.' Those were his words.

"What's worse now is that Carl is the only witness. He's the only one who knows what Ford did that day, and Carl's kinda worried, scared that Ford could do somethin' to him, especially now that the sheriff has been around askin' questions. And now the womenfolk got their own made-up speculations goin up and down the damn mountain on both sides all the way up to North Hollow!

"Dad, I gotta tell ya—Carl didn't do nothin' wrong. He's bein' railroaded, tarred, and feathered. All he wants to do is marry Mamie and start a family, that's all. God knows he's had a hard time of it so far. How can I—I mean we—help him now?"

"My lord, son, this is very incriminating information, I can see now why it's of such great concern to you and Carl, and to me as well." He held his head for a long moment. "I've dwelled on this while you relayed the story. I've formulated some facts that I believe could work in everyone's favor. First order of our business—and just hear me on this—is that Ford is a very important person here in the community. Much of the commerce and employment of folks depends on his enterprises. A lot of folks need him in one way or another.

"What he did in that barnyard may have been justified or even self-defense, and not necessarily below the law. More than likely it was not justified to that extreme, but we will never know. I don't believe it's in the community's interest or Carl's to disclose Mr. Ford's secret, or to start a scandal based on rumors and assumptions."

Mr. Shirley held both hands on either side of his head, massaging his temples in deep contemplation. "Mr. Ford will have to answer for his actions someday to a much higher authority than the good Sheriff Trunske, and so will Mr. Burke, for that matter."

"It seems that no one witnessed the actual event except perhaps Mrs. Ford, who is also a woman of prominence and stature here in town, but she is also not in town and has not been interviewed by the sheriff. Neither has Carl. Therefore, the lawman does not have the facts to formulate any kind of case worthy of prosecution.

"As far as Carl's word over Mr. Ford's on the mountain, that could be dangerous for Carl, given his simple, quiet nature. There's only a few folks who understand him and his heartfelt manner—you, mother, Mamie, and now myself being those select few.

"Son, please don't take me wrong about this, and know that I do not condone Ford's taking advantage of Carl Morse any more than you do. But I don't believe it would be in anyone's interest to allow this news to become inflated more than it has within the gossip circles. Do you agree?"

Elwin nodded.

"My reasons are simple: As of this moment nothing is substantiated. Those women's gossip and speculations are nothing more than hearsay, folklore that within another week's time will dissipate into yesterday's news and be replaced by some new topic soon to be forgotten."

"Not many people would take Carl's word seriously if he were to announce his witness of burying Burke, especially now that he made his deal accepting Ford's bribe. And yes, he may have been coerced, son, but the fact that he accepted is complicit to accessory. Even the good sheriff would have only Carl's word pit against a man of Ford's stature."

"If Ford were prosecuted and found guilty beyond doubt, a highly unlikely scenario is that Carl could be found guilty by association or implicated also. However, the sheriff cannot act or implement the law without any physical evidence. Do you follow me on this so far, son?"

Elwin nodded, intrigued by his dad's vast perceptions. "So Pop, what would you suggest Carl do? I mean people are now talkin' about him, not about Ford!"

"Well, son, my personal advice is for everyone to just relax a bit, take some deep breaths, go about their business, and let this storm just blow out. Time heals." Scratching his head, he continued, "If Carl is in a panic, feeling uncomfortable around the folks here in town, perhaps he could leave for a while—take a job down near Hancock or someplace else for a while."

"I may seek a personal meeting with Mr. Ford on Carl's behalf as emissary, but only with your permission," said Mr. Shirley. "Would that sit well with you as Carl's voice and counsel?"

Elwin said, "I s'pose so. I just don't think Mom should know 'bout this because of those old biddies who started all the hearsay. Would that sit with you in agreement, Dad?"

Mr. Shirley half-smiled. "Under the circumstance I agree that would be prudent for the time being. Let us also agree that this piece of important business be contained strictly between you and me as pillars of the community."

"Thanks, sir," Elwin said, "I am now feelin' relieved, looking on it from the way you point it out."

The strap of bells hanging on the store door jingled as it announced the entrance of another patron. The ring of the bells seemed to be a perfect conclusion to the father–son discussion. Elwin felt much less weight on his shoulders compared to yesterday.

45 Dime Novels

These last few days had been extremely exciting, Elwin reflected to himself, what with the appearance of the sheriff here in town, and his invitation to go along and learn how an investigation works. The observations alone from a lawman's perspective were intriguing. He felt lucky to be able to just play a part in the lawman's work, feeling as if he was in fact deputized in a way.

Continuing his daydream some more, sitting at the kitchen table, Elwin envisioned himself as the sheriff. He would be looked upon as the ultimate authority, dispatching a savvy and practical sense commanding resolutions to domestic conflicts whereby both parties in dispute would respect his counsel and arbitration.

The pursuit of harder criminals would require skills in gunmanship and cunning tactics of apprehension or even stealthy ambush. He would have deputies of staunch conviction of the law and skills of the same mindset.

He imagined a scenario in his mind, being called out into a gunfight like in the dime novels he got to read as the new editions come to the store every month. He was to face off at sunrise with a black vested, studded hat outlaw of underhanded reputation. While he stood tall, unafraid with his white hat, badge shining and 44-caliber Colt strapped to his leg at the ready, his eyes remained fully focused on his opponent who was spewing belittlements and curses in a show of ego to build courage he did not have.

After the display of puffed struts and pomp, the silent moment arrives. The pistol hand shakes ever so slightly as the varmint pulls back the tail side of his duster coat. The outlander licks his parched lips of the white spittle and froth at the corners of his mouth, the outlaw raises his hand up above his belly-holstered revolver slightly, another fatal mistake in timing of the draw.

Noticing all his opponent's flaws, including the outlaw's stance being ever so slightly off balance, and the forward lean in advance of the reach. His own right arm was the only part of his body to instinctively and effortlessly slide back. His hand fluidly formed the pistol handle as they became one with each other. The pistol's slide from its holster in the same motion as his arm and hand. The tip of the barrel barely cleared from the holster, his left foot simultaneously slips forward a few inches, reverting all weight on his right rear leg, perfectly balanced on the ball and toes of his foot.

If one could shoot a bullet from the index finger, it would hit the target where it pointed every time. The same is true when a pistol barrel is substituted for the finger point, knowledge that was practiced and taught in the gunslingers' circles.

His finger grazes the trigger slightly in the same fluid motion as the revolver points straight at the outlaw from a position just forward of his hip. The smoke emerges from the barrel's tip and a slight thud or thwack is heard as the slug hit the chest of its target. Delayed slightly, the report finally echoes in the still air.

The outlaw's pistol reports a second later, with blue smoke billowing out in a cloud. The impact of the bullet buckled his body as his pistol was discharged, causing any intentional aim to go awry.

Store clerks, bystanders, and audience leaning on their porch rails and windowsills flinched and ducked in reflex to the bandit's gun hand flailing at its discharge. The bullet went wildly toward the blacksmith sign, splintering shards of wood from its painted border edge. The outlaw's feet launched a few inches off the dirt as he was propelled backward, landing on his back in the mud of the wagon-rutted street.

He stood up straight from his firing posture, slowly surveyed the surroundings, being ever vigilant, and holstered his pistol once the absence of danger was clear. Elwin envisioned himself as the humble lawman, dismayed with the outcome of this encounter, preferring to have apprehended the outlaw and contained him in the jail for prosecution by judge and jury.

Taking a man's life, no matter how vile he is, does not set well within him, and dispositions him in a place well below his character. He hides his shame on the matter well as he walks slowly toward his office, maintaining his integrity with the town folk. Once inside, he will pour a coffee tin or two full of whiskey kept in the bottom drawer. "Drinking in" would calm his nerves to better reflect in solitude some before completing the necessary paperwork required for submission to his peers.

Elwin snapped awake from his fantasy, pondered the events of the last three days and came to the realization that he had in fact achieved more investigative information on the Burke case than the good Sherriff Trunske. He went back outside, stood in front of the bulletin board, cocking his head slightly, contemplating the live colors of the new army recruiting poster.

46   Rebellion Run

Pete Hubbard thought he herd the creaking hinge of the rear door. Eyes half open in his slumber, he knew it was not yet sunrise. Then he heard the wind gust up again outside. He rolled over onto his side to a more comfortable position to allow his higher being back to the realm of unburdened sleep.

Events of the previous evening proved to be way too much anguish between his wife and Mamie, and without any resolution they all went to sleep in separate bunks. He knew the animosity would continue in the morning and that he would have to be the arbitrator, not something that he relished doing.

Trying to force the peace and release of sleep to an out-of-body state cannot be achieved easily unless there is surrender of the physical baggage of thoughts. So he focused on a new, more comfortable fetal position, and concentrated on breathing only slow and steady deep breaths.

He remembered what his own mother taught when he was younger. "Petey," she would say, "Just breathe in the things you want and breathe out the things you don't want. Only then will you find rest and peace."

The morning sunlight warmed his face, and the sensation brought him back to physical reality. The body feels heavier coming from a deep sleep, so he lay motionless for just a few more moments, reflecting on any dreams he might have had but this morning he was unable to retain.

Sitting up in the bunk he forced himself to swing the legs over the edge and onto the floor, rubbed his eyes and reached for the suspenders of his trousers hanging on the peg on the post near the bunk. After some coffee he figured he would sit the two women in his life at the table and resolve the previous night's conflict with a whole new perspective.

Pete looked over at his wife still bundled and sleeping in their normal bed. She was the first to arise most mornings, hitting the privy out the back door, then stoking the cook stove from still smoldering embers. Not this morning. Emily was exhausted from her own rantings the night before and a subconscious guilt deep within her being.

Pete gazed up at Mamie's bunk, with only the bedding and wool blanket crumpled in one corner of the bunk. It was vacant.

With her pack slung over one shoulder, a pair of wool plaid pants, wool shawl and a yarn-knit hat that fit her head tightly, she was plenty warm enough in the predawn air for the hike up trail to Carl's house. He would be very surprised at her arrival she figured but wouldn't mind if she snuggled with him for a while. She reflected on the comfort a few nights ago sleeping with him together for the first time. With somber quiet, she might be able to catch some much-needed peaceful sleep. She planned on just a brief explanation about the argument with her mother and the crazy rantings, and the reason she was unannounced. After a nap she would tell him about her Mom's betrayal and the rumors now circulating.

Scared and confused as to how her mother could have the power over her to come between her and Carl, her rebellious nature kicked in just after the betrayal her mother displayed. Thinking about that and the lost bond with her Mom brought tears welling up again as she walked a faster pace in the moonlight.

The whole episode last evening presented an unsettling catalyst, driving her to seek out the only person who could provide comfort, understanding, and nurturing. Carl Morse was the only one she had in her world this given day. Her mind continued to reel, and forgiveness was not on the table.

Wiping the tears from her eyes as she walked, her realization was that reflecting on the previous evening's event would do her no good in planning the choices she would need to make next.

Passing the bar way leading to Ford's farm and glancing down the trailhead to it, her mother's rantings about Burke and Carl and old Ford welled up in her again. Maybe we could just run off together down to Rochester, she thought. We could get married there and come back to our own cabin to set up house.

Her thoughts of this relieved some anxiety. *I would invite only my Dad up to our new home after we get settled in*, she thought. As for her Mother, she decided to let her anger toward her prevail. We will not speak until Mother decides to present herself in a humble and apologetic manner. Her fantasy continued. There might be a day in the future when she and mother would be back on speaking terms, but like broken china, one can glue it back together, but the crack will always be there.

Her pace quickened on the dirt trail.

47 Lovers Confide

It was about five in the morning. The sun was just peeking over the horizon. Mamie decided to better compose herself before knocking at Carl's door.

From his slumber the light knock on the heavy solid wood door was very distant; it came again to his waking consciousness. This time he accepted it as his local woodpecker grubbing for bugs on the outside beams of his cabin. That was a good thing in a way because insects can and will deteriorate the timber frames of a dwelling over time, and if nature wants to even that score with no labor on anyone's part well, so be it!

He always welcomed the sounds of wildlife in the early morning: birds chirping, wild turkey gobbles off in the distance, crickets and tree frogs, and peepers all sounding their spring mating calls. The woodpecker was just a little more prominent this morn.

Then the door squeaked on its hinge, clear and concise, a very familiar sound, that one point exactly at the spot when the door is half open with all its solid oak weight stressing the wrought-iron hinges, and it sounded again when the door was closing.

He had been meaning to put some bacon grease on it as his Pop used to do every so often. Then he heard the gentle, whispered voice faintly, "Carl...Carl." It sounded like his mother's voice when she would wake him to get ready to head to school or to get ready for a chore she needed. Becoming a little more awake, he rolled onto the side of the bunk where he was able to sit up and roll out for the day.

It was no dream what he had heard, as he cocked his head to the side, hearing the whisper again. Sitting up, he let out a low groaning "whoa" sound as he realized that somebody was in the cabin calling to him!

With no idea yet as to who it was, he swung his legs over into an upright posture and tried to focus his eyes into the dark room. Rubbing them with both hands, then refocusing, a silhouette of a girl appeared standing just inside the door.

The soft voice was familiar, but not at first. He still had the dream state of his mother's voice softly calling in his head. He wondered if it were some vision of his Mom's youthful features coming to him or if he were actually awake.

"Good morning, Carl. It's me—sorry I woke you. I needed to come here and be with you."

His mouth went agape, managing to utter her name. "Mamie? Whoa!" He looked around the room, realizing he was fully awake but completely off guard. The next thought was, *This is better than the dream!*

Dropping her pack, tears streaming down, she launched herself embracing and kissing him with her wet tears. Off balance, they fell back onto the bunk.

Thinking he had somehow overslept, still holding her distraught embrace, she started sobbing uncontrollably. With his hands on both sides of her face to demonstrate his affection and concern, she was able to calm herself.

"Mame, let me wake up here a bit. What time of day is it?" He looked at the window, not seeing any real daylight just yet.

"Okay—okay, come, shhhh, let's get quiet now," he said in a bit of a whisper. "Here, lie back now." He took the wool blanket and tucked it in around her. She still had a slight quiver, murmuring, "I'm sorry, I'm sorry. I'll be all right. I just need a while."

Satisfied that she was feeling safer, Carl slowly got upright and restoked the potbelly wood stove to keep the chill off, then lit the kindling in the small cook stove, putting the teapot on top. "Mamie, you just lay there fer a spell. I'm gonna hit the privy. I'll be right back," he was still whispering, his way to keep her calm.

Pulling his suspenders onto his shoulders he headed out the back door, somewhat confused at the hour. Once on the stoop he realized it was just at the crack of dawn. "Oh boy," he muttered to himself, "Somethin's goin on here. Guess I'm about to find out!" The little squirrel came in his gut again, that uneasy pit in his stomach, a sensation he began to know well enough—a prelude to when something or someone dear to him was about to bring negative energy. His sensitivity was at peak performance.

Mamie was dozed out when he returned, so he brought the teacup over to the bedside and nudged her from her slumber. She half sat up, placing her head on his shoulder as he held the cup to her lips wrapping her hand around his on the cup.

"I want to stay here with you! I'm never going back to that crazy lady! Don't care 'bout that place no more. Tell me you love me, please, tell me true. Say it out loud." She started crying again, snuggled in closer, already knowing the answer. She sipped more of the tea and waited for Carl's response.

It took him a moment to get composed, deciphering why the pit in his gut had anything to do with his lover here in his arms and his dream of her being

191

his wife, a dream that at this moment seemed about to come true.

"You know I do, Mames, I do want you—need you as my wife, my love, and my friend. That's why I gave you my Mom's ring." He held her face again. "Not that I'm complaining, girl, but what is it that has brought you to me this early in the morning?" His smile was meant to lighten her mood.

Sunrise brought a crystal blue magenta hue skyline with just a few whispers of low lenticular clouds way off hovering over near the tops of two high mountain peaks, truly one of God's signature portraits.

They sat on the wooden chairs on the porch, Carl just stared at the two clouds, taking in the subtlety of nature's pastels—blues, off-whites, and multiple shades of green emerging from the mountain's foliage.

He was trying to contemplate Mamie's story, her previous night, her mother's new perceptions of him, and her proposal to run off to get married. The folklore now spreading about the mountain community with him and Mamie smack in the middle of it was unnerving to say the least.

Holding Mamie's hand, he stared at the distant sky picturing her father, Pete, coming into his barnyard to retrieve Mamie—something that at any moment could become a possibility.

It now seemed that everything he wanted just yesterday with Mamie was here at his doorstep, all he needed to do was open it, but at what price or consequence? Looking at her innocent features, noticing the youth in her face, his older soul came forward, and he felt like her father figure or a guardian of sorts. An inner wisdom came over him at that moment. He realized that decisions that day needed to be carefully made with full contemplation.

"Mame, sometimes things are not what or how they first appear when we are upset or angry. Sometimes we need to stop and look at the bigger picture from a higher perspective. It's better to do that when we are calm and centered and quiet inside. That's what my Mum taught me, understand?"

She squeezed his hand tighter in acknowledgment.

Running to Rochester to get married would break the pact that he had made with Pete Hubbard, and men of stature do not break their word. Carl decided in his mind that he dare not deplete his relationship with the senior Hubbards any more just yet. As for Mrs. Hubbard, maybe she was not a stable woman after all, he caught glimpses and sensed some of her skittish traits a few times, revealing a very fearful, negative, and analytical personality that he did not much care for.

Remembering what Elwin said about truth, his flash thought was finally to reveal to Mamie as to what really happened that evening at Fords.

Mamie had finally calmed herself; the short nap did her a world of good.

Although he was enchanted by her appearance and her decision to just run off down to Rochester even today, he recognized right off that she was not thinking rationally. Her description of her mother's "crazy" behavior was mixed with emotions of anger and fear—and her perception of betrayal by her mother.

Carl's inner intuitive senses kicked in and he could see or "feel" that both mother and daughter were not able to relay their feelings properly, causing their conflicting dramas to escalate. Nevertheless he was happy that she was here with him and excited by her demonstration of affection and need to be with only him.

Most of Mame's mother's rantings and speculations involving himself were not even close to the truth, at least by Mamie's version of it. She was coming from a distraught frame of mind when she explained it to him that early morning and the reason she ran up to his house.

He pointed out to Mamie that even the good sheriff was not interested in this scandal any more. She understood better after he told her what happened on the trail when he and Elwin caught up with the sheriff later that morning after she left to go home.

He thought to himself, perhaps now was the time to relieve his secret burden to her, to bring her into his confidence. Maybe now was the time to tell her the truth about that dastardly Ford, what he did to Burke and what he did to me!

Somehow, he thought that she, being his lover, could redeem him of the burden. She would be the only other person in the world who would know that Ford was in fact the true perpetrator, no one except himself, Mamie, and Elwin. They were closest to him in his world, and they could redeem him.

Carl looked at her half-smiling, gazing at her pretty features. She smiled back at him cocking her head questioning his silent stare. "What?" she said.

"You feeling better now?"

She cooed in response, smiling warmly with her starry eyes in a sort of wonderment.

"I know you had a pretty rough night, we're gonna take it a little slow from here today, now let's go feed the critters. I think they're about starved."

They got up holding hands, "A little while later we're gonna have a sit down. I got a story I been meaning to share with you for a long while. I suppose now it's time; it's a secret that only you, me, and Elwin will have."

She smiled in wonderment again enchanted by the mystery.

In the corner of the horse shed, half-covered by an old burlap grain sack, the wooden box that used to contain wrought-iron nails protruded by just one little corner from under the burlap. Not much larger than a cigar box, it sat there barely noticeable. A coil of rusted chains with four closed critter traps at each end were loosely strewn over the burlap as if they belonged inside the sac.

Hidden there in plain sight, who would possibly suspect its contents?

Carl glanced at it as Mamie scooped some grain from the open sack of oats just two feet from the corner. The oats sack was hung suspended off the dirt floor by two of the very wrought-iron nails that used to be the box's cargo.

His flash thought was to bring it out of its hiding, set it on the table in the house and have her open it to reveal its contents, with hopes of making the desired impression that would impress upon her a strong sense of security for their future. He speculated she would be in awe when she opened this simple box. Inside it, the assortment of silver and two gold coins, the folded bills of paper money and the deed titles of the land represented a small treasure trove.

The combined sum included the meager savings of his dad's years of hard labors—a small nest egg he had kept to be used only in hard times and on any very special occasions.

Along with the installment from old Ford, representing the purchase of Carl's silence, the combined value inside this simple wooden box was far more than a normal family man could earn in a lifetime of work.

Quietly and nonchalantly he reached down and pulled the box out of its seclusion, setting it on the rail of the stall, ready to bring inside as soon as the animals were all fed. He did it in such a way that Mamie did not even notice.

They retired finally into the small kitchen and restoked the cookstove from the still-glowing embers. The cast iron teapot began to steam up to a boil. He took both of Mamie's hands and held them on top of the oak table, the wooden nail box just sitting on the corner of the table. "Mame, I need you—I want you—to open this box. When you see what's inside you'll know me and you, our future, is gonna be okay. But there's a story inside it that needs to be told. You are the only other person in my world who can understand—the only one that I can share it with."

"This box is heavy!" She looked at him slightly confused, then half-smiling she reached and untwisted the wire latch, releasing its sealed lid.

48 Puppy Love

Pete Hubbard never put any stock into the hearsays and lore that women folk yakked about in their circles and gatherings. In fact, he rarely paid full attention to it at the dinner table unless the topic included some opportunity for trade or barter or news from the outside world. Most of the time he tuned it out altogether and pretended to be listening to his wife, all the while planning chores and manifestations for his personal well-being and his family obligations.

This particular morning, though, he had to listen to his wife; he had to deal with her behavior of the previous evening. Now her fear and "poor me" approach of Mamie's departure irked him to no end. It fell to him to go and find her before she did something rash. Irritated, he now had to act out of his character. With severe conviction he reprimanded Emily for causing everything that was needlessly disrupting the morning's quiet enjoyment. Now he had to consider the obvious—Mamie could very well at this moment be on her way out of his life.

He liked Carl Morse, his quiet manner and direct posture on things. The young fella was in a strong monetary position with some integrity to go with the dowry for his daughter's future. Pairing Mamie with this Morse boy would insure keeping his daughter close to home. His love for her these days was in fact stronger than his love for Emily.

Pete was impressed with Carl's approach on the marriage proposal and agreement that they made that day. He honestly wanted to include this young man in with the family now. Carl would be like the son he'd never had. The prospect of combining their assets of acreage and livestock was immense in a way that would create stability and benefit the next generation—his own grandchildren.

Emily's hysterics might jeopardize the marriage pact they all agreed to. Anger welled up in him a little more. Unsettling was that now he had to change his plans for the day and take time to go up trail to Carl's. He knew where Mamie was; that was clear as daylight. What put him out was the impending conversation he would need to have with Carl to reiterate their courtship agreement man to man.

"Oh God," he mumbled out loud, "Now I'm gonna have to humble myself and appeal to Carl's integrity so he don't just elope off with my little girl." Perturbed, he grabbed his wool plaid jacket and beelined out the door without closing it.

Struggling with the wire that was wrapped around the square head nail, Mamie lifted open the lid of the wooden box. Another piece of thick burlap custom cut to fit perfectly the inside perimeter of the chest again covered the contents.

Mamie gently lifted one corner of it and peeked under as if to relish the moment of surprise. Peeling it back slowly and setting it on the table just aside the case, she revealed a thick leather letter pouch bound with a wrapped tie strap, two square tobacco tins, and a piece of red plaid cloth bundled around something oval and tied off at the top with a leather shoelace. Under those items laid flat were some neatly folded pieces of thick parchment papers, then finally another layer of the thick custom-cut burlap to serve as a cushion to cradle the precious heirlooms.

Mamie stared at Carl in wonderment, knowing that there was some importance as to what was about to be revealed in these canisters.

She lifted one of the tins out and set it on the table. It was of some unexpected heft.

"Go ahead open it up," he said. "That's the first one you should see."

She pried the lid off. Inside were some large silver coins, five coins in three stacks that fit perfectly inside the round tin. "These are my Mum's and Pop's life savings, Mame. They're silver dollars—15 of 'em. Pop worked all his life saving 'em up. Now they're ours."

Her mouth went wide open in bewilderment. Setting her back straighter in in the chair, feeling somewhat important and businesslike for the first time, her smile dissipated to just a straight line as she lifted the next tin out and set it on the table. Prying the lid open revealed only two coins much smaller in diameter compared to the silver. The color was different, though, at first glance. The only real gold she had ever seen before was the little vial of flakes that the old prospector Fred Bagley showed them at the streamside. Lifting one out, it was as heavy as the larger silver ones were and less than half the size. "Those are about a quarter ounce each, Mame."

"These were from your daddy?" she inquired.

"Not exactly," he stammered a little. "They come from my great-grand-pappy way down south somewhere—Louisiana, I think. Handed down directly to my Mum. She told me she was his favorite of four sisters. He chose her 'cause she had the gift, same as him."

Mamie, not quite comprehending, squinted slightly.

He thought to himself for a moment, then tried to explain. "It's the *trai'teurs'* gift. Cajun healers have it. My mum had it. I think I have it, too."

Still fondling the gold piece, she inquired, "What's a *trai'teur*?"

"Well, girl, that's another whole story. I suppose I'll have to get to that shortly." He reached in the box and gently slid the parchment documents from under the leather pouch and cloth bundle. Unfolding them carefully, he explained, "Mame, these are land title grants—the deeds to the acreage. These papers show that whoever holds 'em owns the ground, the dirt we're standin' on.

"If a man don't have land then he don't have anything of value, 'cause God ain't makin' any more of it.' That's what my Pop used to say to my Mum all the time. These papers are 'inherited.' It says right here," and he pointed to the words, 'heirs and assigns forever.' I'm an heir right now," he glowed, looking up from the forms. "When you and I are married, that will make you an heir, too!"

Folding the parchments back to their creases, he placed them on the table off to the side. Mamie had the brown leather pouch, already unraveling the wrapped ties. She lifted the fold of the half flap gleefully looking at him in that girlish way, anticipating another treasure.

Pulling the short stock of colorized printed bills from the pouch she set them on the table and opened both of her hands in a questioning gesture.

Carl grasped both her hands for a moment, then reached to the cloth bundle.

The coins inside jingled as they dropped on the table, and he unraveled the shoelace tie and like a flower pulled open the cloth.

He spread the bills open like a deck of cards and grabbed Mamie's still-open hands again, this time holding on.

"This is the hard part of the story, Mame. So far, the story behind each of these other items is 'inheritance,' understand?" He looked square into her eyes.

She nodded: "Uh, huh."

"But this stuff, the bills and silver," he said, sliding them away from the other pile in a gesture of separation, "are not inheritance. This alone is a lot of money, more than any normal grown man has these days, I think." He stared at the ceiling, "I can't say the way it came to me was earned, either."

A quiver of his voice, "Mamie—" he paused. "This," cupping his hands around the bundles, "was shoved on me by Old Man Ford! Remember that last time you helped me at his barn yard?"

"Yeah, I think so," she rolled her eyes side to side.

"Remember Ford coming back early, then that shot after we left?"

Her mouth dropped open, then formed a half-open shape.

It took over an hour. Every detail of what happened after the shot, that's where he began the tale. It was etched in his soul. His description of that day was as vivid to Mamie as it was to Carl, and she hung on every word. With Burke falling out of a manure wagon, the bribe money sitting here on the table, the drunken stupor of the sheriff, even Jenny the chestnut mare. She felt emotions welling in her she never knew she had.

He paced the floor to and fro, while she sat on the edge of the heavy maple chair. Then he would collapse back into the chair trying to suppress tears that were welling up. There were spells of anger as well, especially over the entrapment Ford put him through, burying Burke up there in the corner of that meadow and tilling the field over like it was for potatoes. Both of their emotions soared in his description of all the events—every event leading up to this moment at this table. Mamie was absolutely stunned.

The visions of the catamount, his gift of insights, the pangs in his stomach, the "trai'teurs" of his great-grandfather and mother, auras of colors around people—all mystical taboo topics to be disclosed only to close loved ones. He held her face with both hands. "Mame—you are the only one who knows how I work inside. You and Elwin are the only people who know the truth about Burke and Ford. Even the sheriff don't know and don't care!"

It was the deepest of revelations. She just blinked her eyes for a few seconds trying to absorb the intense spiritual meaning, visions, catamounts, colors, and healing by just a touch of hands. She wasn't sure if she wanted to be part of it. It was a realm that she somewhat feared. Knowing he had something unique within him, that deeper part of him was what intrigued her, and up till now she was content with the mystery of it.

She was still trying only to grasp the entire turn of events about Burke and the money, which was overwhelming enough. She found she agreed with the predicament; she was a big part of it after all. She felt how the turmoil was eating him inside. Her relationship just became convoluted.

At that moment a personal revelation came. She removed herself momentarily from the emotion of the last hour's discussion. It now seemed that perhaps her mother's hysterical rantings were not that unfounded. Maybe the innuendos and rumors were not that far off. Unconsciously she changed her posture and her inner demeanor. Carl sensed the change in her body language. The pit in his stomach welled; the catamount flashed into his higher mind. Subtle as it was, he could feel the energy shift between them.

There was a long awkward silence in the room. Mamie stared at the far wall in contemplation, her eyes shifting side to side, focused on nothing. Carl stared at the floor, cloaked in quilt, feeling exposed and vulnerable as to how she was about to react. It was a blunt reality: he had actually buried Burke and kept it a secret from her until now. Did she feel he had violated her trust? Her body language said as much, confirming that intuition.

The silence finally was broken by the sound of Jenny and Sadie whinnying out in the corral, a sound they made only when another horse approached the yard.

It wasn't difficult for Pete Hubbard to see Mamie's boot prints in the moist muddy sections of the trail, confirming her destination in the dark predawn hours. Pete and Marley quietly entered the barnyard at the Morse place, except for the horses sounding off. Wrapping the reins around the coral fence rail so the three horses could interact, he slowly walked over and stepped up onto the simple plank porch deck.

Pete took a deep breath and knocked gently on the heavy oaken door. Unsure of what they were engaged in on the other side of it, he decided that a gentle knock would indicate his peaceful intent.

He might have to demonstrate some patience, he thought to himself, to give them some time to collect themselves, so he resolved to wait a few moments before knocking again. As he raised his hand up to strike the second attempt, he heard the latch lift. The hinge squeaked at the mid-open point and the door opened with Carl standing there, unsurprised.

They both nodded, awkwardly acknowledging each other.

"Top of the morning to you, Carl."

"Morning to you, Mr. Hubbard, sir," Carl responded.

"Pardon the intrusion. I came to talk with you both, on family matters of some import. I come as your friend and her father."

He kept his voice calm and monotone, glancing over at Mamie still sitting at the table. Pete was relieved that she was fully dressed. "Is this a good time to have a discussion?" It was his way of asking permission and demonstrating integrity on an adult level.

Carl glanced at Mamie for her approval, dependent on her loyalty in keeping his secret. She nodded slightly, having no conflict with her dad. She half expected his arrival sooner or later anyway.

"Yes, sir. We was—I was—kinda 'spectin' ya to be stopping in." Carl hastily leaned over the nail box and scooped everything loosely back into it, in a nonchalant manner he closed the lid and set it on the floor, hoping Pete didn't notice it. As he did so he looked at Mamie intent on her keeping the confidence, still looking at her, he pushed it a little farther with his foot till it touched hers. Then he gestured to Pete to come and sit at the table.

After a few pleasantries Pete looked straight at Mamie, leaned over, and gave her a hug, caressing the back of her head. She nuzzled her chin into his chest. His meaning was directed at her, but he looked at Carl when the embrace ended.

"How are you two holding up today? S'pose it's been quite the morning here. We certainly had a long night in our house," he said, looking at Mamie again.

She stared at the floor.

"Well, I s'pose y'all know why I came up today," rubbing his eyes with one hand displaying some frustration. He looked at Carl, "The Missus gets a little out of control sometimes, and she says things later to be regretted. I s'pose Mames told you all about it?"

"Yes, sir, yup! It was a good story. I got her calmed and she got a good nap, so I think we're all thinkin straight 'bout now."

"You two making any fast decisions I should know about?" Pete just blurted it out to kind of cut to the chase.

Mamie responded first, "No, Daddy, not anymore, but earlier we was ready to go off somewhere. I mean I was ready, but Carl calmed me down, Daddy. He's not like Mom thinks he is."

"Mr. Hubbard, sir, the stuff Mame told me 'bout what her Mom said, I mean 'bout me and all—is that why you're here? To break us up?"

"No, no, not at all. I'm here just to talk with the both of you, to try and patch a few things up between Mame and her mother. I'm sort of stuck in the middle of it and we—I just want her to know that it will all pass." He looked at Mamie. "Mother wanted me to retrieve you, Mame, but I want to leave that decision to you, girl. I'm just your poor ol' dad doing what dads are supposed to do. I know you're in good hands here with Carl today. I see that, but I needed to talk to Carl 'bout our bargain that we made not too long ago up by my spring. Can I depend on you to honor that?" By presenting the option, Pete appealed to Carl's integrity.

"Yes, sir, that is still our intention," Carl said, as he looked at Mamie, feeling somewhat torn.

It was quite late in the afternoon. Among the three individuals, all pleasantries were displayed, truths were revealed, privacies withheld, integrities were retained, and respect was given.

Pete Hubbard stood up from the table, acknowledging Carl and Mamie as his equals, in a subtle silence of thanks for their ear and bond. He decided it be best to allow these two young adults to make their final decisions and plans in the comfort of personal privacy.

Taking out his only cherished personal possession, flipping the lid open at arm's length with full extension of its silver chain, he viewed the hands of the pocket watch as a gesture of conclusion and his departure.

With his confidence restored in that his family structure was still intact as it was two days ago, with no words spoken, he held both hands open, making eye contact with Mamie first, then with Carl.

His gaze dropped to the box under the table near Mamie's feet, for only a split moment, if that; then it returned to Carl's. He nodded slightly, turned and reached for the latch of the door.

As Pete closed the door behind himself, he could not help but notice its thick solid oak weight and dense mass. He mounted Marley, clicked his cheeks for her to walk on, and proceeded out the barnyard.

Mamie stood up from the table with her straight back in rigid posture, leaned over and placed a chicken peck kiss on his cheek, and grabbed her wool shawl and hat. Slinging her canvas sack over her shoulder, she exited the cabin.

Carl jumped up. "Where you going, Mame? Stay with me for supper! We need to finish our talkin'!"

She stopped and turned, stared at him momentarily and diverted her eyes toward the ground. "I best be goin' back. Come and call on me later; we can talk more on it then."

Mamie turned on her heel and ran to toward the bar way, stopped and turned, looking at him again as if in a silent, final farewell. Carl stood stunned on his plank wood porch. As he watched her silhouette fade from his view, he felt drained and deflated.

Pete was just 20 yards beyond the simple bar way, and automatically his arm reined in Marley as he heard it. "Daddy—wait!"

Feeling abandoned and powerless, Carl stood there for over ten minutes staring at the now void bar way with only the trail's darker outline seemingly forming a black hole into which her silhouette had disappeared.

He could not fathom what to do next, what action to take, or how to process her abrupt departure. He could only surrender to it. "It's done," he murmured to himself. Revealing the Burke story to her may have been too much for her to comprehend. Maybe it wasn't the right time, he thought. Maybe he should have just showed her the money. The Burke story had changed her mood. "But I can't change it or take it back now," he murmured. "It's done."

Only upon that reflection did he realize Mamie was just a girl child, she would need time—the time that he and Pete discussed and agreed.

He turned and walked the few steps back to the little porch, sat on the stoop, and held his now-pounding head in his hands.

A new revelation came to him. It felt as if there were some curse on him, or that there was karmic debt he had to endure.

Every single time his hopes, dreams or goals were within reach or he got enchanted with something that could bring him joy, it got torn away. Within a matter of hours, someone or some circumstance occurred that disintegrated his happiness. His sense of trust in humanity was beginning to diminish. "Guess I don't deserve to be happy in this world," he muttered to himself.

He decided that he would wait two days, then call on Mamie at her folks' place.

He realized that being with her was the only dream reality he had to hold onto in the world. She was his only salvation, his only redemption, his only grasp and hope of something "good" to come to manifest, the only manifestation that can provide safety, comfort and pleasure in this life.

Holding his pounding head with both hands, he dismissed the negative thought that this, too, would be under the curse. He would know for sure soon enough.

In this moment, the quiet of his solitude became more prevalent, just the slight breeze whispering through the tree limbs seemed to bring a little harmony back. His mind went blank for a short time and he felt somewhat centered, connected only to nature, the wind and the blue sky.

Tired of fighting for every little thing, he closed his eyes and breathed in full and deep, then released the breaths slow. It was his inborn method of surrender.

49 Torn Apart

Elwin finished his chores at the store and decided to head up trail to catch up with Carl. "I haven't seen hide nor hair of him," he laughed to himself. "Best to go check in on him and just go do something, even if it's wrong."

He felt pretty good with the solace his Pop provided, the inside path, and the approach Pop was going to take in meeting with old man Ford. Elwin's confidence that the senior men would absolve his best friend from any more worry and emotion with the Burke matter. He knew they could change the old biddies' perceptions in the gossip quarters as well, absolving all of the problems for Carl Morse in itself.

Just past the Patterson trail split off 100 yards or so was the schoolhouse, where all the younger kids were at their sessions. The older teens were not required to be in attendance this earlier part of the spring due to the chores at the homesteads and some of the planting preparations for gardens and certain crops requiring a man and a boy.

Elwin could see some of the "little rascals" in there through the window, he reflected that they were probably just pretending to focus on lessons, he laughed again to himself, at least some of the boys, anyway.

The girls were always a little more attentive as he remembered some of his own antics when he was at their age. That wooden ruler on the knuckles would always regain the focus promptly if he got caught "dilly-dallying" in class, not to mention the embarrassment with his friends.

Just on the bend at the knoll in the trail he had to rein his horse in from the trot. "Whoa it up, boy," he commanded, as they came head to face with the one-horse buggy.

It was Mrs. Hubbard and Mamie. Elwin tipped his hat at Mrs. Hubbard. "Top of the day to you, ma'am" he said, and, "Hey, there, Ms. Mamie! How are you two ladies this fine sunny day?"

"We are just fine Mr. Elwin Shirley. Hope all is well with you and your folks," Emily Hubbard responded. Elwin looked at Mamie again, half expecting her smiling eyes.

Instead she just stared at the bottom of the buggy, not in her jovial character at all. He glanced at the suitcase near her feet.

It proved to be an awkward moment; one could feel the thickness in the air. Mrs. Hubbard clicked her tongue on her cheek. "Well, good day to you, Elwin," and snapped the reins on her horse's back, lunging the buggy forward again.

Elwin's horse just stepped sideways and backward slightly to get out of the way. "Whoa," he said not referring to his horse.

It was two days past since Mamie had appeared in the wee hours of the morn and disappeared the same late afternoon. It was two opposite mindsets of her demeanor as well. Carl chose to wait the extra day before heading down trail to call on her, hoping to give her the space and time to take in and reflect on how he could be a good provider.

He showed her how he could take care of all their needs when they entered into a life together; now his hope was for that to happen sooner rather than later, while still upholding the commitment to her father and fulfilling her own idea to run off. A compromise in the timing of that was his mind.

Today he would call on her and try to confirm that arrangement. He saddled up Jenny the younger chestnut mare, grained all the other animals and he held Sadie's head with her nuzzle in his chest. She wanted to come with him and Jenny, so he whispered to her, "Yes, sweetie, I know, I know. I'll be back later girl; you just relax today. Next trip will be your turn."

Like a child she kept pushing her nose into his chest trying to get her way. He took her out to the grass clearing and hooked her halter to the rope and lengthened the line another ten feet from the center pin to give her the fresh grass in a 40-foot circle for her to graze while he was gone.

He and Jenny headed down trail with his pack strapped to the back of the saddle containing his denim jacket and some fresh eggs for Mrs. Hubbard.

"Should never go to visitations empty handed," he said to himself, and he added a mason jar of venison strips that he pulled from under the compost pile.

Halfway down the trail at a full trot rounding the same bend on the slight knoll where he encountered the catamount, they came head to head. Both riders had to rein the horses in abruptly, as both were at the same full velocity eager to get to their destinations.

"Hey, there, old man!" Elwin shouted, just as surprised as Carl was. "I was just comin' to see your old hide!

"You always seem to be sneakin' up on people like a damn Indian," Carl responded, happy to see Elwin.

They both needed to settle the two horses down from the fidgeting and side stepping, "Where you headin?"

"Goin' down to Mame's. Then was thinkin' of takin' her down to your store for a treat."

Elwin shifted his eyes to the side. "I don't think she's gonna be there, old friend. I just saw her and her Mum buggy'in down trail a way. They was movin', too! Mamie didn't look too smiley, either."

Carl's heart felt like a rock in his chest. It was then he realized they were standing in the exact spot where he had been face-to-face with the cat.

"Well, guess I'll just drop this stuff off anyway and leave a note or somethin'." Carl dismissed his initial fear that Mamie was running off somewhere, so he quickly tried to compose himself before Elwin noticed his look of worry. "Guess they're just going to the store or over to Farr's or somethin'." Then he kind of snapped out of the dark thought and manned up by shaking his head and arching his back straighter. "Come on, then, it's only round the bend there," he pointed in the general direction. If nobody's around, we'll head back to my place, but I wouldn't mind to see if Mr. Hubbard is around to talk to 'bout somethin'."

As they walked the horses along, Carl told Elwin about Mamie's early morning visit and everything that transpired at his cabin two days ago. He even told him about the nail box and its contents. He had no discomfort sharing everything because Elwin was his best and only friend.

Elwin listened intently. He couldn't help but wonder how so much emotion and intensity could occur in one day. He tried to place himself in Carl's boots, envisioning himself and Lola going through the same scenario.

Elwin concurred about the spread of gossip going around and surmised why Mamie's mom was acting so standoffish. He never really cared for Mrs. Hubbard, anyway. She seemed to be way too analytical about people at the functions or when she visited the store.

They entered the bar way at the Hubbards' place, and the horses seemed to walk slower along the long access trail, at least in Carl's mind. As he wondered about where Mamie went, too, the barnyard loomed into view and smoke was still puffing out the chimney of the cabin.

Pete Hubbard was out back of the barn splitting some wood. They could hear the axe fall with the faint echo bouncing from the hillside. Hitching the horses, the two boys walked around the barn. Carl stuttered, "Morning, Mr. Hubbard. Come to see you, sir, and to call on Mamie, too. I—I—brought the missus over some eggs and venison."

Pete looked up briefly, nodded his head and went back to chopping. He swung the axe with virtuosity, splitting the chunk clean, then grabbed another, splitting it with one motion, then another, without one word.

Sweating, he suddenly stopped and just stared at the wood, breathing heavily.

Then he swung the axe down with one hand into the chopping block and walked past the two of them, motioning for them to follow. He kicked out the chair on the porch and plunked himself down on it, indicating wordlessly that they were to sit in the two vacant chairs. He was angry.

"Let's get some water! You fellas want some water? I need some water!" He raised his voice slightly. Pete abruptly stood up walked through the open door. He retrieved the pewter pitcher of spring water from the table along with three pewter mugs and poured out the cups, spilling them slightly as he handed them to the boys.

Elwin and Carl just looked at each other. Bewildered and not really wanting the water, they just stared at Pete. Elwin at first was amused; then he became intrigued with what was about to unfold.

Carl, also perplexed, felt the hard pit in his abdomen. He knew intuitively that Pete's behavior had something to do with Mamie, and he could feel that it was about to have some effect on him. He glanced back at Elwin with a sort of helpless expression, then looked back at Pete. Carl was still awkwardly holding the jar of venison and the cloth-wrapped eggs.

Pete sat back down and set the pitcher on the porch deck by the side of the chair, took in a deep breath, "Well, Mamie's gone! Just lost my little girl. Won't be back any time soon, neither—probably not for a year if I'm guessin' right.

"God-damn women o' mine just won't let things lie. Got it in her head to put my Mamie in that finishing school; then the two of 'em decided to up and go. Decided it yesterday while I was at the log company. Just weren't no talkin' sense to either of 'em when I got home! No, sirree. Bolted out of here just an hour ago or so. Mamie said it was her choice but put it on me to explain it to you.

"I didn't expect you today, Mr. Morse. Guess you can tell I'm not thinkin' too straight right now—thinkin' the missus caused all this with her God-damn crazy rantings listenin' to those chatterin' biddies and their gossips! They're like geese—squawk, squawk, squawkin' all the damn time!"

He finally sat back and took another drink from his cup after gesturing cheers to them raising his cup slightly forward in sarcasm. "I s'pose you two don't care to hear 'bout this old man's problems, now do you!"

He took another deep breath, exhaled loudly, "Thinkin' I shoulda made her stay up there with you the other day. We all would've been better situated. Now I gotta deal with Emily, actin' crazier every day, without my little girl to keep me happy."

"Oh, here, before I forget—I'm s'posed to give this to you." He reached in his pocket and pulled out Carl's mother's ring. He held it out in the palm of his hand toward Carl. "Sorry son—guess you and me are in the same boat. Mamie said you'll know."

Carl just stared blankly. His lower lip quivered.

"Whoa, man, what the hell!" Elwin gawked at Carl, imagining it was his own girl Lola who took off, leaving him to his devastation. Out of general concern for his friend, he put his hand on Carl's shoulder to prohibit him from an outrageous reaction that was probably about to occur in the next few moments.

After a few hard-choking swallows, which were his effort to suppress the multiple emotions of loss and abandonment, and a few really deep breaths exhaling as almost a sigh, he stared at the porch deck for a real long moment, realizing that his earlier intuitions were dead on.

He decided then in that brief moment of contemplation that no one close to him could be trusted with matters of the heart, and that acquaintances and strangers should be kept at a distance for lack of trust and hidden motives.

He decided to try to project some type of manly integrity before Pete Hubbard and Elwin, as he stood up from the chair, staring at his mother's ring in the center of his palm. He set his jaw firm, then took a deep breath or two and simply said, "Feelin' a little worse off than you are, Mr. Hubbard!" Glancing at Elwin, he saw his eyes were bloodshot red. "I suppose I'll be goin' now. Sorry if it was me brought this on in some way, Mr. Hubbard. Least she be comin' back to you, and at least you have a wife to come home to."

He was holding hard to maintain the façade of calmness and a monotone in his voice to keep the bravery of manhood of his outward expressions. He wanted only to get on Jenny and gallop down trail to catch her up. He started off the porch toward the horses tied on the fence rail.

Elwin quickly bid Pete Hubbard farewell, reaching out and shaking his hand, all the while watching Carl briskly walking to the horses. He knew he needed to stick with his friend to keep him from doing anything stupid to himself or just making a spectacle of things.

"Better stay with 'im to calm 'im down, sir. I think he's hurtin' pretty bad inside 'bout now. You take care now!"

Elwin raced after Carl who was already mounted and heading out the bar way. "Hold up, Carl! I'm comin' with you!" he yelled, slightly out of breath. He managed to mount up, murmuring to himself, "...whether you like it or not, damn it!" and yelling out, "Better hold up, or I'll kick your ass when I catch you!"

Carl was at a full gallop some 30 yards ahead, and he veered left at the gateway in the direction of the buggy. It was a quarter mile down trail before Elwin was able to catch him up, and that was only because of the huge log sledge being hauled down the trail by Diana, the steam tractor, taking up most of the trail width.

Carl had to rein Jenny in from the full gallop since he departed Pete Hubbard's barnyard. The mare was frothing at the corners of her mouth and her flanks and shoulders were sweat wet from the hard pace.

Elwin caught up at the narrow, pulling up alongside Carl, reaching down in one motion without a word and grabbed the reins at Jenny's bit. Totally out of breath, he glared at Carl, insinuating that he ain't goin' nowhere just yet.

Still gasping, Elwin managed to blurt out, "Now you need to knock it off! I know you ain't thinkin' straight right now—chargin' off to catch her like some fool! You'll probably break your damn neck before you get to her anyway, like you almost just did!

"You better listen to me good right now. We're gonna go down to the brook over there," as he pointed to the little grass spot next to the stream bed. "We're gonna water you and the horses down for a spell and you are gonna listen to what I got to say!

"If you give me any of that poor-me lip, I will be obliged to slap you! So let's go." He clicked his cheeks and directed the horses to walk on.

Carl remained in saddle. Surrendered some, he cold-stared at Elwin and released the reins by thrusting both hands up in defiance.

Elwin led both horses by the reins to the grassy spot. Carl just sat like he was cargo.

"Have yourself a seat," said Elwin, pointing at the three-foot round log situated in the toll grass clearing. Elwin tethered both horses off in a way that they could reach the stream water and nibble the grass too.

"It's pretty much over, you know—you and Mamie. She left on her own accord! Ain't nothing you can do about it 'cept to hope she changes her mind. She knows everythin' about you, but you don't know everythin' about her, and you chase her down heading towards some confrontation in the middle of a trail road. You can only be makin' a spectacle of yourself! I don't know what changed her, Carl, I truly don't, but you need to get a grip on a way bigger picture here."

Carl mumbled, "Shouldn't have told her 'bout Burke."

"Well, speaking of Burke—I got a couple things you need to know 'bout. It's the whole reason I was coming up to see you in the first place. I know you're feelin' pretty broke up right now 'bout Mamie, but you can't control it, so sit here or someplace else and have yourself a good cry. Hell, I'll even cry with you some. Oh wait," he cocked his head sideways. "Did you just say you told her 'bout buryin' Burke?"

Carl nodded. "Yeah, I told her the whole story just like I told you. She wanted to run off and get married, showed up at my place middle of the night or sometime, so yeah, I told her the whole truth." Tears welled up and his lower lip quivered.

He started to breathe with short breaths as he thought to himself that his whole world was tumbling down. All kinds of fears ran through his mind as he began to mumble, again making no sense.

"Well, then it ain't any wonder why she run off, damn it!" Shaking him by the shoulders to get his attention, Elwin took charge of the talking again. "You told her that stuff, and all it did was confirm the gossip goin' 'round the dag nab mountain!

"I'm here to tell you that that's all gonna be taken care of; it's all gonna release you from it and with some time it's all gonna be behind you, so you need to start walking around like there ain't no burden anymore!"

Withdrawn into his own depression, all Carl's thoughts were negative and consuming. He barely heard the words Elwin was speaking.

Had he been listening, his attention would have been focused on the new prospects.

Elwin noticed his lack of comprehension. "Come on, Morse, breathe in deep a few times. Take a few minutes here, then we'll go down to the store right from here today. "I'm gonna have you sit down with my Pop. We'll have some good hot supper and you can stay right at my place tonight. We're gonna clear a few things up fer you and help you with real good advice; it's already in the works. You need a change, for sure, maybe an adventure or somethin'. Maybe get the hell out of Granville!"

Elwin remembered the army poster. "Come on, I got somethin' to show you when we get to the store."

Carl finally looked up at Elwin, taking his hands off his head and just nodded. "Hurtin' real bad inside, you know! Can't get her out of my head."

It was over an hour since he sat on that log in the grass next to the stream.

Carl stood up briefly and took a couple of steps toward the horses. It was now mid-day and the morning events had taken an emotional toll on him. He fell on his knees in the grass holding his head with both hands and then laid on his back, oblivious to Elwin, who just watched in amazement.

The catamount flashed again in full vision consuming his mind and thoughts with a renewed presence of power. All fear-based thoughts were gone just like the first time he saw the big cat. There were no words, but the message was clear: Look within to manifest, focus only on yourself, stay in the moment and observe all actions and people; allow no fear to enter your mind. Remain ever vigilant. Like the cat!

Carl got up. Another half hour had passed.

Elwin was now sitting on the big log staring at the stream bed, letting him have his quiet and trying to decide if he should continue to coax his friend any further or just let him go stew off alone somewhere.

He first heard Carl brushing the grass from his canvas pants, then turned around still sitting on the log to see Carl standing there with his jaw firmly set. Elwin remained silent to contemplate if Carl was still distraught. There was a long moment of silence between the two friends.

"Guess I'm ready to head out now, El. Sorry I went loony bin on ya there. Thanks for hangin' with me through that spectacle. I weren't thinkin' straight."

Elwin smiled. "Welcome back to the world, Morse. Thought you was goin' off the deep end on me for a bit. That kinda crap can be rough on any one ya know, I mean losin' your woman an all, but maybe ya didn't lose her yet, they're all purdy fickle creatures ya know! Once she starts missin' yer ugly hairy ass, she might just come sneakin' back!" He laughed in that Elwin way on purpose to keep the moment light and nonchalant for Carl's sake so as not to lose the mood.

They both meandered over to the horses where they were tethered and had managed to nibble every blade of grass with full circumference of their reach straight down to the dirt.

"Guess I'm just damn jinxed, huh, El?"

Elwin clicked his cheek, "Don't know 'bout that; I'd say you been pretty lucky so far! That's if ya really think about it! Jinx stuff is only in yer head!" This time they both chuckled and headed down to the general store at a walking pace. "Mother ought to have some pretty good supper, and I'm witherin' away to nothing 'bout now."

50 Fishin'

Two work wagons and one buggy were sitting out front of the store, so it looked busy as Carl and Elwin pulled in. They tethered the horses on the rail next to one of the other store patrons. Elwin went inside to inform Mother that he and Carl were back for supper. Carl came through the doorway, and the bell jingled again as he opened it. At least five people turned and looked—the typical curiosity folks have in a public place. It was probably the busiest he had ever seen. For some reason, he did not feel comfortable about it, so he just stood near the door, not sure what to do next.

Mr. Shirley peered up over his specs, noticing Carl standing near the door as he was entering one of the local patron's credit account in the ledger book. He knew then it would be a long evening, most likely talking with Carl and Elwin after supper.

Some of the other customers were still placing goods on the large counter top in their separate piles, others were just trying to pick up mail or post letters out. He wouldn't close the door until everyone had been waited on, so it was going to be a long evening at the store.

Elwin reached in the door from the outside and grabbed Carl by the shirt-sleeve, pulling him out onto the porch. "Come on, give me a hand with putting some of the displays away!" Just then old Fred Latham came out with a voucher for a sack of oats, so Elwin handed it to Carl to retrieve the 50-pound sack from the shed. It was good to keep Carl busy with something.

Six o'clock or past came around and the last of the customers was loading up his supplies on the old work wagon. All the display items were put away for the night or under canvas cover, the animals were all tended to, and you could smell Mrs. Shirley's roasted chicken supper wafting through the evening air.

It was a comfort to Carl, reminding him of his Mom's meals all prepared after a long day of work, school, or hunting. Sitting down at a table with both Mum and Pop, hearing and discussing the events of the day or some latest hearsay of the town folks, brought up some emotions in him.

He missed it fiercely, especially after these long months of fending for himself.

Smelling the chicken again he briefly felt some emotion well up as he reflected on his loss of people he loved. Then Mamie popped into his head again; he looked up and the sun was just setting over the top of the western peaks.

It was light conversation at the supper table starting out with generalities and polite gestures.

"Your Mom and Pop were good people. Hope you are getting along with things at the cabin. If you need anything at all, the credit account here at the store is extended to you."

There was an undercurrent at the table, though, thick enough to cut with a butter knife. Mrs. Shirley was up on all the current gossip. Mr. Shirley had just concluded his discussions with Mr. Ford and was eager to sit with the two boys in private. Elwin had spent an emotional day keeping his best friend from going off the deep end, and Carl was still reeling from his shattered heart over Mamie. Each had topics that should not be brought up at the table.

It was Carl who finally broke the ice a little just by making a simple comment, "Thank you, Mrs. Shirley, and you all for the home cookin', and the invite. Reminded me of my Mum and Pop at home a while back. I don't get it much like this anymore."

It was noticeable to them all while the small talk continued during the supper that Carl was stressing and withdrawn even more than his usual quiet self. There were a few awkward moments of silence broken only by Elwin's humor.

"Hey, maybe before dark you and me head over to the bowl mill and drop a line in the river!" he smiled at Carl waiting for the response.

"Sure, guess so, if you got an extra pole."

Mr. Shirley announced that he wouldn't mind tagging along, too. In his mind it would be a perfect opportunity to have the talk regarding his meeting and discussions with Mr. Ford and others, resolving most of Carl's fears.

Mr. Shirley had fulfilled his promise to his son by orchestrating some basic political maneuvers, all in the best interest of Carl and the community as a whole, whereby everybody would win and the breeze of gossip and hearsay would cease.

Mr. Shirley was a savvy strategist. The three of them sat on the embankment of the White River baiting their hooks. "I have some interesting developments that will be releasing you, Mr. Morse, of some recent concerns regarding Mr. Ford and Mr. Burke. I would like you both to listen very carefully."

Carl's mouth just gaped open as he looked at Elwin.

Elwin looked at Pop with approval. "Carl, I'm thinking you're going to like this part."

Carl's mouth stayed open, enough for a horsefly to go in.

Evening has a subtle way of slowing time to a crawl; it settles the mind and washes away fear, anxiety, and anger. It soothes and quiets a man's mind as the natural earth's energy shifts dramatically, placing most creatures into a quiet dreamlike state of mind and body, and providing a closer connection to the cosmic reality of existence. It occurs every day, and many of us take it for granted and forget to acknowledge the power of its subtlety.

The fire they made on the grassy embankment soothed Carl's soul as he lay in the grass and stared up at the twinkling stars. The sun and moon had just taken turns. Mr. Shirley's soft tone of voice and calming wisdom of his chosen words were a revelation as he began to explain his endeavors over the last ten days.

The fishing resulted in just a few bites of a couple of finger trout hiding in the small deep pool, a hole in the ledge rock formation where the steep rocky mountain slope met the valley floor. They were small and promptly released to grow larger for another day.

The three men regrouped on the grass embankment where Mr. Shirley had remained fishing while Elwin and Carl headed downstream. He had built a small fire there with some of the dry river driftwood gathered from the stony sand bar at the river bend. A fire is always a welcome gesture and helps keep the bugs and "no-see-'ems" away. It was part of Pop Shirley's plan for Carl's benefit.

Elwin's hook was taken deep by one of the nine-inch speckles, so as they all sat around the fire in the grass, Carl whittled a point on a straight stick and poked it through and slowly roasted the morsel for a shared quick dessert.

"I know about your troubles, Carl. Elwin here came to me in private confidence a couple weeks ago concerned with your well-being and the sheriff's inquiry. I want you to know first off that El was not willing to disclose or betray your trusted confidence until I made a pact with him in your best interest. It is very disconcerting that two adults such as Mr. Burke and Mr. Ford could not have resolved their dispute, and it's even worse to have involved you in that sordid affair.

"You were not the only one, however. It seems there were two grown Frenchmen who were sent back to Canada, which has caused a disruption and a grievance amongst the French community that came close to shutting down the log camps."

Carl lay back and closed his eyes. He felt a sense of security and solace that someone much wiser was looking after his well-being. So he closed his eyes and listened to his peer's perspective.

"You see, fellas, there's much more at stake here than just the anguish this affair has caused for Carl. As a matter of fact, most of the community can and will be affected. Entire livelihoods could be in jeopardy should Mr. Ford's enterprise collapse. Do you both comprehend my meaning, gentlemen?"

Elwin and Carl just looked at each other, bewildered.

"Well, let me briefly paint this out for your understanding. If, for example, Mr. Ford should be indicted by the law, and if the lawman can prove what he did to Burke was unjustified, or even if he is simply implicated by any further investigations and detained, all his operations would cease, which would affect many local employees and their families regarding income all around the town. It would have a drastic impact on all the additional shops and trades and could cause a collapse of the Granville local economy, which fortunately is still stable while the entire country is under The Great Panic of economic depression. God only knows that we do not need one here in Granville.

"So after my initial meeting with Mr. Ford, we have come to an understanding that will behoove the entire community. What occurred between Burke and Ford will remain between them and God. Our newly appointed deputy sheriff will very shortly dispose of the investigation of Burke in a very—how should I put this?" he mumbled—"Ah, yes, let me put it to you both this way: in a very politically legal manner.

"Once that is done and becomes public, the rumor mill, gossip and innuendos will fade into memory and the busybodies will move on to their next topic of trivia. There will be no interruption of employ, commerce, or routine for folks here in our town. As for yourself, Mr. Morse, Mr. Ford owes you a debt of gratitude and an apology for using you the way he did. As I understand it correctly, he does not owe you any further compensation for your silence?"

Carl looked at Elwin again and nodded with a mumble of shame, "No, sir, he does not, and I would gladly return it if only to ease or release my burden sir."

"It should not come to that, Carl. You have my word and Ford's, as I am witness, that you will be exonerated by him should this matter ever resurface in his lifetime. As for the hearsay circulating about the mountain, that I cannot immediately control or dispense; only time can do that."

"None of this is gonna bring Mamie back, sir. That's all I really care 'bout right now!" Elwin piped up. Gesturing with his hand for Carl to calm down, Elwin stood up from the fire and continued informing his father of the hard upset Carl endured earlier in the day, with Mamie and her Mom bolting off to a private school, leaving Carl abandoned, jilted, and destroyed. His courtship, engagement, and dreams were shattered.

"That's why I brought him down to stay with us tonight. He ain't got no one now, no family to be with or nuthin'. I think he just needs some rest. All he's got now, Pop, is a couple of chickens, two horses, a barnyard and me! That's it. Everythin' else that matters has been ripped away from him, so we need to get his head cleared out."

"I agree," Mr. Shirley said.

Carl laid back down in the grass holding his head again with both hands, Elwin poked at the fire with one of the sticks.

"This is what I suggest for now, Carl." Mr. Shirley pushed his glasses down on his nose, peering over them at Carl. "The proposition is this: You're in good hands tonight here with us and for as long as you need. Tomorrow, you two head back to your place and tend to your stock. Elwin will stay with you there each night you choose. Do that for the next week and stay here every other night for 'family time' and home cookin'.

"Then I want you to consider a new adventure of sorts, an opportunity if you will, that will take you out of Granville to the outside world. My recommendation is to let this negativity dissipate, and let my political plan engage while you are gone for a while. It can open you up to new horizons.

"Tomorrow morning after breakfast on your way up to your place I want you to pay special attention to a new poster on the porch bulletin board. You have a lot of special skills, son—skills and expertise that go unappreciated here in this small town, where they could be wasted or untapped. If there is nothing here for you or any young man to hold on to, then the adventure of going into the outside world beckons you.

"You already have your land and financial stability. Your chances of finding a new lady love are far better beyond Granville. Perhaps later you will reunite with Mamie—no one knows that future—but all manifestations are possible for you.

"So that's my proposal. Take a week or two, set your routine and your affairs in order for now and contemplate the future opportunities that await."

It all made perfect sense, it was sound advice coming from a very savvy man who had the prowess to make things happen in the town—in fact, he had already initiated the sequencing of it with others in the community.

Elwin felt proud to be an integral part of it all, and better still, he felt it to be the best solution for his best friend. Placing his hand on Carl's shoulder, he said, "Come on, you must be exhausted! Let's all head back to the house and catch some sleep! God knows I'm beat!"

With that, the three of them headed back across the White River over the catwalk just across from the log companies' Puddle Dock pond.

It was a soft bed, the latest version of comfort offered by Sears and Roebuck, a goose-down-filled mattress mounted on coils of boxed springs and a goose-down-filled pillow. The fine-woven light wool blanket took the night chill off with little effort.

Carl succumbed to the deep-earned sleep, an out-of-body experience he had not felt in a long time. None of the events of physical life entered that realm this night.

The early morning sun danced on his face from the light breeze subtly moving the curtain in the window. He tried to hold the dream state and lightness of body, but the warmth and light of the sun beams beckoned him to the reality of conscious thought and awareness.

At first, he had no recognition of where he was. The level of comfort was unfamiliar, and it took a moment to regain the full consciousness and memory of his surroundings. It had been dark, after all, when he had entered his room the night before, lit only by the dim oil lamp on the bedside shelf. The room had been prepared by Mrs. Shirley while the men were fishing across the way.

He could have just slept in a little longer, or all day for that matter. But, he thought to himself, he could do that back at his own place in quiet solitude.

Remembering the discussions at the campfire he decided to arise, feeling somewhat excited at the prospects that they had spoken of.

51 Horizons

He was eager to see the poster on the bulletin board. Feeling refreshed, the anticipation of some new adventure energized his body. Not wanting to be a burden helping with morning chores was foremost on his mind.

Finally standing vertical, his bladder was about full to the brim; first order of business was out to the privy! That simple release was a comfort.

The morning went by quickly. Being occupied in a different surrounding kept his mind free of the depressing events of the last couple days. After they set up the store front and tended to the animals, Elwin's mom cooked up some taters, salt bacon with maple syrup drizzled over it and the scram eggs with an array of veggies cooked all together in the skillet.

"How do ya like those chicken embryos!" Elwin joked, laughing in his jovial way and drawing a scornful look from mother.

Looking up from the plate reluctantly, hesitating long enough to swallow, Carl said, "This has got to be the best breakfast I ever ate. Can't thank you enough Mrs. S. If you're not careful you might be adoptin' me here permanent, whether you want me or not!"

"I'll take that as a compliment, Mr. Morse, but for the appreciation of the help and chores, we have to keep you boys fit and strong. That's how life comes to full circle." She smiled subtly as if there were a deeper meaning.

"Well, boys, there's still a few things need attending to before you all go gallivanting off." Peering over his specs, Mr. Shirley handed Elwin a folded notepaper he had prepared earlier that morning. His businesslike tone was meant to reiterate his seriousness and instructions from the night before.

Carl had forgotten most of the anxiety from yesterday and was eager to start fresh, so he offered to help clean up the breakfast table. The Missus declined, freeing them up for the outside tasks, which entailed assembling one of the new displays.

It was a small new-style galvanized metal evaporator from Sears Roebuck with flow compartments meant for any family farm operation to boil down maple syrup. It would be a big seller at the general store. It just needed the leg stands assembled to complete the promotion that the representatives at Sears offered for free to the store owners. After selling ten units the owner could option to sell the display unit and keep a 50 percent split fee from the supply house.

The boys dove straight into the task.

The full-color army recruiting poster was on the notice board just under the evaporator display were they were working. Carl was mesmerized by its alluring features and detail. He found it hard to focus on the assembly, constantly looking at the colorful details of the poster and envisioning himself in it.

Elwin saw him staring at it. "See, I told ya, Carl, me boy! There's a whole world to be seen out yonder there," as he pointed off to the south. "You could put some of those shootin' skills to good use with those army boys!"

"Think I'd rather tend to the horses an' stock, ya know, keep 'em safe an' calm an' healthy," said Carl, picturing himself behind the battle lines whispering to the stressed animals in his way amidst the excitement. "Besides," he said, "the animals don't shoot back!"

"Yeah, but with that eye of yours you could pick off the bad guys and still stay outta range. Oh yeah, the army will draw out your talents an' put 'em to good use fer sure!" Now they were both sloughin' off, daydreaming, as that poster came to life.

"Wonder how ya go 'bout joinin' up?" Carl posed the question.

"Oh, that's fairly simple," Elwin said. "Pop has papers inside. It's an Army Enlistment form that ya sign your name an' age and where ya live. Think ya got to be 18 years old, though, but you look older than that anyway, so no one would know if ya told a small fib!"

"Then I think ya got' a go up to Montpelier to report in with your horse and gear. Pop must send the form in once a month, and they send him back a notice where the volunteers are to report to. I heard him telling one of the older fellas who signed up a couple months ago how it all works, somethin' 'bout a trainin' camp where they test ya out to bring out your best abilities."

"They send ya down to that camp on a train with a bunch of the Green Mountain Boys—that's what they call the Vermonters. They keep all the Vermont boys together 'cause they fight better that way an' look after their own kind."

Carl gazed out at the horizon totally enthralled, "Jeez, Green Mountain Boys! Damn! That really sounds like somethin!"

"Yeah, they're pretty famous for courage an outsmartin' the enemy all the time. Ya don't want ta mess with the Green Mountain Boys in a fight! That's what I been hearin' an readin' about."

"Oh, yeah!" he shouted, slapping his thigh.

They both stared at the poster for another ten seconds in silence, each with a fantasy energized by the lure, the adventure, the camaraderie, and the uniforms.

Kneeling back down to keep the assembly going (they had to refocus on the evaporator project), Carl looked up at the poster a couple more times, his mind reeling from the thought of it all. He was hooked.

The painted poster had done its job psychologically as it was meant to do.

Carl now was anxious to get back home and square things away, if he joined up there would be a lot of preparation; he would be gone for a few years at best. Holding the red-painted legs in place, Elwin put the square-head bolts through the holes and tightened the square nuts with the special wrench that came with it.

The evaporator was a thing of beauty, with its red legs and pastel blue trims. They both admired it, stepping back a few steps to view the accomplishment. A slight twist and a slide into final position on the store front porch made it stand out to pique anyone's interest. The final touch was the colorful display poster with the Sears Roebuck emblem, some specs, and a silhouette of two fellows in hats with sleeves rolled up. One was pouring the sap in on top tray and one was at the spigot with a pail.

The boys went out back to saddle the horses, returning to the storefront. Three customers were already admiring the evaporator. Elwin's dad puffed his pipe, nodding in approval of the display and the potential customer orders.

"Thanks fer everythin' Mr. Shirley. We're headin' back up to my place to tend the critters and get a few things situated. Think I'd like to talk to ya some about the sign-up forms," he gestured to the poster, "maybe tomorrow or the day after."

Leaving the customers to the display, Mr. Shirley excused himself and walked up to the horses, stroking their noses and ears.

"Some family folk just arrived in town looking for work and a place to stay. They may be the perfect people to rent your farm and tend all your animals if you decide to enlist. Once you make the final commitment you should have about a week, I believe, before the rendezvous at the train station. I'll check the dates. You should plan on being back here within three days anyway just to go over all the terms."

He was always very straight and to the point in his manners, Carl thought to himself. He could feel he was in good honest advisement.

"Oh, Elwin! Before I forget," Mr. Shirley stepped on the store front porch and grabbed the big leather satchel. "Here—you might as well bring the mail up mountain while you're on the way. Speaking of which," he peered over his spectacles at Carl again, "it may please you to know that you might be able to correspond with Mamie while you're off in the service. I'm sure we can obtain her current address if you wish." It wasn't really a question, but more of a suggestion—a seed of something that could ease a young man's mind during trying times ahead.

"Yes, sir. I been considering getting in touch with her for some needed words."

It was way too soon to stop at Hubbards' and try to talk to Mame's dad, Pete, though he considered it as they rode past the bar way—besides his embarrassment was powerfully overwhelming.

Elwin didn't have to talk long to persuade him out of it. "Nope, not a good idea, no!" That's all he had to say, reading Carl's mind when he reined up at the gate way.

All the chores got done quickly with two of them, leaving a little time to laze around in the afternoon sun. The old porch chairs seemed to suck them both into the concaved embrace and the hot tea just set things right.

"So ya really gonna join the army? Man o' man, I mean it sounds a lot better than tryin' to eke out a livin here in Granville! I'd go with ya, but Mum an' Pop talked to me 'bout taking over things here at the store, ya know. They want to slow down on the pace it demands on them, anyway."

"Yeah," Carl said, "you got some good things to latch onto here, and there's Lola! She's got an eye fer you, no doubt 'bout it! I'm picturin' you two all settled in a couple years, 'bout the time I come rollin' back into town with a line of fine breedin' horses in tow!

"Yup, think I'm gonna do it. Mamie took the wind outta me, leavin' like that." His voice started to quiver, chocking back his emotion. "Her mother ain't right in the head anyway, and Pete Hubbard—well, I took to like'n' him," he muttered.

"You an' your folks are right. I got nothing but hard people here and nuthin' to hold me down, so maybe those new folks would like to rent here for a couple years, tend to the keep the till in, and Sadie. I'll take Jenny with me 'cause she's a lot younger.

"You gonna stay here tonight, El? All I got is beans 'n' bacon for supper if you are."

"Naw, I'm thinking of headin' back unless you need the company. You ain't gonna go off the deep end again on me, are ya? 'Cause now ya got me thinking on Lola, an' I might take to lookin' her up in the morning!"

Carl put his hand on Elwin's shoulder, "Thanks for all the help and such. I'll be down in a day or so to set up the affairs. Just gonna take tonight an' tomorrow, get my head screwed back on, ya know. Some quiet think time is good for the soul!"

He watched Elwin trot his horse out the bar way, reflecting on how Elwin was truly a loyal friend, one who always seemed to stand behind him through the tough times, someone who had seen him at his worst and always showed up just when the chips were down.

The next two days were a spiritual healing, allotting him the time to just stay in quiet solitude. Sleep came easy and deep, with dreams of Mother and Pop as if they were still home going about their routines.

He kept his thoughts of Mamie only on the affections and tender moments at their secret rendezvous place in that sugar maple stand. That lone pine tree in the middle of the maple grove with its boughs sweeping down low would hide them well from view. They would lie in the bed of soft pine needles and caress each other, exploring their bodies without guilt or fear of consequence.

52 Gifted Ways

Carl thought about the things his Mom spoke of with insights and his great grandfather, who could put his hands on people and heal them. And how he himself saw, heard, and felt a person's true nature.

The faint colors he could see around folk's bodies as they talk or just stand nearby him were starting to make sense now in his ability to read a person's demeanor.

His intuition or knowingness of folks was different from animals. With animals there was almost an unspoken language, he reflected. It was as if he were the creature and could somehow sense its fear, anxiety, or hurt and what was causing it. He knew that the animal could sense his gift and connection. It was a spontaneous knowingness between the animal and himself.

Carl always was more comfortable with the four-legged creatures, way better than with human strangers. With them he just saw the colors around them and the changes of colors, reds and browns when they were angry and fearful or upset. He remembered Mamie when she was feeling love and comfort. She projected tones of light blues and yellows out of her that seemed to circle out of her breasts and back around through the top of her head.

Then he thought of the catamount, that huge black mountain lion that appeared to him whenever dangers were looming or a situation of consequence. The cat was his protector.

He reflected on these things in the quietness of his mind. In revelation the human betrayals were not worthy of his insights. To him, trust, like Elwin's came hard earned. The animals were the only creatures that would display loyalty and appreciation.

Four full days had passed. Carl enjoyed the solitude, completing the daily chores and his preparation tasks for his trip to wherever the army corps was going to send him. This included separating the important papers and money left from his parents from the ill-gotten coins and currency received from Mr. Ford.

The brown leather pouch—the same one he showed to Mamie—took some pondering as what he should do with it. After some moments he decided to bury it for some good cause in some future day, or never to be used again. Let it stay forgotten forever! It had brought nothing but trouble and heartbreak since he came into its possession. First Pop died, then Mum, then Sheriff Trunske investigating things, then Mamie leaving suddenly.

Holding the pouch, he murmured out loud, "Damn! This is jinxed money! It's cursed money! It will only bring bad things to anyone who finds it or spends it."

So the decision was made then and there. The spade hanging in the barn had not been used since Mother was out in her little garden. It didn't seem right to put it anywhere near the cabin or the barn, nor did he want to desecrate either of his parents' graves with it.

As the last shovels of dirt went back over the nail tin box, suddenly came a whistle, then a man's voice shouting, "Walk on—walk on," commands to the horses from the wagon driver. Peering through the foliage and trees he saw they were just down slope of the stone wall he was at. The pastel green and red wagon had some folks aboard and one lone rider on horseback was in the lead.

He quickly replaced the flat stones at the corner of the stone wall that marked the property boundary, making sure to place the weathered moss sides back the same way they came apart so there would be no indication.

The folks in the wagon pulled into his barnyard; he could hear the familiar voice of Elwin shouting, "Hey, Carl Morse! Got some visitors for ya! Carl Morse!"

He circled around back of the barn and emerged out front with the shovel still in hand as if he were cleaning the stalls.

"Hi folks! Hey, Elwin Shirley! Heard ya the first time, El." The half-smile was meant as a razz of camaraderie.

"Hey, Carl," Elwin gestured to the three people in the wagon, "This here is the Lamphere family, the folks my Pop mentioned to ya 'bout rentin' out yer farmstead here whilst yer off to foreign lands! Thought I'd bring em up to meet ya an let em see the place for themselves."

"And we got the notice from the recruit office for the draft volunteers an' where they need to report in!" Elwin was talking all exited the whole time as he dismounted his horse. He flung the leather mail satchel off the saddle towards Carl almost in one motion as if it were routine.

"So you would be pleased to meet Howard here, and Daniela, gesturing to his wife, and young Miss Josie, who is soon to be the prettiest eight-year-old young lady in all of these mountains!"

Josie blushed, then giggled.

The Lamphere family dismounted the wagon, shaking hands and going through all the pleasantry exchanges. Elwin served as the moderator, explaining their history briefly and as to how they came to Granville. He also spoke some about Carl's background and his most recent venture to depart for service in the army, thus his need for live-in folks to look after his estate.

They all agreed as to the unique synchronicity and timing of the coincidence.

Josie excitedly said, "I don't know what coincidence is, or synchronicity, either—but the angels say it was all meant to be." She trotted off in the barnyard investigating things, starting first with Sadie at the rail of the corral. Carl smiled at her, nodding in approval. He connected intuitively with her and could sense her innocent strong connection and gift. Her aura was a light blue and soft yellow hue.

Suddenly her father's voice jolted him from his brief focus. "Oh, don't pay no mind to Josie. She'll come out with stuff like that from time to time." Defensive and smiling awkwardly, Howard was feeling embarrassed by his daughter, afraid of leaving a wrong impression. "It's mostly her imagination ya know, she talks to her make-believe friends a lot lately. S'pose we might have to make her a little brother to play with!" He glanced at his wife, then shifted his eyes to the ground.

After a disconcerting look at her husband, Daniela said, "So, Mr. Morse, would it be possible to see the inside of the house, sir?" With that subtle word, she shifted the visitation back on course.

Carl, already impressed, glanced at Josie again and then gestured holding his hand out towards the cabin, nodding approvingly with another smile and nod at Elwin. These folks were the embodiment of his own dream and vision of a family now just beyond his own reach.

At the conclusion of the visit, and acclamations with the property, an agreement was finalized. The Lamphere family would take possession in about five days, allowing Carl some more quiet time and a better chance to organize his personal affairs. They would remain at their campsite just down trail alongside the White River. Howard would interview with a few potential employers, including Rob Ford. Seems he may have a couple of positions open right about now!

Carl would rendezvous with the train by way of and over the Braintree Gap Road just off North Hollow Trail. That would put him into East Granville just were the Jonesville Trail intersects at the top of Braintree Mountain. Once down the eastern slope along the east branch of the White River, he would travel north another twenty or so miles on that valley road into Roxbury. There he would catch the train, Old Number 88, at the station.

The train would accommodate his horse and one duffel bag of personal gear and provide a hot meal during the trip down to White River Junction. There would be a five-day orientation, issuance of uniforms, personal gear, and rifle. All non-essential personal items would be mailed or shipped back to the enlistee's home address.

These were the instructions that were mailed back to the Granville general store along with his one-way army train pass. He figured the trip would take all day, so just to be sure he would leave two days before the departure time at the train depot. In the meantime he would spend his last evening at the Shirleys' place just to secure all his financial affairs and holdings with his best (and only) friend, Elwin.

Some of his money, along with the land deed and the new lease agreement would be held in safekeeping until his return as a safe deposit to be locked in the eight-by-eight safe in the back of the general store, which also held the town clerk's records and documents. Carl's annual taxes would come out of the rental payments from his new tenants, payable directly to the town clerk, who happened to be Elwin's Pop, or direct to his appointed beneficiary, Elwin himself. There wasn't much he needed to worry about in Granville while he was absent.

Carl reflected on these things while viewing the different shades of greens of the landscape from out the train window. He had no insight as to how his special skills would soon place him in France—a European conflict, the very first stages of World War One.

53 Uncle Sam

Four years of Carl's military life, including two deployed in France, under duress and anxiety of combat conditions can and will affect a man's demeanor and values.

The first year of army training was spent finding a recruit's aptitude, applying brainwashing tactics to utilize a soldier's highest potential to their application. It was enduring but ineffective on Carl L. Morse. He could sense and see through their tactics and decided to demonstrate his abilities both on the rifle range and with the livestock as well by using a one-on-one personal connection with his superiors throughout his training. He learned quickly how to connect to his commanding officer's highest inner being, planting a seed in that person, gaining a higher respect over the others, and causing Carl to shine and stand out more somehow above others in the unit.

One such occasion occurred when a string of draft horses and four mules got spooked by a clap of thunder and a lightning bolt at the top of a distant mountain peak that makes its own weather. The assigned handlers could not control the ruckus and the entanglement of the tether lines. Two mules went down, dragged by the potential stampede.

Carl raced to the dominant horse in the herd, the one horse that the rest seemed to follow. He held his hands outward facing the black Morgan stallion while the other handlers were yanking less-dominant horses by their halter lines and shouting directives and angry absurdities.

Carl stood without anger or fear and gained in a moment the Morgan's eye contact and attention. The Morgan stopped his thrashing and immediately became calm. Carl approached and cupped the stallion's long face with both hands.

He spoke in a monotone voice almost above a whisper. "Now what's all this? You're much too brave and smart to let a little thunder upset everyone. It's passed now, anyway; it always passes by. Now you and me, let's get the others calmed down." Then Carl took a deep breath and exhaled slowly and methodically on the Morgan's nose. Within moments the black Morgan turned to face the frantic members of the tethered herd straining the lines. Like magic they all suddenly stopped the thrashing.

The staff sergeant witnessed the entire event. For some reason he could not fathom, he remained strictly focused on Carl when he saw him approach the horses. It was watching a flicker show with the camera on the main character. The sergeant's decision was made, and he appointed Carl as lead handler the following morning.

It was the same demonstration with the sharpshooting abilities. Time and again Carl outperformed the others by applying his secret knowledge utilizing windage effect, powder grain and caliber of the bullets or projectiles. He also had a sixth sense of even humidity's effect on how the bullet would travel to its target. His breath exhaled and held prior to the soft squeeze of the trigger was all part of his natural techniques.

Carl endured many things that no man should have to endure in France, bearing witness to human atrocities that no man would choose to witness. The cruelties of war, especially regarding his beloved animals, caused him to withdraw within his being. He would attempt only to place these memories in a small compartment of the mind upon his return to the States.

Debriefed and with an honorable discharge from his service in the elite army unit, he began his trek back to the Green Mountains of Vermont. On the train looking out the window somewhere in Pennsylvania he dropped his medals of valor and bravery out the train car window and let them bounce off the tracks somewhere near an Amish farmer's field where a farmer was planting his corn with a horse-drawn planter, in his white shirt, suspenders, and large brimmed straw hat.

For him there was no honor in any of it. For Carl, the travesties were a detriment to human evolution in this age of ignorance. The country rejoiced and called it "victory."

Carl L. Morse returned to Granville, devastated by human travesty and betrayals. He chose to remain only true within himself, to live in peace and harmony and savor the quiet moments of daily life.

There was a surreal sensation as he entered into Granville from the Hancock side of Texas Gap, passing the falls. A couple of Hancock farmsteads and the small school building were missing—or was it just his lack of memory as to their location? "Well, it's been four or five years!" he murmured to himself.

Texas Gap trail leading to his old homestead was grown over from disuse; water ruts and erosion painted a clear picture as he approached where his own homestead was supposed to be. Instead of the cabin and barn that his Mom and Pop built all those years ago, where he was raised and had grown up, where he was to marry Mamie and raise his family, stood nothing but the stone foundations and charred remains of post and beams in a heap spewed at the foundation floors.

This was indeed the ultimate human betrayal, to desecrate a man's abode or dwelling. Even ancient native peoples would never enter another lodge or teepee if not invited, or if the entrance was closed or marked with crossed sticks. To do so was a sacrilege, bringing repercussions back on the perpetrator spiritually.

For Carl, the burned homestead cemented his decision to now remain disengaged with untrustworthy humans. He sat on the corner of the stone foundation and contemplated and pondered for half the day. The light breeze hit his face gently, the blue wispy sky and the green hues of the distant vista caused his focus only on nature's energy, the only energy that matters, as he came to realize in that moment. In the quietness of the moment, a deep peace and tranquility set into his existence. It went straight to the marrow of his bones.

Carl camped there that night, the stars filling the night with ambient celestial light. Visions of how he would rebuild filled both his waking and inner mind. The daybreak brought the rustling of a moose and two deer bedded in the grass clearing nearby.

After exploring through the rubble, he found he would need tools. He made his list and after three days he headed down to Elwin's general store to try to get an understanding of what had happened here.

The year was 1918. Carl spent most of the summer building a smaller log cabin starting with a six-foot-deep stone foundation nestled into the side of a knoll just a few yards or so from the Texas Falls Trail Road. He could not bear to rebuild the older homestead after learning how it came to be burned down.

Instead he would utilize and salvage some of the timbers and foundation stones to create his one-room cabin and his small horse barn stalls and a sugar shack with same evaporator unit that he and Elwin assembled before his departure to the army.

Such was the beginning of Carl Morse's new life of solace living in nature's peaceful solitude, after making a few adjustments and a few minor hardships, and a few mid-season trips with his new horse, also fondly renamed Sadie, along with wagon to acquire gear, tools, and supplies, he would rapidly set his new routines and realize a deeper connection to nature's rhythms, animals, and the intuitive power of spirit and earth's energy.

The "Hermit" as he was now referred to by local folks, had acquired a talent to intuitively communicate with animals. Deer, rabbits, squirrels, turkey, moose, partridge, and black bear would frequent and bed in his small hay lot clearing just near the barn. Daytime and evenings alike they were not intimidated by his presence.

54 Twenty Years Withdrawn

With an armload of wood, his right foot nudged the small cabin door open. It took a moment for his eyes to adjust to the dark interior of the newly constructed one-room abode. Instinctively he felt the box of wooden strike-head matches. It lit with one strike on the side of the thick maple plank table. The oil lamp soon glowed to life and illuminated the small room.

Kneeling on one knee, he lifted the wood stove door slightly, then swung it open, revealing the glowing coals. The handful of shavings made good fire-starter kindling. A soft couple of long breath blows ignited the shavings. Four or five dry pine sticks topped off with two good splits of birch would rekindle nicely for a couple hours.

His body was fatigued. It had been a long day of small accomplishments, putting some finishing touches on the exterior of the cabin. Sitting in his handmade wood chair the Sears Roebuck catalog was nearby sitting on the table. He thumbed through the pages, locating the exact tool to add to his list.

The tea pot began to whistle. It suddenly reminded him of the day the train pulled into Rutland station all those years ago. He reflected how his army uniform was adorned with badges and a few medals and how eager he was to get back to his mountain farmstead.

He reflected on the twenty years gone by since his departure from home in 1907. Now at age 36 and maybe one-half years old, (he couldn't be sure), this evening in the year 1927 his body felt all of 70. He chuckled to himself, "Oh, well—a good night's sleep will cure that.

"Ah ha! There's that wood rasp I'll be needin'," he quickly jotted the catalog number down on his neatly written essentials list. The thick pencil that he kept sharp with the six-inch Buck knife mounted in the scabbard on his belt just near his right hip was about half of its original length. The sharp knife took two peels off the tip, exposing the newer lead. Even the pencil peelings he neatly placed in the tin tinderbox.

Sipping his tea and munching from the wooden bowl of dried grains, hickory nuts, and some maple syrup, he began to doze off from the simple supper.

A few more staves of split oak on the wood fire should last most of the night, keeping the chill off, and the soft down-filled mattress and pillow felt very welcome and pretty much coddled him under the wool blanket. The only sound in the now-dark twilight was the symphony of crickets, peepers, tree frogs and linnets. And then he dreamed.

Morning routine had become systematic in his solitude. In the darkness he could slip on the boots placed just at the end of the bunk over the leggings of the cotton long john underwear.

Four paces to the left was the ever-ready pile of kindling staves. Reaching with one hand, he could clutch four of the thin strips. The spring-coil stove door handle was never as hot as the stove's cast iron, so with a slight lift and pull he opened the door to reveal the embers still glowing, awaiting the kindling to fuel its morning flame.

The wooden latch of the cabin door slid sideways from its cleat; the pathway to the privy was fifteen paces from the cut granite door stoop. The two buttons at the long john rear flap were unhinged easily with two fingers enroute to the privy. The wooden handmade seat was always cold no matter what season in the year.

Birch bark paper, always abundant in the forest, was kept stacked neatly alongside the bench seat. He could walk back to the cabin door with eyes closed if need be, the wood fire crackling as the embers again became flame.

A large stave of hickory or oak would sustain for the tea pot to boil the natural spring water and sizzle two strips of bacon or venison. The hot water would feel refreshing on the morning face, and the tin cupful was just enough for the pig hair toothbrush dipped in the spearmint twig bark shavings and baking soda paste.

The last of the hot water, still in the pot, went well with a handful of the raw oats in the tin cup mixed with a spoon of maple syrup from the large mason jar on the simple shelf he called his pantry.

Slipping his boots off while sitting in his hickory chair, he pulled on his green wool pants with eyes-closed ease; suspenders still attached would stretch up and over the shoulders. The Montgomery Ward wool long-sleeve green plaid shirt would take off the morning chill every time.

The worn path to the horse stall now stood out in the morning light as the sun illuminated the outside world. His eyes took a moment to focus from the darker cabin interior.

He poured a small bucket of oats into the wooden trough for his horse, Sadie.

The galvanized pail he would dip into the rain water tank and set on the ground for her, too. Then he would slide the two cedar rails from the simple gate so she could forage at her free will in the grassy clearing down slope from the cabin.

The two almost-tame deer in the far corner of the meadow, with their heads and ears perked up at attention, knew they were next in line for a morsel treat from the oats pail. From his pocket he would hold out two handfuls of grain for the deer, who would run up to him at the cedar gate and nibble from his open palms.

That was a typical morning routine in all four seasons for the last 20 years since his return home from the war. It was interrupted only by inclement weather. The solitude of his chosen lifestyle brought him peace and tranquility, as his daily chores and tasks were strictly at his own pace and related only towards the gathering and preparation of food stuffs, chopping wood, and simple upkeep of his cabin and grounds to supplement himself and his one horse.

The wild livestock consisted of his local flock of turkeys, a couple pair of snowshoe rabbits, a pair of young white-tail bucks that he'd found as spotted fawns, and the covey of some six or eight partridge, or as some prefer, grouse.

Even the occasional coyotes that ran in a pack of five would come around in the clearing hoping for a handout. There always seemed to be a solo red fox also seemingly living in the same type of solitude, so he would cater to the fox with some table scraps in the winter months just to help him through.

There were daily and weekly visits from these wild creatures who for some reason were drawn to the human hermit. They would appear and stay around his small clearing and barnyard, allowing Carl to walk among them without fear. He truly had a connection with the wild creatures.

He reveled in the ability to interact with them and that every day, and at every distance his eyes could look, he could see and focus only on natural beauty—from valley vistas on top of a high vantage to the close-up patterns of lines in the bark of an oak or maple tree. He learned over the years of wilderness living that all things in nature were symmetrical in shape and in cycle. He knew he was connected to nature and the rhythms of the earth.

Each season was a welcome change, with its benefits of new beginning and harvest usefulness. The fresh clean air would lift one's energy with every lung full, the clear spring water purified his body with every sip, refreshing every cell, hydrating and revitalizing his entire being.

These are the things most people would take for granted in the civilized world just seven or so miles away. He savored his quiet solitude. The interaction with other humans had proved to bring only heartache and conflict. He did not miss the interaction with other people these days.

He remained leery of any strangers who might come around or venture near his cabin. On some occasions passersby traveling on the Texas Falls gap road that meandered 100 yards from his cabin at its closest point would stop to get some water or directions, encounters that he choose to keep distant and elusive with minimal but quiet politeness in his nature.

Encounters like that had a way of shattering his daily routines and occasionally cause him to retreat into the cabin or to seclude himself deeper into the forest at one of his special pristine places to withdraw from the encounter and regain his centered solace.

It was for good reason what with his past experiences with human beings and witness of what they could be capable in causing harm and anguish to one another, but mostly it was the vexatious betrayals that they always seemed to bestow.

55 Recluse

It was spring time in 1929, and winter snows receded rapidly, melting daily now with torrents filling the stream beds. Nighttime snow showers changed to rain by sunup. The forest was beginning to spring to life, morphing with buds of silver and pink tips. Red buds were the first sign of sap flows awakening the maples.

Carl Morse was also breaking from the routines of cabin fever, and he planned his bittersweet annual trek down trail to Shirley's general store. Elwin was now and had been the town clerk, postmaster and proprietor of the flourishing store along with Lola, his wife. His Mom and Pop now were long deceased.

Bittersweet for our hermit in that he would have to trek with his horse and wagon all that way, only to encounter god knows how many strangers, and or now estranged town folk whom he once knew years ago. Not out of fear, but only that his insights and sensibilities were increased tenfold because of his meditative lifestyle.

The rumors and hearsay town folk circulated about him now were that he was a seer. "There's an odd individual who lives in seclusion somewhere high up on the mountain," they would say. By the folklore alone he piqued the curiosity of folks whenever the subject came up. Some said he could talk with the animals.

The sweet part of the venture down to town was the prospect of picking up as many supplies as possible and his new tools and essentials that he could order from the Montgomery Ward and Sears Roebuck catalogs. The trip was a huge emotional seasonal event for him.

He kept a meticulous longhand-written list with the exact catalog number on each item consisting of clothing, tools, hardware, and the occasional toy and sweets that can bring a man simple pleasure. All his personal effects were available over the counter. Items he had ordered last fall would be in the back room awaiting his arrival for pick up.

The trip would also allow him to conduct all his connection business with his only trusting friend, Elwin, who handled his monetary affairs. Lola also had an understanding of his nature and the hardships he had endured. She had good energy and his brief words with her were always soothing and nurturing. She was the only female he knew and trusted.

This trip he was excited about obtaining ten more taps and collecting buckets to add to and increase his maple syrup operation. Yes, he did get an improved version of the Sears Roebuck evaporator a few years ago—in fact it was the discounted display model that Elwin and he had assembled on the porch of the store all those years ago. He considered it as one of his toys!

He also had ordered the Burrell's Corn Sheller apparatus, a hand-crank machine made by Gould's Manufacturing Co. in Seneca Falls, New York. The hand crank would spin a heavy internal flywheel and keep its revolutions by perpetual motion with little effort once its inertia was started. He would place the ear of hard corn or feed corn in the port at the top; the dull teeth on the flywheel would press against the smooth internal plate and remove the kernels from the entire cob. The kernels would disperse from the bottom funnel, shoot into the collection pail, and the husked cob would spit out the opposite port into the wooden collection box. It was ingenious and simple.

Carl used the cobs as fire starters for his woodstove and fireplace. He also made his corn cob pipes, but more important, the grain would sustain his horse most of the winter. Finally, he always reserved some of the kernels for replant in the spring.

His multicolored wool-lined denim jacket sleeves were worn through on both elbows, and there were a few holes of wear on the front bottom corners from the years of picking and lifting and carrying routines. It was time for a new one.

He was not enchanted about the trip down trail with the wagon. He had already replaced two of the wheel spokes that had rotted from sitting most of the year without use. He had disassembled the entire wheel and whittled out and shaped the new spokes from some harder wood of locust tree limbs, but the originals were made of oak. His concern was that ruts in the trail could cause additional wear and tear on the hubs and spokes with the weight of his supplies on the way back.

The wagon was used only once or twice in the summer to bring in his wood from his stand of oak and maple at the far corner of his piece of acreage.

Vigilance of planning and preparation was instilled in his daily life. It was a trek he had made hundreds of times growing up, back and forth from school or down to Ford's or the Hubbards'. Farr's turkey farm was even farther down trail from his house, but all those destinations were relatively easy on horseback.

One would plan on an hour or so each direction if one were not in a hurry, and no one ever really was unless it were some emergency. The trek all the way down to the general store or the bowl mill or the log company was always twice the distance off the upper mountain community and especially difficult in a lumbering wagon, cart or buggy.

Carl always took the rifle with him these days. He had made a unique scabbard for it that he could lash to sideboard of the wagon next to the plank seat with long strips of soft deer hide leather passed through three holes he drilled through with his maple tree tap auger.

That way he could always mount it on the saddle or even sling it over his shoulder. Usually and more comfortably it would be across his back for walking in the woods hands free. He made a stiff leather ring out of a piece of old harness sewn in just at the top inside the softer deer hide so the rifle could easily slide in and out in one motion.

"Well, that works real slick!" he told himself the day he modified it, admiring its finished version and feeling proud of his innovation.

So off he went, snapping the rains on old Sadie's back lightly, "Come on, Sadie girl, walk on now! Nice 'n' easy now! Ain't no hurry, ain't no hurry."

Just before he hooked the wagon harness up, while walking back to the cabin to get the day pack that he had prepared the night before, he noticed a small hole in the top side of the right rubber boot, revealing why his wool sock was damp and wet occasionally after he was in a stream bed or just getting water from his spring sump. "Well now, there's the culprit!" he said. It had started out as a pin hole but now it had evolved to the size of a spike nail.

He immediately retrieved a small thumb tack from his tin box inside. Just after contemplating a solution, the answer came quickly to his entrepreneurial mind: a tack with its round head on the inside poking outward and a gob of spruce gum sap from the spruce just near the barn. He warmed the ball of sap with a match flame and plugged it in just over the tack pin poking up around the whole area. The sap adhered nicely, regaining its gummy flexibility, and sealed the hole perfectly.

56   Ghost Town

He passed the Ford bar way, the memory of the event there now just a crack in the vase of china. He looked up the overgrown lane briefly and shook his head in disgust, not wishing to review any of it, as he had already done hundreds of times over the years.

Inevitably passing the old Hubbard place, with its gate long rotted away and just the remnants of the two posts, half as high as they once were. The long access way was now grown over from non-use with brush and small trees encroaching in on each side. The Hubbard farmstead was now reduced to just its stone foundation.

This was also one of the bitter parts of the annual trek into the Granville Valley, the reflections of his return from the army expecting to find his family homestead intact, and his neighbors enjoying their prosperity in a small bustling community as he had left it all those years ago.

Instead, he found most of the farms razed to the ground including his own—lands, fields, and timber lots all seized by the government. The U.S. Forest Service agency during the prelude to and on through the Great Depression, bought out all the town's tax liens—back taxes owed by the farmers that demanded payment in hard currency—a commodity hard to come by for most.

Once the agency purchased the tax lien, it would then foreclose on the landowner, forcing him to relinquish his title and deed. There was no negotiation or flexibility. The government had an eye for the natural resources. Some say it was the timber—straight pines and spruce that could grow fast in those cleared fields and harvest well for masts of ships in just a few years' time.

Some farmers were conned by agents into planting these seedlings instead of viable crops with the promise of a large monetary return in ten or twenty years. The seedling money (hard currency) was loaned to the farmer, placing him deeper in debt, posting land parcels as collateral. The bottom quickly fell out of the timber market with the advent of the improved steam engine for ships. Loans were called, and land parcels were seized and foreclosed for non-payment.

Others said there was another natural resource up in the Green Mountains, a mineral that was found in outcroppings throughout the forested landscape in Granville. They said the government under the guise of the Forest Service was planning on mining this new mineral, barium, for its use in industry. The clear-cutting of vast areas may have been in preparation for these exploiting these deposits.

Tax liens were foreclosed, government loans were called, land and farmsteads were seized, and armed agents forced evictions. Other finance agents lured and coerced the sale of folks' land for pennies on the dollar, taking advantage of the hard times starting with the recession known as the Great Panic. That recession evolved into the Great Depression. Folks were in one way or another methodically forced to sell and move out.

This took place throughout all of Addison County and other counties in Vermont. It might have been an elaborate scam just to claim the land for the Forest Service to fund its own agency at a time when government funding was on the list of budget cuts. Or it might have started that way.

Franklin Roosevelt then took office and created the New Deal, whereby many folks throughout the U.S. were employed building the country's national parks, roadways, trail systems and reserve areas to the great benefit of the nation. The sanctioned harvesting of timber resources continued through the 1920s and over the last nine decades in Granville, some of which is under State Forest supervision to manage and thin some areas for wildlife preservation. But clear-cutting vast regions continued on the U.S. Forest Service land.

Many believe this to be exploitation of the forests themselves all for governmental level monetary gain—pristine forests that the agency was charged to protect! It continues to this day and was something that Carl Morse was extremely aware of intuitively and by firsthand experience even then. It was the seer in him, his deep vision into the future of the landscape and the diminished heritage of Granville.

He reflected on the day he returned to his farmstead. It was to be his first stop off the Texas Gap trail traveling from Middlebury over the long Ripton trail. He was eager to get to his childhood home and start his life over after leaving army life behind. At first, he thought he was disorientated with his whereabouts, but there were Mum's and Pop's headstones, the old spring and hand pump—all the landmarks were intact. But the house and barn were gone! Only the stone foundations and the stone chimney were left with charred debris in the bottom cellars of what used to be structural handcrafted post and beams, pegged and dowel timbers. What had occurred there he could not fathom. Did the place catch fire? Why the barn? Was it abandoned by the tenants? Was it intentional?

He made a temporary camp, utilizing the old chimney fireplace. The truth finally was revealed by Elwin when Carl got to the general store for supplies.

237

57   Government Scam

Elwin and Lola were surprised when he first arrived, heavily bearded, still wearing a partial army uniform. He stood, quiet and humble, just inside the store door, not making eye contact with the other customers, who eyed him as some stranger. He did not speak or move until all had finally departed with their wares.

Still he did not speak or move from his stance next to the door; he looked up from the floor. Elwin peered over his specs just as his father had done, and asked, "How can I help you sir?" He said it nonchalantly after the quick glance at the stranger, then went back to his ledger, finishing his note in the leather-bound book.

There was a moment's pause. Elwin refocused on the stranger's form, squinting some, looking beyond the disheveled appearance of the man.

"Lola!" he said in a raised voice. "Lola!" He said again even louder, "You need to come out here!" He closed his ledger and removed the specs from his face. Lola emerged from the back room, curious. Elwin walked from behind the counter with both hands extended towards Carl, who received Elwin's right hand with his in a firm shake. Lola did not recognize the stranger. She could not conceive why her husband was embracing this vagabond.

El latched onto him with another genuine full embrace that lasted a few uncomfortable moments longer than it perhaps should have. Hesitant at first, Carl responded with his awkward man bear hug. The feeling of rekindled camaraderie took those few moments to return.

Lola, still confused, finally questioned her observation by smiling at Elwin and eyeing Carl up and down. "El? Who might this quiet person of your obvious acquaintance be?" She continued her smile, staring apprehensively.

Not taking his eyes off his old friend, Elwin grinned, now holding Carl by the shoulders at full-arms' distance. "My dear devoted wife, this is none other than my good friend, Mr. Carl L. Morse, back from the dead!"

"Oh, my God!" Lola exclaimed. "We all thought you had perished in that terrible war! Did you not get our letters?"

Carl's hands began to shake. He had still not spoken. Unable to muster words, he could only process the overwhelming feeling of genuine love and friendship coming from them both with their elation at his appearance—sensations he had not felt from others for the past seven years.

The look in his eyes already revealed the answer to the question. All he could do was to look downward again and shake his head twice side to side.

He started to stutter some words, in mind torn between simple pleasantries and the burning question of what happened to his homestead. His hand fell into his coat pocket and found the simple list of items he had hastily put together that morning. Hand still quivering, he handed it to Elwin, and he put his hand palm up in the air to gain a moment to collect himself. Elwin glanced at the list, recognizing that the tools listed had an intended use.

"Come and sit down, my friend; there's a lot to discuss. Lola, can you please lock up? We need to talk with Carl here undisturbed." He took Carl's elbow and herded him towards the long maple table.

Carl's first whispered words were, "You look well, Elwin Shirley."

Lola put some tea water on the cookstove and sat next to her husband.

"There have been some major changes here in town since you left," said Elwin. "We sent you multiple letters, some of which came back, and many did not. So we were not sure of your survival. The army correspondence office was elusive as to your whereabouts and well-being. I wrote them many times, to no avail."

Carl could only muster out a whisper in his next question, "El, what happened to my home?" He stuttered every third word.

Lola and Elwin recognized the intense emotion, and trauma, now evident in his manner from the person he was seven and a half years ago.

Elwin put his hand over his on the table. "Carl, I have handled your affairs here on your behalf, as executor and beneficiary of your estate just as you instructed me when you departed for the army. It is gonna take us all some time to explain the occurrences over these last few years, so I'm insisting and will have nothing other than your presence here this evening with a nice hot home-cooked meal, and a warm bed and morning breakfast.

"I will start by reintroducing Lola here as my beautiful wife of four years now! She was reluctant at first," he said, smiling, "so I had to resort to a kidnapping."

Lola blushed.

The tea was good and hot, and set well with Carl. He started to feel a little bit more comfortable and somewhat at home with the only familiar family folks left in his life. Throughout the evening, Elwin tried a few times to get him to talk about the army experience, only to receive a teary-eyed reaction, shaking his head side to side, not as a "no," but more as a memory he wished to deny.

Carl flashed memories of the mortar attack in France on his elite unit. The only words he stuttered out were, "Couldn't save my animals—the horses—tried hard, El. Couldn't save em in that place over there." He dropped his head in shame and a tear fell on the table.

Elwin looked at Lola, deciding not to pursue any more questions of that subject.

Over the rest of the evening Elwin explained how the government agents from the Forest Service arrived and posted a notice on the board at the store. "They were offering to purchase cleared land and acreage at 'fair market value' for 100-acre parcels or more. They would also offer any farm with 50-acre cleared parcels to plant white pine saplings that they would supply, along with a payment advance loan.

"Many sold out to pursue a simpler life in bigger towns or tried to maintain on their smaller tree-farm parcels. Many of them did, only to endure the demand of payment on the government loans and foreclosure just three years later."

Elwin continued to explain what no one noticed, was the purchase of tax liens on delinquent taxes—situations that many folks were in because of the country's recession. Liens were selected and purchased by the government agent who appeared one day and intentionally went through the public record and began to methodically purchase the liens with government funds, then immediately sent a foreclosure notice to the owners.

Most of these properties were well over 200 acres and sometimes 500-acre parcels that were original land grants to the owner's father or grandfather before the state became annexed.

The agents then proceeded to force evictions and burned the homesteads down so no one could return or squat back in again. They wanted to get the acreage by any means. They focused on vast regions of parcels throughout the township with the established trails and roads as access ways.

Carl's farm and estate fell into both categories—large acreage and a delinquent tax payment. His tenants, the Lampheres, fell onto hard times soon after they moved in. The first winter for them was brutal. Howard Lamphere took a job at the bowl mill but could not continue the job so they moved on shortly after the second year. That's when Elwin adopted Old Sadie, who sadly died in Elwin's small corral in the back of the store, probably out of heartbreak, as Elwin put it.

Elwin had the money for the taxes in Carl's reserve trust, but the agent targeted the land and tried to slip it into the lien purchases. Elwin caught it in time and thwarted the foreclosure.

The log company sold much of its land holdings to the government soon after the timber industry took a decline; thus the private timber lots went as well. This brought the entire logging community to a rapid standstill economically.

Government crews were shortly called in and with no public notice began to burn the acquired farmsteads down, plumes of smoke would appear on the horizon sending the public into a rage, men and women alike.

No one could fathom why they were in such a hurry to extinguish their heritage. Emergency town meetings were held, alliances were made, and town folk banded together ever closer. A community effort and vigilant protest took place—a community spirit not seen since the times of their forefathers.

Confrontations, fisticuffs, and even gun discharges were endured. The appointed sheriff was torn trying to maintain the peace. Carl's homestead and barns were razed to the ground because of a "boundary line mistake" by the burn crew agent on some makeshift map. That mistake allowed Elwin to negotiate better terms of purchase.

Following his personal inspection, Elwin negotiated with the purchase agent on Carl's behalf and sold off some 300 acres of the rougher terrain adjacent to and including the burned farmstead, for which he demanded a healthy market value. This enabled Carl to retain some 200 acres for a homestead should he return from the war. Lola and Elwin explained that they had not received any return correspondence from their multiple letters to him. Naturally, they began to think that he had not survived.

Elwin said smiling, "Hey ol' friend, look at ya standin' here. I always knew ya was too tough an' ornery ta up an die over there!" It was El's attempt to lighten the mood a little, to no real avail.

Carl slept in the same comfortable bunk as the night he had left for the army all those years ago. In the morning, with few words, he loaded his supplies paid for out of the surplus account. He bid Elwin and Lola good day in just a few whispered words.

They all stood on the store porch, recognizing that Carl Morse was now a changed, withdrawn man. They could feel his connection with them as trusted friends and others as not. When he stood in the doorway for twenty minutes without speaking a single word, that alone spoke eloquently of the trauma he had endured.

Elwin knew just by the tools and the new woodstove he added to the list that he was going to rebuild. Carl shook Elwin's hand and managed to murmur, "Guess I'll come back by fall." He was satisfied with his leather pouch containing land deeds, transaction documents, and certificates of monetary funds that he chose Elwin and Lola to handle on his behalf—an agreement they had worked out the evening before. As far as the rest of society, he could not bear any close human contact. With his heightened sensibilities, his clairvoyance was overwhelming for him. Closed-minded thinking in most adults he found distasteful and avoided. Children he did not mind so much.

This event with the government land possession under a fabricated ruling called Eminent Domain, as Elwin explained it, changed the entire character of Granville. To Carl, it was a massive betrayal by the very government he had just put his life on the line for. It was a crossroad, and his new path was clear.

Whispering, "Much obliged to you both; got some work needs doin'," his steel grey eyes told Elwin all he needed to know, revealing that he did not need or want any help or intrusions in his life.

Mr. Morse snapped the reins and instructed the horse to "walk on." And so began one man's conscious choice to live life with simply "quiet solitude."

58   France Remembered

It was Fall 1934, 25 years since Carl Morse rebuilt his cabin. It was a chilly October morning; leaves were in full foliage of colors. Every distance the eye can focus on from any high point revealed magnificent vistas.

Carl completed all the morning routines of personal hygiene and tending to his animal friends. With the rifle scabbard slung over his back, and the small army canvas daypack, today's focus was to head up and over to deer hollow.

A yearling button buck would suffice this day for his needs to replenish the venison in his small pantry. Carl would not take a doe; it was not in his religion. The rule was simple, "No does, no babies." Preservation of the deer herd depended on it.

The harsh winter months would take its toll on the deer population's ability to survive, deep snows alone would limit their ability to defend from timber wolf, coyote, and catamount. Natural predators would take advantage of the starved weaker and younger, those restricted in their agility of movement and escape.

Foraging for food was also an impediment. Buds, acorns, and beechnuts were all either buried well below the deep snows or too high on the trees themselves for younger ones to reach. Carl witnessed firsthand how the moose would strip the bark and consume the beech nuts off an entire tree up over eight feet high where even the biggest buck could not reach, even standing on his hind legs.

The smaller yearlings, unfortunate to be born in very late spring, mostly could not survive these harsh winters. Spring carcasses always revealed this fact, just the skeletal remains on which even the mice would feast in the end. Most of these would be found just under a thick grove of white pine or hemlock stand where a small winter herd would congregate, taking advantage of the shallower snow accumulations and the protective cover from the elements. A small group could better fend off predator attack with antler and hooves if need be, but even the biggest bucks' antlers drop and shed during and about the end of January. So this day our Hermit would save one from a worse fate, taking only what he could use for his own winter survival.

Carl was like a ghost in the woods. He would walk in steps of six or ten paces, careful not to shuffle leaves or snap ground twigs. Then he would stand perfectly still using the terrain, pine scrub, brush, or trees to obscure his silhouette. He would crouch, kneel or even lie belly down before the next steps. Movement, he knew, would draw attention from all creatures of the forest. Birds would stop chirping, red squirrels would sound an alarm that echoed in all directions. Carl knew if he moved as the deer or the rabbit, with short steps and then stand still, ever vigilant, utilizing all his senses, he could become one with the forest.

Off in the distance he heard the unusual crunch of the leaves and snaps of dead branches. It was no form of wildlife; deer and moose would not continue in their initial leaps after being spooked. It was human—another hunter tromping through the woods, probably hell bent to get to some location or to rendezvous with a companion.

The human walked within ten yards of the large hemlock obscuring Carl's presence, then just walked on by, stopping for less than one minute with his back to Carl's position. Carl was irritated with the hunter's intrusion, disrupting the natural stillness throughout the area. The wind was also at the man's back flowing in the general direction he was heading, spreading his scent before his noisy arrival.

Carl just shook his head in disgust, then decided to use this fellow's lumbering to his advantage. He would circle in a half-moon arch about a tenth of a mile upwind in his same direction, letting this fellow drive any deer directly toward his new position.

A half hour went by. Then to his disbelief, while he stood on the ridge looking down into the hardwood stand at the fellow still walking through the leaves, shots echoed through the air, three in under a half minute.

The shots came from beyond the fellow in his view, then the shouts, back and forth, again breaking the stillness. Carl saw the two white tails straight up as they bounded over the ridge line out of sight. Still the un-aimed shots again discharged from the man's rifle nearest to him. The bullets whizzed through the air over his head making the all familiar whistle as they cut through the beech leaves. He leaned against the back side of the large maple tree. Two deer stood motionless the same as he did—two does, just twenty yards away in a shallow dell.

The war in France suddenly filled his mind; the shots, the shouting, the whistling bullets overhead triggered the memory. Carl and his trusted French assistant worked frantically under fire to move their beloved string of horses and mules back deeper into the tree line. Their artillery unit, all American specialists, came under fire in a remote field in southern France where they were training the French allies in the use of the American-made Howitzer 8-inch M190 and 6-inch Model 1908 Hydro spring-recoil long-range cannons.

It was a mechanized unit for the most part, but the positioning of supply wagons and equipment utilized the horses. Most of the twenty-odd men in the unit were Southern Baptists, quite discriminatory regarding men of color.

His assistant, Joval, a younger boy of French heritage about three years below Carl's age, was a French citizen and recruit with the resistance forces. He had a similar gift with the horses in a way that calmed them. The young black man was under constant criticism since his assignment with the Americans. The southern boys belittled and disrespected him as inferior from almost the very first day—something he did not understand and had never experienced, being born French. There all were equal and accepted, respected for their own attributes and talents. Like Carl, he preferred working with the livestock.

Carl took notice of this boy almost immediately, the way he could whisper with the horses, his gentle touch and the subtle, calming manner of his speech. His accented broken English was unique, pleasurable to the ear. Carl liked him from the first, sensing this young man to be like himself.

Carl witnessed one harsh encounter with a particular redneck sergeant on the ninth day of Joval's arrival. He kicked Joval on the backside, knocking him down, because the coil of rope he carried knocked over the sergeant's tin cup of coffee. Swearing and cursing, standing over the thin boy, the sergeant went to hit him again with a back hand toward his head. Carl intercepted the strike. He threw the sergeant backward four feet with a swift palm square under the jaw.

"That will be enough!" he said, pointing down at him. "Ya touch my friend again an' ya not gonna be goin' home vertical!" Carl's penetrating steel-eyed stare spoke so much more. "Out there," Carl pointed toward the front, "are plenty of guys your own size you can pick on." Carl helped Joval up and brushed him off.

The sergeant started to rant, citing his rank. Carl went nose to nose. "We kicked your asses once already. It was called a civil war, you ignorant soma bitch. Don't make me do it again."

Carl was respected in the unit amongst the men. His skill with the long-range rifle was deadly accurate and they knew it. He was their key sharpshooter, a secret weapon.

Still stunned, the sergeant backed away. Suddenly mortars began to explode fifty yards ahead of their position, and bullets whizzed and cut through the air. Everyone scrambled for cover except Carl, Joval, and the cook. They all headed straight to the horses tethered at the tree line behind the mess tent.

They worked in unison and led the three strings of animals farther into the wooded area by another fifty yards, safer from bullets and shrapnel. It was the sound of explosions they could not control that kept the horses and livestock on edge.

The soft talking and whispers of Joval and Carl were the only soothing sounds among the chaos. As Carl taught them, all three of them would whisper or speak softly in each animal's ear directly to give it the sense that it was being cared for, protected individually.

A small contingent of Huns basically had stumbled on their position from their flanks, and hastily launched a mortar attack, catching the main French defense legion off guard, focused as they were toward the front lines.

Carl headed back to the main American Howitzer battery after the horses were secured in the woods. Before he left, he noticed the direction of the rifle bullets whizzing through the air at the tree line and that they were coming from a small knoll. He saw movement up there with his keen eye.

Grabbing the 1903 M1 Springfield 30-06, he laid amongst some mess supply crates and used his Warner/Swazey MI 1910 scope to better view the enemy position and their number.

He then proceeded downslope to where some of his unit's men were still in confusion. None of them at that point had verified where the fire was coming from.

He rallied four men with rifles and the two men who manned the Stephen model 1907 machine gun. Two of the Frenchmen volunteered also and grabbed up a Hotchkiss model 1914 MLE French machine gun. The sergeant was nowhere to be found in the confusion and the smoke.

Carl led the eight men back to the mess crates. They rapidly set up their defense with the French machine gun on the right and the American machine gun thirty yards to the left. The riflemen were set up in the middle and Carl took his position at the tree line between two round haystacks.

His scope brought the enemy mortar position into full view. With his M1 Springfield special sights system he took out one of the two-man crew. The plan was that at the report of his rifle the American and French would open a basic cross-fire.

The Huns were unaware of the American team as they were mistakenly focused on the Howitzer line of cannon facing toward the trenches at the front lines.

Carl's Vermont hunting tactics worked very well this day, utilizing the terrain, tree lines, natural cover, and stealth. In a time where frontal trench-style battles were prominent, and straight-up charge assaults only won a few hours of peace, the improvised "special force" tactic proved to be innovative and well before its time. It later won him a useless and hollow citation.

The Warner/Swasey scope was intended to be mounted on the M1 rifle but its dependability was not perfected very well then, so most sharpshooters learned to use the scopes only to calculate distance and magnify the targets as spotter devices. Through the scope Carl was able to see the 15-man enemy unit and their squad commander shouting and pointing directives toward the Howitzers in the distance behind Carl and his men.

He brought his small team up into range inside the tree line to the rear of the mess tent, which happened to be at the same elevation as the enemy position. From that advantage they could view the entire enemy unit and still remain unnoticed.

Carl wished that he did not witness the carnage they inflicted on the enemy unit that day. It made him feel ashamed to be a human being.

He returned to the horses, Joval, and Angus the cook, where they waited, anxious for his safe return. In his southern drawl Angus reported that the stock were okay, then asked, "What happened out there?"

Carl stared up at the sky for a long moment and muttered, "Out of all of nature's creatures in the world, humans are the worst. They are the only animals not in balance or harmony with the earth." He stared at Angus with steel-grey eyes. Then he sat down cross-legged on the ground. Being with the horses was his only solace and retreat from the daily carnage.

It was fate that threw them all together—Joval, Carl, and the unit's cook, Angus, also from the states. Carl Morse met him when he was first assigned to this unit down in Hamilton, Virginia just after basic training. Angus was of the same mindset as Carl. They both had an inner knowingness of things, a certain sensitivity with people and surroundings. Angus took a lot of heat from some of the closed-minded men, especially those who liked to criticize the meal of the day. He took it personally after he had put his heart into the preparations.

On one occasion that Carl witnessed, a southern redneck soldier who didn't like carrots or cabbage decided to intimidate Angus by throwing the stew bowl on him as a personal attack. The intimidator tried to instill fear, but it was repelled when Angus just turned sideways and stared straight ahead, ignoring the verbal assault.

Carl saw the red hue energy from the soldier slide past Angus and dissipate; it did not draw the response or create the fear to feed the intimidator's control drama. Instead it had the opposite effect, leaving the private baffled and confused.

Now with his back toward the intimidator, Angus grabbed two armloads of carrots, celery stalks, and a few heads of cabbage, proceeded to the string line of horses and dumped them into the feed troughs.

Carl leaned in toward the redneck private still in awe with his mouth agape.

"You must be a special kinda fool! Ya gotta wonder what he might put in your special bowl of soup next time. S'pose ya didn't think that all the way through, now, did ya!" Carl winked at him with a slight jab of the elbow. After that he admired and befriended the cook, and whenever possible Angus would slip veggies to the horses as treats.

"You see the colors, can't you," Angus blurted out, handing the crate of carrots to him.

Carl just stared in his eyes for a moment. "Yeah, sometimes it feels like a curse."

"No, no, it's a blessing, I think, keeps me knowin' who's who."

"That was somethin' with that Southern boy the other day," Carl said.

"Oh, you noticed that, did ya? I learned that a long time ago. Just turn sideways. Let their hate just pass on by. That way they can't steal your energy. They can't drain you out through fear, then they don't know what ta do next. Keeps em guessin'! Ha!"

Carl and Angus shook hands and sealed their friendship and camaraderie that day. Besides following orders from the superiors, they kept pretty much to themselves within the unit throughout the rest of the training down south.

Being an elite unit, with the newer long-range versions of Howitzer artillery and the precision marksmanship of the gunners, there came a time when some higher officials paid a visit to the facility.

Their unit was selected as the best of the best. The request came down for specialist volunteers to ship overseas into France and work with the French army artillery teams to introduce the new cannon designs and retrain the French with their improved tactics, features, and support teams for the Howitzer weapon systems.

The army pay for this deployment was double the regular wages—quite the incentive for almost all the men. Carl and Angus made their decisions based on the pride and the adventure of going to a foreign land.

Carl had nothing to hold him here, anyway. He was proud to be recognized as part of an elite team, to which he was integral in that he was the only sharpshooter. He could speak some limited French words that his mother taught him from the French quarter in Louisiana.

Carl was asked personally by his commander be a part of this group because of his skills and abilities. "Never seen anyone work with those horses the way you can, Mr. Morse. We need more men like you and God knows so do the French."

Carl's ultimate decision though, was truly due to his staunch convictions in the "just cause of the war" and the need to take care of his beloved horses, his only real family.

59 Tap Sap and Syrup

Spring 1939: Maple sap flows heavy in the 40-degree morning temperature and flows even more as the midday temps rise to 50 or more. This morning was the start of sap collection: the day would consist of pouring all 45 buckets hanging on the taps into the galvanized tank he'd placed in the back of the buckboard wagon.

The buckets held about two gallons when full, but they would average maybe a gallon or so over 24 hours. That process had started just the other day when Carl hammered in the taps and hung the pails in his small sugar tree grove just down trail from the cabin.

He would fill the 100-gallon tank by late afternoon, then bring the wagon back to his small evaporator shed and siphon the sap into the larger elevated tank so gravity could feed the evaporator with his control valve. The wagon was positioned just up on a knoll, its height just above the larger holding tank.

This strategy saved hours of transferring by bucket from one to the other.

Once the first load was complete, he would go out and collect one or two more loads over the course of three days. Then the boiling down would begin.

It was a labor of pure love for Carl, just being in the sugar grove alone with the peace and quiet and the warmth of the spring sun. The nectar of the sap flowing from the ground up through the life veins of the maple trees was a miracle.

The sweet sap during the boil-down filled the air with an aroma unlike any other. The finished syrup product was the most gratifying of treats. The process was an art form of timing to boil down the sap to just the right consistency, texture, and amber—entirely worth the labor that replaced the cabin fever that could creep in at this time of year.

Nature provides bounties in many ways, some less obvious than others.

Honey bees transform sweet nectars from wildflowers, plants, and tree buds into honey. Apples when pressed provide sweet cider that naturally ferments into a tasty hard cider treat and then, after final fermentation, into vinegar, with its cleansing and medicinal us es. The maple sap in its season converts to the sweet syrup. All these bounties utilize a certain technique and art form, knowledge handed down to each generation.

Even Sadie seemed satisfied to be pulling the wagon into the sugar grove. Carl would unhitch her and let her roam free while he collected the pails from the taps. The work was done in about a foot of snow still on the ground with drifts in spots of maybe two feet, so snowshoes were essential.

Sadie would walk along with him from tree to tree stealing an occasional lick of the sweet sap from a bucket purposely set sturdy in the snow. Carl would smile to himself at Sadie's excitement while he retrieved the second bucket.

Two buckets at a time went back to the wagon; then he carried the empties back to rehang on the taps. By mid-afternoon Sadie would volunteer to the hitch, knowing they were to head back to the comfort of her stall.

At midday break in the sugar grove, Carl would set out his canvas on a snow-bank, break out some of his sourdough bread, and drizzle some of last year's syrup over it. He would customarily bake a large loaf of bread each week in his cookstove oven. He always kept and nurtured the starter dough "mother" in the cupboard at the cabin, keeping it wrapped in a damp cloth for its yeasts to continuously grow.

Relishing the flavors and absorbing the warm spring sun on his face, he spoke out loud to Sadie standing just a few feet away with her ears perked straight forward. "Sadie, this is the best batch so far, girl, if I don't say so myself!" He then broke off a small piece and she would nibble it off his open palm. Lying back and closing his eyes with the sun beating down and the still-cool air filling his lungs, he slightly dozed into the memory of himself and Mamie sneaking to this special spot and caressing each other. He relished the tender moments when neither had any need for words.

He flashed back to a time just after his return from France. As an officer in charge of a new horse unit, he was sent back to Rutland, Vermont, by train to collect a half dozen strings of 100 or so quality horses purchased for the army war effort, some of which he thought to come from of all places, Rob Ford's ranch. He then collected some back mail he'd not received when he was down south and deployed in France.

Three letters were dated from one year after he left Granville and the second and third each at six-month intervals, all from Elwin. The first two were just light local news and inquiries as to how he was doing. The third contained important updates and happenings in Granville, along with disheartening news about Mamie.

Dear Carl L. Morse,

We hope this letter reaches and finds you well. We write to assure you that your financial holdings and assets are being managed on your behalf entirely in your best interest.

There have been many significant changes here in Granville since your departure some two years ago regarding land and farm acquisitions by the federal government and the general state of economic downturn throughout the nation.

Many folks of your acquaintance have endured financial duress, choosing to transition land titles and departing Granville to seek alternate lifestyles. To date, your tenants, Howard and Daniela Lamphere, remain in occupancy.

The Lumber Company is now on verge of relocation. Your rental income now comes only in form of property upkeep. I fear the tenants will soon seek a warmer climate. We will continue property management without any further intrusions.

It saddens me to announce that the Hubbards held a small ceremony at their farm in which your beloved Mamie entered matrimony with a decent fellow from Rutland. They are to head west to pursue work in his trade. Pete Hubbard and his wife have succumbed to pursuits of the government buyout and conceded their land grant holdings.

Your farm and acreage now falls in scope of government acquisition through a bid process based on tax valuations. Please advise your instruction.

> *Very sincerely yours,*
> *Elwin W. Shirley*
> *Postmaster - Clerk*
> *Granville, VT*

This letter never reached Carl in Hamilton, Virginia, or in France. His special unit was deemed Covert Operations and no correspondence was permitted during training that could jeopardize Intel regarding secret deployment and the equipment into France. Carl received not one caring letter from home during those years.

Sadie nudged her muzzle into his dozing cheek and ear, exhaling her warm breath with a bit of snort that snapped him out of his half-slumber daydream. He dismissed the depression and his missing her.

"Okay, okay, girl," he mumbled. "Yup, I know it's time, I'm ready ta head back."

Picking himself up from the snowbank, he gathered everything together into

251

the wagon. Sadie positioned herself just near the hitch, eager to get back, too.

They spent the rest of the afternoon transferring the sap into the larger tank at the evaporator. He announced out loud, "Well, guess this is all set for morning! We'll start the boil down early." He even had the kindling stoked under the pan ready to start the fire. The seasoned dry maple wood was meticulously stacked and covered with the same canvas he us ed at the sugar grove.

Back on his short porch overhang, he had a single shaved thin willow stick mounted on the post. He glanced at its position pointing straight out with a slight curve upward. It indicated fair to good weather for tomorrow. If the willow bough were arching downward, it would indicate rain or snow or some degree of precipitation. That was guaranteed!

It was an art to utilize willow boughs in the shape of a Y as a divining rod to locate underground water sources. The straight part of the rod would draw itself downward at any water vein underground, no matter how hard the person held the Y ends in his upturned grip.

Carl learned the technique years ago when old man Bagley was looking to dig an artesian well at his new Bagleyville barn just off West Hill where it meets the Patterson Road just down from the Farr Turkey Farm. It was amazing, almost magical, how it could peel the bark from the strongest grip.

The same principle with a thin pine or willow bough about one foot long being mounted on his porch post could predict the weather, he found. Carl learned to read the stick's angles with precision. Slightly upward meant fair weather for the next six to twelve hours. Straight out or upward arcs indicated variations on dry and sunny; acute downward arcs meant storms were brewing. Other varieties of pine would react the same, but willow worked best overall as a weather predictor and certainly a divining rod.

Its position this evening was straight out with a subtle curvature upward indicating morning sun. "Hmm," he acknowledged to himself, "looks like a good earn day." In satisfaction he retreated in for the night. Enjoying some warm supper and thumbing through the Sears Roebuck Catalog was the only evening agenda.

60 Summer Pastime, 1941

Morning chores included collecting two pails of spring water from the underground stream where it bubbled to the surface at the base of a hill some 100 yards from the cabin. The water was so pristine and clear that, some years before, he had placed a large reservoir of stone at its base with a two-inch section of bent copper pipe protruding out. He lined the inside of the stone with clay as an impermeable barrier.

It took him three days to move the three-foot circular flat stone into place as the cover. He used a long bar and slid the stone downhill from the ledges about 400 feet above the spring. He would place a series of flat stones down first as a sort of "track" about six feet long, then glide the larger heavy cover stone over the track in increments so it would not hang up in the soft soil and mud.

Clear mountain spring water flowed from the pipe all year 'round with its excess overflow continuing its underground course just five feet downslope from his pipe outlet. He made a nice stone bench and stone steps to provide some creature comfort. He would sometimes sit there on his bench for hours and just listen to the soothing sound of the stream trickling through the rocks.

Carl was also intrigued with smaller stones that he would find in the stream beds. Worn smooth from eons of water wear, tumbling against each other, they formed fascinating shapes that somehow had meaning to him. They were like small treasures, each with some earthly energy that made him feel whole again.

It was a great adventure just to go travel in the middle of a summer stream bed from hole to hole and ledge to ledge, investigating the sinks and crevices that clutched the gems in their ancient grasps. Many occasions panning the fine sands and gravels extracted from the deep pools at the base of a four- or five-foot waterfall he would collect the fine flakes and rice-size particles of gold. It was his favorite pastime, collecting heart-shaped rocks, red and blue gems, and the revelation of gold particles from the panning.

Significant only to himself, he would place these collected stones here and thereabouts, little stacks at and around his most favorite parts of the forest, places where he would spend quiet time just communing with nature and being connected to the earth and something greater than himself. His religion was to increase vibration, feel connected, and be part of nature's energy as a human being.

The pathway was well worn, crossing the Texas Gap trail leading up to the secluded cabin. There he had a small water barrel along with another barrel to collect rain water off the roof. That water was used mainly for washing, laundry and latrine.

He also went to his compost pile nestled into the embankment near the horse stall and retrieved two canned jars of venison buried under. The compost stayed at a constant temperature all year round and served well as a root cellar system to keep fruits, vegetables and cured meats fresh most of a year.

This morning upon his return to the cabin, hands full with water pail and mason jar, there at his stoop was the black catamount lying in the grass. A welcomed friend, it was awaiting tidbits and morsels of the jarred venison Carl was carrying.

It was one of the two or so monthly visits from this powerful creature whom he has known since that day many years ago heading to school. It had become custom now that catamount would appear on a morning like this and walk alongside Carl with his daily routines and treks in the woods, whether hunting, fishing, or collecting stones during a day.

Catamount would always seem to appear when Carl was seeking a deeper connection to nature's rhythms or when he spent more quiet time sitting near the stream bed.

The times of quiet were the only relief from the tormenting thoughts, memories, and vivid nightmares of travesties he had witnessed in the war—the pain and screams, not of men, but of his beloved horses on both sides of the battle lines. It was the inability to save them or tend to them that caused him the most anguish.

Then there were the constant betrayals of humans and the witness of what they could inflict upon each other out of greed, hate, and fear. He did not care anymore if they killed each other.

The dreams would sometimes put him into a cold sweat, intense anxiety waking him to the dark cabin, crying aloud for the defenseless dying and wounded animals.

It was his life's burden to endure the nightmares and memories and he conceded that it was his task to be the one to consciously care for all of them by savoring their memories, even after years gone by.

Even Sadie had no anxiety with the cat's presence. It was not there with intention to hunt. It was a pure and simple spiritual relationship due to Carl's heightened ability to communicate with animals.

The catamount walked along with Carl into deer hollow this day to collect blackberries alongside the edges of older clear-cut areas now beginning to grow back in with younger vegetation. Saplings of maple and beech were now three and four inches at the base.

The thorny blackberry bushes were thick on these embankments and knolls. A favorite spot for the black bears, moose, deer and Carl. One could smell the ripe berries in the air from a distance.

Two hours of concentrated picking with three burlap shoulder-strap-style handmade baskets near full and the cat lounging in the tall grass just nearby.

Carl spoke out loud to the cat. "Well, that should just about do it for a batch of jam for tomorrow's boil down!"

Just then off in the distance they both heard a high-pitched bleat. Catamount zoomed straight in on the direction. Carl, too, headed towards the call of distress. He knew the bleating call of a young fawn, and sure enough, just under a thick thorny blackberry bush it stood alone, wobbly on its legs. Then it would lie back down for a moment and attempt to get back up, restricted by the brushy thicket. Its rear leg seemed lame and painful.

The cat did not react as one would expect, pouncing on the helpless fawn for an easy kill. Instead the big cat just stood aside as Carl reached into the thicket and gently coaxed the fawn out, talking smoothly to it the whole time. It was only a few days' young, with no mother doe in sight.

It struggled a little so Carl put an extra burlap over its head, which seemed to calm it down. He slung the berries over his shoulders and cradled the fawn as he carried the fawn back to the cabin to nurture it back to health.

These were the kind of things that occurred when the catamount appeared and walked along for the day. Days like this were always spiritual events.

Though folks would occasionally travel over the Texas Gap trail just a couple of hundred yards from his cabin, there was far less traffic since the U.S. Forest Service had acquired all the farmsteads and acreage. It was used now only as a thoroughfare trail from the neighboring town of Hancock.

Most folks nowadays used the newer valley road, now known as Route 100, but then it was just a dirt road maintained by both towns. It was much shorter and more direct to travel to Rochester or Middlebury from the junction in Hancock up and over the Ripton trail.

Carl could feel the presence of passersby, just a knowingness that someone was around the area. He would get the sensation and stop what he was doing so as not to draw attention or make any noise that could attract curiosity.

This time he sat quietly in his little clearing near the garden to wait for them to pass by, most likely two or three folks heading to Granville on the old known trail or taking a day hike to conduct some business there. Intuition told him they were on some form of business.

They continued by with no awareness of his habitation. He sat quiet and relieved, suppressing any anxiety of what he would do should someone decide to stop in.

He had become so accustomed now to living in solitude with his own thoughts and sensitivities that he was not sure he could utter words to common folks or answer sociable questions. He certainly did not wish to reveal his name or be in any way inviting with his business of living.

He kept a journal, a manuscript of writings about his revelations with nature and the animals and how he found his sensibilities heighten in the quiet and solitude. His writings were of how all of nature speaks to us, if one truly attunes oneself to hear, feel, and listen.

He walked swiftly to the cabin to make the notations of his intuition with the passers on the trail. It was important to outline these events, he felt; perhaps someday others might read about his life-altering revelations and the extreme choices of humanity.

His manuscript was now at this stage more than seventy pages, insights from connections in three different dimensions of reality.

He had darned his cotton-lined denim jacket this morning. The insulation was a masterpiece of one-inch striped colors of different earth-tone pastels. Ingeniously, it was reversible, so the colored lining could be worn on the outside for a social gathering and the denim side out for working.

This early morning had a damp chill in the air justifying its use. He kept the lining on the inside for the warmth of it. The Carnation milk mix was well received by the little fawn, along with some of Sadie's oats and grain.

With all of the morning chores and routines completed, he prepped the wood stove fires to boil down the berries to make the Famous blackberry jam, as he called it out loud, talking to the little fawn that now seemed to just hover near his side as if Carl were its newfound mother.

The big cat was off somewhere this morning. After spending a full day with Carl all through the return with the fawn back to camp, it seemed the cat was now tending to its needs. Of course, the cat also received some canned venison morsels.

Just at dusk when Carl was ready to retreat inside, bringing the fawn in with him, the cat got up from his relaxed position, made eye contact with Carl as if to bid good day and slowly walked out of sight into the wilderness.

He knew Catamount would be back in a week or so, as all the other critters seemed to do; they just came and went at different intervals. Carl thought the other couple of deer that were tamed to his barnyard would be good for his newfound fawn.

He stared out into the woods while smelling one of the pots of blackberries on the outside tripod with the Dutch oven pot over the fire pit. While the aroma wafted into the air and filled his nostrils, he made a mental calling to the two older bucks to come in for a visit.

Satisfied with the message, he let it go and resumed his concentration on the three pots of blackberries boiling down simultaneously. Within a matter of two hours, two deer appeared at the tree line with their ears perked inquisitively forward. Not so wobbly anymore, the young fawn let out a bleat, and the introductions were made. This young buckling would grow and mature and proved to be Carl's most loyal visitor for many years.

61   Empowered by the Badge

The two deer were not the only critters attracted into the yard from the aromas stewing on an outside fire pits. Carl's intuition of the folks on the trail was very perceptive. They were in fact heading to the Granville clerk's office on business of survey and identification of U.S. Forest Service mapping and charting an outline of Wilderness Boundaries and Sustainable Forest Woodland previously owned by private farmsteads. They were part of a team of volunteers headed up by two Forest Service agents armed with very rough sketches of parcels depicting purchased acreage.

The U.S. Forest Service would bring the volunteers up to an area and point them into a certain direction with a compass heading and have them nail four-inch round star-shaped tags in trees along a penciled in line on a vague chart for a paced off distance. The stamped tag read, U.S. Forest/ Wilderness Boundary Survey. It was all just an eyeball guesstimate, mostly a close assumption by the agents in charge.

The visit at the clerk's office with Elwin was to verify the private landowners properties that still abutted the forest areas. While one of the agents in charge was generally concerned about the correct correlations from known landmarks and roads or trails, the second, shorter agent was arrogant and abrasive toward the process. Elwin noticed he seemed "empowered by his badge." Elwin favored the more professional agent with review of the maps that they copied at the storefront table. Unknown to Elwin, each would take a different section of territory and split the group of volunteers up to accomplish the task. The shorter, abrasive one seemed only interested in expediting the project in order to bilk the government for the billable hours under his subcontract as a temporary agent.

Elwin had an immediate dislike of this deputized arrogant man, "He kinda made the hairs on the back of my neck stand up!" he reported to his wife after they all left for the day.

As bad luck would have it, the short arrogant agent, William Mulholland, chose for this day the upper section of Texas Gap trail with his group of four young volunteers.

Carl was just finishing the blackberry jam in its thickness state when again the sudden pit in his belly reared up. His mason jars were set to cool and he thought he should dowse the fires, because he could sense the presence of someone up on the trail.

Mulholland had already set his volunteers off through the woods in his guessed direction, and he was determined to go find a place to catch a nap rather than work alongside them. In his laziness he figured he would catch up to them later at the intersection of West Hill and the gap trail and sign off the paperwork on that section of forest.

The smoke of the fire first caught his attention, then the aroma of blackberry jam, so his mischievous curiosity took hold. All the critters in Carl's yard were now suddenly vacant, even the little fawn who had taken up with the two older bucks.

As the agent wandered off the trail toward the scent of smoke, Carl's stomach pit deepened. He decided to head down towards the stream bench just out of view and gain an overview of his cabin by circling back uphill to a wooded knoll.

Sure enough, the silhouette of a lone man appeared at the edge of Carl's clearing. Sadie was untethered there with smoke still smoldering in the fire pits.

Carl watched as this little intruder rummaged around his cabin and barnyard, first circling the cabin, peering into the windows; then, against all ancient custom, he opened the door and stepped inside.

He emerged after a minute or so and skulked around the barn stall and then the small evaporator shack. With rifle in hand Carl watched intently, knowing that this man was here to cause some trouble. From his very aura Carl could see the dark black and brown colors mixed with dark reds in a swirl.

When the man had the audacity to open one of the jars of jam and stick his fingers in and taste his creation uninvited, Carl walked out to the open edge of the clearing and pointed the rifle at him with intent. He stood silent for another full minute in contemplation of sending this evil presence back to the creator for redemption.

When the agent finally noticed Carl standing there, startled at first, he pulled open his coat flap and flashed the forest service badge. Putting his hand up in a halt type of gesture he proclaimed, "Hold, friend, I'm Forest Service authority."

This meant nothing to Carl, and he stood silent, not wishing to engage him. Authority or not, no man has the right to enter a man's camp or home and just walk in and violate the privacy of a closed door or sample supplies uninvited.

Mulholland looked around to see if anyone else was near. Concluding not, he boldly tried to enforce his authority again. "Appears you've been here for quite some time. This is U.S. government land whether you know it or not!"

Carl just stared at him with his steel grey eyes; he then proceeded to walk up to this short fellow without blinking, summoning and choosing carefully seven words, "It is you who are wrongfully mistaken." He just stared.

"I don't know who you are, friend, but I'm William Mulholland. I'm a government agent with authority here, and I believe you are a squatter in violation of Forest Service land!" His voice quivered at first, then became a little brasher.

Carl responded, "Proof."

"Say what?" the agent inquired. "My word is the proof! You been cutting firewood and looks like you been tappin' maples by that evaporator over there." He pulled the pencil sketch map from his pocket and flashed it in front of Carl. "This is the proof, Squatter!"

Carl knew his boundaries and rights; he had been living here in peace since the war and well before that, as he glanced up in the direction of the original homestead, mistakenly or intentionally burned to the ground by the same type of ignorance that stood before him. Carl did not want to tolerate belittlement from this little closed-minded bastard playing out his control drama of intimidation.

Anger at this man's behavior began to replace Carl's long years of comfort.

He towered over the shorter man, looking down on him in close proximity, and quietly instructed this Mulholland, "Get off my land. The records are clear at the clerk's office."

Mulholland reached for his pistol and pointed it at Carl just after he had turned away. "I'm evicting you from these premises here and now until you can prove your legitimacy." His hand shook with fear.

Carl reacted swiftly and with precision. In one movement he grabbed the pistol hand at the wrist and with the other palm pushed the pistol barrel into the little man's face, then swung his same arm under his extended arm still holding the wrist, arm locked. A swift kick behind his right leg sent the agent hard to the ground. A powerful blow to the left rib was followed by another blow to the solar plexus, knocking all wind out. As Mulholland lay gasping, Carl's final blow to the right lower jaw rendered him unconscious.

The army training in the special unit and the actual hand-to-hand combat experience was automatic, swift, and effective. When and if your life is in danger with close proximity, do not think! If you do, you can end up dead!

Those words were instilled along with the technique of arms, legs, and situational balance over any opponent.

Carl knew this little man was not going to react to reasoning or dialog; he was only looking to play out his intimidator control drama, expecting Carl to succumb to fear and be drawn out, giving the agent a temporary boost and sense of domination.

It backfired in a painful way. Had Mulholland been an enemy combatant, Carl could have broken his neck with his next reflexive motion, but he hesitated, fortunately for the arrogant man empowered by his badge.

It was an invasive intrusion to Carl's quiet solitude, another human betrayal. so now, bound and gagged, Mulholland had to deal with the situation. Carl waited for his consciousness to return while he contemplated what to do next.

It seemed inevitable that Carl make an unscheduled trip down mountain to the general store, giving the agent water and a directive not to speak when the gag was removed. After it was ignored, he was promptly regagged and tossed him the in the wagon. Carl tied him to a tree just off the trail a quarter mile from the bowl mill.

Carl entered the store to obtain his list of supplies, then in private, quiet tones with Elwin he explained the circumstances with the agent Mulholland, giving Elwin the heads up on his provocations, and his impending release from bonds on his way back up the mountain. Carl would keep the man's pistol because he could be a danger to others with it. It was agreed that all agents henceforth would be well advised to stay clear of the Morse real estate.

Upon returning to unbind him, Carl had a few directives for the arrogant deputy agent William Mulholland. He addressed him calmly and assertively. "Do not attempt to return to my abode on pain of death. Do not speak; just nod if you agree." Mulholland nodded in a gesture of affirmation. Carl loosened the rope on his hands just enough for him to wriggle free. Then he calmly put his forefinger to his lips to indicate his keeping silent about the affair. The fear in the agent's eyes was proof enough for Carl that this lowly creature would not bother him again. Then the odor arose. Carl backed off a distance, staring with steel grey eyes. Mulholland had shat himself.

"Well, Sadie!" said Carl. "Don't know 'bout you, but that was enough for today, methinks."

Elwin Shirley was not surprised when Mulholland stumbled into the store.

He was a little surprised at his condition—being very "barked up" and lame all over with a dislocated shoulder and two broken ribs.

"Perhaps this agent should seek out a doctor when he gets back to Rutland." Elwin said as he leaned into Lola with a half-smile,

"Oh, my apologies," he responded when the agent requested a room for the night. "We did not expect you. Ironically all our rooms are in occupancy, but you can bunk in the haystack behind the horse stall if you wish."

When the other agent and the volunteers came back to the office the next day, Elwin promptly displayed the property maps and deeds that depicted all the private landholders' estates that bordered the forest lands. He did it for clarification.

Not all were so concerned with Mulholland's condition. Elwin even heard one of the interns chuckling about it. The other more professional agent just sort of shook his head at him when he learned of the encounter.

He privately told Elwin that he requested his peers at the Forest Service head-quarters to screen the personalities of these deputy agents to be people-friendly, sensitive, and respectful of the privacy and cooperation of clerks and citizens.

Elwin just peered over his specs, saying, "It could have turned out much different."

62   Mountain Treks Healing

Spring 1946: A lot had occurred in the world—economic downturns, the on-set of World War II, vast improvements in automobiles, aircraft, and other technologies dependent on fuels and electricity.

Carl's daily and seasonal routines did not change. The spring and fall treks down to the store were the biggest social events in his reclusive life.

At the head of the White River, just along the embankment near the east side of the bowl mill, he would stop and groom his beard with a scissor and a small mirror. It took him almost an hour of primping and trimming his hair, but mostly he would spend this time just to recharge his mindset to enter the public forum after being in total solitude with no need to speak aloud.

His meticulously written list, neatly folded in his binder folder, was prepared well in advance. However, he would always allow for contingencies like sweet treats and a new shirt or woolen socks.

It took a lot of courage to make the final steps across the road to the front of the store. He would always try to enter when there was the least number of public nearby or inside. It seemed busier there than ever before, so once inside, he would just stand quietly in the corner of the doorway to allow others to depart first and to glance about at the novelties.

This trip he noticed a new contraption on display on the front porch. It was a hand grinder and screw press for making apple cider from whole apples, along with a type of burlap fabric bag. The broker showed how the whole apple could go through the hand grinder and shoot into the stave basket with the bag and a round solid plug with a metal divot to receive the screw tip would press the juice into a trough tray and drain straight into the pail under the tray.

He had to have one of these! He figured he could use it for berries and even vegetables. Finally the last customer tipped his hat to him on the way out and Elwin emerged from behind the counter with his hand extended.

"Was getting worried 'bout ya there, Mr. Morse. Now that was a hard winter this one past! Down here in the valley we measured snow over six feet in places come February! It had ta be the same up on top."

Carl only nodded in agreement, then handed his list to Elwin. "Lol, my sweet" he called into the back room, "Carl Morse is here! Step out with the girls and say a quick hello!"

Lola appeared smiling with two young women, all pretty and smiling as well—Elwin's daughters, now grown and filled out. "You do remember my beautiful babies, Carl? They always come home occasional just ta have a visit with their old Ma an' Pa for no reason! This is Ruthy, and you remember Eleanor. Elly is just newly engaged to the Norton boy and Ruthy is now Mrs. Ruth Newton for almost a year!"

Carl remembered when Elwin and Lola's girls were just toddlers running about the store. He felt close to them as his own in a way, but now here they were all grown into young women. He wondered if they remembered him with the short moments in the store each year.

Of course, they remembered the stories of Carl growing up and their dad's adventures with him. Now he had become somewhat of a legend of folklore, and they were both many times instructed to be polite about his senilities and gifts.

Lola led Carl by the hand from his position near the door to the store table. "This is an occasion for some nice tea and honey cakes. Now sit here for a rest."

He was able to tip his hat to the younger ladies and barely murmured, "Yes, Ma'am," but his eyes gleamed with joy as he sat at the table feeling awkward.

Elwin rummaged around in the back and emerged with a couple boxes of things Carl had ordered last fall from Montgomery Ward and Sears Roebuck—a new denim cotton-lined jacket, two pair of canvas pants with pockets on the legs hips and rear, one new pair of green suspenders, and his favorite Levi Strauss button-down wool checkered shirts, one blue and green and the other red and black.

Another box had various wood-working tools: chisels, files, a new plane, a hasp. Two boxes of 30-06 cartridges, ball and black powder, and finally a couple of wire sieve pans that he was eager for to sift out the sands and gravels from the stream holes to rectify and refine his gold panning technique.

"I do believe these are all the articles we received from your last order, Carl," Elwin said, as he sat at the table. "We have been speaking 'bout an idea we all had lately regarding your well-being Carl, and that would be perhaps for us to organize mid-season treks up to your place to bring you additional staples and supplies. Our thinking is to organize two or three of us, myself included, to come up midsummer, maybe in July, and then again in January and February.

"Course in the wintertime we would have to use snowshoes and backpacks, and you could always have another list together ready for supplies. What do ya think 'bout that plan?"

Lola emerged from the kitchen with the tea and cakes at that moment and piped in, noticing the apprehension in his eyes and body language.

"I agree with Elwin on this, Carl. Please know that we respect your privacy and your lifestyle, but El and I care about you and feel the need to check in on you from time to time."

"Yeah!" exclaimed Elwin, "An' God only knows I need a break from this store occasionally, so the trek would do me some good, too!"

Carl thought about it for another moment. He finally looked up and nodded in agreement, murmuring, "So be it— just you and some kin. I can't be so good a host, though," he stuttered, "only can make bread for ya all."

"That'll be fine, my friend. It'll be like the ol' days when we used ta visit an' go huntin' a little. You still can make your spring an' fall trip down here an' stay overnight if ya need to."

Eleanor said, "I would like to hike up with you all in the summer sometime. That could be a fun outing, if you don't mind, and in the winter, I bet Denny Beatty would help with backpack stuff. He's pretty strong!"

Elwin smiled. "Sounds like we got an agreement," he said, lightly spitting on his hand and extending it out to shake on the deal.

Another customer pulled up out front, leading his horse in by the halter. Shawn Bugby stepped through the store door and ringing its bell, looking a little bewildered.

Elwin rose from the table. "Hi Bugby! How can we help ya this day?"

"Not sure yet, ta tell the truth. It's my Donny outside, just come up lame, gimpin' on his rear leg 'bout an hour ago, on the way here. He's in some awful pain, so I walked him most of the way in here. Think I'm gonna need some salve or something for him. Now the missus needs sugar an' salt too, an' stuff she put on this list for ya."

Bugby handed the list over the counter as the bell on the door jingled again. Both turned to look, but no one walked in.

Elwin boxed his wife's groceries and entered everything in the ledger on Bugby's account. "Now there, only thing I got is this here Vaseline ointment. This is a sample can, so let's go out an' see about Donny."

They stepped out on to the porch.

Carl Morse was already standing in front of Donny. The reins were untethered. The horse was freestanding with Carl holding his palms on both of Donny's cheeks.

Bugby raised his voice. "Hey, friend. He don't take ta strangers. What are ya doin'?"

Carl continued to hold the horse's cheeks, then nodded and turned without a word, putting up one finger. There was an eerie stillness in the air. Carl leaned into Donny and whispered in the horse's ear.

He turned and gazed at Elwin, then at Bugby, kneeled on one knee and reached up just under the inside of Donny's rear leg, just at the tender crotch area. With one swift motion he removed a two-inch-long piece of bull briar twig. The thorns had lodged in the soft exposed skin between the genitals and leg quarter.

Carl returned to the horse's face and showed the thorny twig to Donny, nodded, then turned and handed it to Bugby. No words were spoken. Carl just took two fingers' worth of salve from the open can that Elwin still held, and reached under again, applying the ointment on the irritation.

"Holy cow!" Bugby exclaimed, "I never seen anything like that before! Donny don't take ta strangers at all, an' least not let ya touch him down there! How'd ya know?" He held the thorn twig looking at it with its minüte prickers.

Carl leaned into Elwin and whispered, "Donny told me."

Carl Morse departed the store with his wagon and supplies. Bugby was enamored with the curing of his horse. Elwin explained Carl's abilities to him and how he lived in solitude up on the mountain. Careful not to reveal too much information or provoke any intrusion on his privacy by strangers, he just mentioned that he has a gift with horses, a horse whisperer.

After Mr. Bugby left, Elwin answered Eleanor and Ruth's barrage of questions about Carl's abilities. They both saw what he did with the horse outside and could feel the subtle calm energy when he held Donny the horse.

Elwin told the girls in confidence all about the tame deer, rabbits, turkeys, and partridge that lived and stayed around Carl's cabin. He had been there and seen them for himself.

"Mr. Morse was my best friend when I was a boy growing up. He was not quiet and aloof as he seems to you today. He was a different person then; now he is a person who has experienced many hardships. I am honored to have known him then and now more honored to know the man he is today. There was a time when I ventured up to his place alone and we chatted and reminisced about things when we were youth, and he opened up to me about his quietness and philosophy of life and some of his views on how to use the magic and energy that surrounds us, all of us!"

"He is a very intelligent man regarding basic principles of living. He has a secret journal that he shared with me that day. It outlines these life principles, along with mystical secrets of existence that reveal a long-forgotten truth.

"He is a man well before his time, I assure you. His promise to me was to entrust me with his manuscript upon his departure of life in hopes that the knowledge within its pages will be published when the time is right.

"There's a lot more to Mr. Morse than what you see at first glance, girls. Do not believe the hearsay about his being just strange and odd."

The young women were totally enchanted by the mystique of Carl Morse the Hermit, as he was now dubbed. They both could not wait to make the trek to bring in his midsummer supplies.

Between the Bugby story and Elwin's daughters, some good folklore started in the community. Most people did not know where he resided miles back up on the mountain, nor did some even know he existed, for that matter.

Folks began to whisper about a mysterious Hermit, the Seer on the mountain who healed and talked with animals and lived way back somewhere up in there, pointing in a general direction. He was a wise old medicine man with a long beard and bushy eyebrows. "He can heal ya by a touch of his hand!"

Unintentionally word spread rapidly of the Seer's horse- and animal-healing abilities. Folks would visit the store frequently requesting Elwin to reveal the Hermit's cabin location, or if he could relay messages to hire his services for their livestock and kin.

The whisper was always subtle and secret. If he could tend to horses and livestock, could he also tend to children or family members in near terminal conditions? In these times, doctors' elixirs were not always reliable for a long-term cure but mainly to remedy the symptoms, and the doc would be the first to admit it as fact. In these circumstances, prayer and alternative solutions were in desperate need.

One farmer, Alton Briggs, was witness to Carl just laying his hands on the mare in her stall when he was supposed to wait outside. His curiosity aroused, he sneaked into the shed, peeking over the stall where Carl had been deeply engaged in the Old Cajun energy technique for quite a while.

Carl knew the farmer was there but did not wish to interrupt the session because everyone's intent was to see this creature restored to health. He had strict rules about human intervention in his healing work, all previously agreed to, with the exclusive arrangements set by Elwin.

The three-year-old mare had been lying down for two days with some internal complication, not a good sign for a young horse.

Within twenty or so minutes Carl had the mare up and standing and taking water from the pail. What Carl Morse did for this horse no one will ever know.

Once he set his touch to them, animals without fail were relieved of their ailments, seemingly without any sign that they had had one. No questions were ever asked, nor did the Hermit ever speak to the farmers directly before or after a session. Compensation was always received by either Elwin or Lola in the form of barter or coin in whatever amount the farmer could afford. In most cases, a sack of grain, rice, oats or some monetary value was credited to

Carl Morse's account in the ledger at the general store.

Elwin and Lola would keep each request in a separate folder, then send them up to him by courier or Elwin himself. Some folks took it upon themselves to amble up trail, desperate to try to find his cabin in hopes of persuading him to come down to the village or to a farm where the ill animal or human patient was.

On many occasions Carl was summoned by Elwin to trek down to the store or to a farmstead to tend to a lame horse, mule, or a high-value breeder bull or boar.

In the folklore of Granville it is said that through certain channels the shaman in the mountain had secretly cured a little girl of eight. She was brought to his cabin by Lola and the girl's mother, Alda Bull. Dr. J. R. Hamlin, who treated the girl, having exhausted even his homeopathic remedies, made the final suggestion to seek out the hermit. The little girl's only comment after the healing was, "His hands are very hot."

63 Panning

It was a hot July day. The sun shone down on the top of the canopy of foliage and wherever it could find its way through to the ground. Ironically the shaded areas were perfectly cool in the dells and streambeds exactly where Carl was playing out one his favorite pastimes.

Bear Wallow was a unique place, with its rocky boulder till and exposed cliff ledges of ancient schist rock mixed with veins of quartz. Here the streambed had cut away some chasms through the sheer rock on the eastern slopes of the mountain.

The gold panning here could be productive, with trace grains caught in the clutches of the ledge crevices that were perpendicular to the stream's flow. The moss on the embankments also held its bounty, but the best sources were always just under the mini waterfalls. Gold remained trapped in the bottoms of these ancient smooth rock bowls for eons.

It was hard work to extract the gravels in these pits, and then to sift or sluice it all out only to find a few slivers perhaps the size of a grain of rice. The deeper one dug, the bigger the pieces were.

Patience was the key, as Carl had learned a long time ago. Once he worked one hole in this stream bed for two days straight, camping on the embankment the first night under the stars. It paid off well then, as he was finding minüte slivers with every pan out the first day, and then two fingernail-size nuggets deeper in the hole the next day.

His small half-pint mason jar was now looking to be pretty promising, he muttered to himself holding it up into the rays of sunlight that filtered through the canopy. He brought it over to show it to Sadie where she was nibbling the sweet grass. "Look Sadie! We're in the chips now! Looks like you're eating oats and alfalfa this winter, girl!"

It was time to pack her back up and head home. He started putting the gear up on the embankment, but it was hard to tear himself away from the potential in the next hole he spotted just downstream, so with the spade and a burlap sack he dug about four shovelfuls from as deep as he could go. Standing in the cool water up to his thighs, he filled the sac with the saturated gravel ore.

"Sadie, my dear, I will ask you carry this additional burden back to home so we can play with this in our own stream tomorrow or another day. It might prove out, so remember this spot, just keep it here in your noggin," he pointed at the side of her head, "Gotta keep these spots secret from folks, ya know!"

That first year, there were two midsummer treks by Elwin up to Texas Gap and two midwinter trips, each on horseback or wagon. The wagon could only get to a certain point on Texas Gap road; then they had to trek the last half mile on horseback or on foot or snowshoes in the winter.

The first time, the two Shirley daughters and Lola, entirely enchanted, made the trip. It was an all-day affair just to get there, and a tent camp overnight in the little meadow just outside of Carl's cabin.

The women all witnessed for themselves the tame wildlife that appeared the next morning. They learned quickly not to ask too many questions of Carl Morse; not that he was antisocial—it was just that too many years of solitude had removed the need for verbal dialog in his world.

It took some getting used to for him to have unfamiliar visitors anyway, so it was a few hours of his adaptation to take effect. Then he finally would with only one or two words answer questions posed earlier mostly by pointing to the example or by showing off his toys by motioning to them to come and walk.

Despite his best effort to communicate mentally with spoken words as he adapted to do with the animals, the women and guests were not open to such wisdom of communication. They just automatically thought he was being rude.

When Ruth asked about how he made the maple syrup, he made eye contact with her; after about three minutes he then took her hand, led her over to the evaporator unit, and opened the lid. The visual and physical display answered her question without his uttering a word.

This went on all day until they all sat outside around the fire pit for a small picnic-style supper while Elwin did most of the explanations and reminiscing of the old days.

Before long on that first afternoon the girls had visited his stone bench at the spring, seen the old foundation of his Pop's original homestead, learned how to make the honey bread, visited his bee hive, and learned to listen some to the quietness in the still moments.

They would notice his body language: in the quiet still moments, he would just lean back, close his eyes and form a half smile, breathing in deeply. The only sound was the subtle breeze, they all could feel a shift in the energy and understood the simple meditation of it.

Elwin would organize the winter trips, bringing up the needed staples and gear that would arrive on the orders he placed from the catalogs. The girls would not make the winter treks, so instead Elwin would choose one of their husbands and in one case two younger fellas capable of donning heavy backpacks and pulling a sled while on snowshoes.

That occasion included Denny Beattie and Billy Parish, who grew up in the homestead just at the base of Texas Gap trail. Billy now lived down near the general store because of the government buy-out. His childhood home up there was now just a stone foundation as well.

Both boys were intrigued with the visit, which had to be an overnight with them bunking on the floor of the Hermit's cabin. Denny noticed the little things about Mr. Morse already being somewhat of a legend down in town. It was the worn sleeves and pockets on the outside of the denim jacket, the inside had a fancy wool or cotton liner with vertical strips of pastel colors about an inch wide. The pencil on the table next to a thick stack of papers was worn down to a stub, mason jars on a simple shelf were full of thumbnail-size pieces of multicolored garnets and crystal clear quartz, greens yellows, reds, and some shades of blueish colors—all unique stones of sorts.

Out on the stoop were stacks of various-size rocks of different colors or ores stacked in knee-high pyramids for no apparent reason or use. Bill thought they were "just for decoration," as he commented later on the way home.

But two things stood out that they both noticed while indoors that evening—the sweet bread Carl had made was out-of-this-world tasty, and his two catalogs were worn clear through about an inch in at the bottom right corners from constant browsing through the pages.

His penmanship was precise and immaculate with any little notes on his list that he went over with Elwin under the oil lamp. The boys even noticed the thumb tacks and spruce sap patches in his rubber boots.

The boys fell fast asleep after the harsh trek through the three-foot snow that day. Elwin and Carl whispered about some type of business the Hermit needed to address with his old friend. Elwin did most of the talking about taxes and deeds and the like.

271

64 Solo Visit

The mid-season visits continued. On one occasion Elwin made the trip alone, just he and his horse on a hot midsummer day. He needed to have a couple of days away from the confinements of the store proprietary life.

The first night he camped out under the stars in a little clearing near Sosamosa's mill after fishing in the upstream holes for trout all day. The native keepers were all of fourteen inches and cooked up nicely over his evening fire.

Business was slow this time of year anyway, but there were other changes in Granville economically, and in general the population of folks in town was ever decreasing.

Many folks were exceeding their credit debts. His ledger accounts were causing some overhead problems, and he had some overstock items that were just not selling as expected. The pay from the postal service and the town clerk position was not always enough to supplement the overhead, nor in his mind should it have been.

The money issues caused some concerns and arguments with Lola, who constantly and unintentionally began to badger him a bit about their own store suppliers and creditors. A discussion of selling out arose a few times also, causing him some emotional anxiety because of the history of the store and his father's legacy of it as the founder. Besides, what the hell would he do with himself if they did sell?

It was hard not to extend credit on the ledgers to folks still behind on their accounts and he hated to have to go out of character by pressuring them or shutting them off. After all, these were folks he had known most of his life.

So it was nice for Elwin to get away from it all and get centered again. Sitting by his fire that evening he thought about the Hermit, his old friend Carl Morse, whose lifestyle seemed to Elwin to be full and peaceful with the exception of a "good woman ta keep ya warm at night an' nag ya durin' the day!" He chuckled to himself.

"No, I'm gonna just go with the flow. Wind always changes direction. I'll change routines a little, cut back on a few things, weather the storm out."

He was now talking out loud to himself without realizing it. "Okee dokee," he murmured again, "and tomorrow we pay old Morse a little visit! Probably learn somethin' from that old boy!"

"You're a legend down in the valley, you know," Elwin informed Carl as he sat back after sharing the simple supper our Hermit had prepared. Carl had had a sense earlier in the afternoon that he might have a visitor, but he dismissed it, being preoccupied with chiseling out a new wooden hinge for his cabin door.

Elwin showed up unannounced but not empty handed. The two 12-inch speckles were the perfect addition to Carl's sourdough biscuit stew.

Elwin arrived and at first stood just off trail on a knoll were he could look down at the cabin and barnyard. He tried to see if he could sneak up on his old friend if he was home or nearby. El could hear the wooden mallet hitting the new wood chisel he had gotten for him just last spring. The tap-tap-tap persisted for a couple minutes. Then—silence. He moved down to get a better look. The mallet and chisel were both setting on the wooden bench, but Carl was gone!

El quietly sneaked down slope a little closer to see where he was. "Nothin'," he mumbled, still looking around keen-eyed. He sat down cross-legged, deciding to just sit and wait. Five minutes or so had passed.

For whatever reason an acorn just dropped out of the sky, landed just in front of Elwin, and bounced to a stop. He turned to see the silhouette ten yards uphill behind him. Exhaling in defeat, he said, "Been there the whole time?"

Carl nodded, then motioned for his old friend to head toward the cabin.

While Carl prepared the trout in the large iron skillet with bacon grease and some wild leeks, they spoke at length about how Elwin needed to get out of the store for a change. Then the discussions went to some of the monetary issues and the many changes down in the little village of Granville. Elwin explained that things had gone downhill since the timber company's departure and that Old Diana had been decommissioned. People had moved out. The population was decreasing, and work opportunities these days were farther away.

"Everybody comes in with some form of complaint day after day. Beginning ta think you got the right idea, living up here in the quiet and peace, somethin' 'bout this simplicity, I'm thinking, just seems ta set right for a man bein' here this way." A long gaze of concern was followed by a nod of acknowledgment.

As town clerk, Elwin had set up the Carl Morse fund with some of the moneys that resulted from the government land sale on the Hermit's behalf. It was an interest-bearing account for Carl's use in acquiring his supplies and staples, but there were still the taxes.

"So sooner or later it's going to cause a deficit," Carl whispered, describing in soft tones a plan that made perfect sense; then he meticulously wrote it out with timelines that would provide a perfect investment and protection solution. Elwin nodded off, still sitting in the chair.

Elwin departed for home the next morning after having some tea and sweetbread. Over breakfast they discussed Carl's manuscript and how he wanted Elwin to have his writings after he was dead to pass down and preserve the insights within its pages.

The agreement was made, and Elwin headed back home with yet another list of certain supplies and gear that Carl had prepared. The next trip would entail the Hermit's trek down to town in mid-October. In the meantime hunting was on both of their minds.

65 Bears

A few weeks had passed, and the hunting routines had kicked in with the hermit: early morning till about 10, then a quick break or nap right under a looming pine, then a different area in the afternoon until dusk.

The October hunts were mostly about partridge or as some folks prefer, grouse. These large birds were found feeding near the wild apples and along the sides of streambeds where they could get the sands and gravels for their gizzards.

He preferred to shoot them with his rifle, aiming to nip off the heads, because if they flew or were flushed, they required a shotgun with some No. 6 or No. 7 shot.

They flew very fast, close to 40 miles per hour when flushed, so one had to be quick and take a three- to four-foot lead on them to be successful. His preferred method, using his 4/10 over-and-under Winchester, was to spot them on the ground feeding in a covey of birds, pick out one and plink off the head with the 22-caliber top rifle barrel on the instrument. This approach was quiet and efficient enough that the other birds in the covey would barely spook. Then he would just lie in wait and choose another fat one—plenty for one sole Hermit's dinner.

It was just another week or so when he made yet another trek down to the general store. He wanted to do it before the snow started to fly heavy. Sadie was starting to get a little long in the tooth and greying out on her facial areas some, so her footing was not going to be as sure in any snow accumulation.

They gathered the supplies after Carl had stopped at the river embankment—a favorite grassy spot that so happened to be the same as all those years ago when Elwin chased him down and consoled him when Mamie had left.

He always thought of her, remembering her pretty features, her sassy nature, and the warmth of her body against his at their secret rendezvous spot in that sugar maple grove.

This time he wondered how she would look with age of years as he looked at his own reflection in the small mirror he had packed just for this riverside ritual of trimming his beard and preening his long hair before presenting himself at the store.

With the gear and supplies loaded and after just a short visit, he was for some reason eager to get back up trail. Perhaps it was because there were a few folks milling inside getting their articles. Carl just stood quietly at the door not making eye contact.

After another gentleman came in, Carl decided to wait outside, near where Sadie was tethered alongside another patron's horse. He preferred the company of the animals over the humans anyway, but he did hear one of the women-folk inside lean over to her husband and half-whisper, "That's that Seer feller lives up in the mountain over there!" She glanced at him inquisitively and then her husband did the same. They spoke as if he were not there, afraid of his presence and/or the lore of him.

He went outdoors at that point to avoid an inquisition.

Glad to have finally departed with only a few words with Elwin, he headed back. About a mile and a half from the cabin, just around a sharp bend, Sadie became all anxious and reared up, stopping all forward motion. The black silhouette stood up on its hind legs and appeared to weigh more than 250 pounds.

The huge male black bear was not willing to yield the trail to Sadie. She tried to bolt in the opposite direction, but was prevented by the wagon's harness, which caused the whole thing to go over on its side, knocking Carl clear out of it, with him and all the gear down on the stony trail.

Still spooked, Sadie dragged the wagon on its side down through some pines and wedged it up good enough to break the undercarriage. It's a wonder that she didn't drag the whole wagon over the top of him as well, Carl reflected later. So his outcome was a banged-up knee and left shoulder, but it could have been a lot worse, a whole lot worse.

It took him most of the next day to reload the gear on Sadie with him hobbling around like a gimp, but the soreness dissipated within a few days, and Sadie got back to her subtle self. The wagon was going to take some extensive time to repair, however, so he resolved to save the work for one of the spring tasks.

Black bears in late October are focused only on fatting themselves up for winter hibernation. They can become aggressive during these times as they forage hard for any and all they can find to eat. Being carnivorous, they will feed on deer, squirrel, rabbit, fish, and domestic livestock when the opportunity presents itself. Same is true with all other carnivores in the mountains of Vermont.

Bobcat, coyote, timber wolf, badger, red fox and finally the elusive catamount are all hunter-stalker meat eaters, but the black bear is the only creature that ravages during its waking months and whose metabolism slows into reverse during the long winter hibernation.

Bears will, if given the chance, take down a horse in its stall. So will a catamount, but the catamount that frequented the Hermit would not jeopardize its relationship with Carl, so Sadie was off limits. That also went for any of the other wild animals that frequented his barnyard sanctuary. It was a spiritual agreement.

This particular bear would roam an expanded territory on both sides of the White River's lower and upper ridges for the next month or so, foraging on crab apples clinging to the trees, salamanders under rocks near the streambeds, and grubs and worms dug up under and inside old tree trunks. Then he would return to the upper elevations to his winter den.

The winter of 1952 was extremely harsh. Snow depths blew in from the first of November consistently through February, and Carl's trek down to town was tedious using only the horse, with the wagon beyond his energy to repair it.

The supplies he desired, and the quantities, were limited to what old Sadie could carry. He loaded her up and walked in lead the entire uphill eight miles as the crow flies on under-maintained trails and roads—more like ten miles considering all the obstacles like fallen windblown trees, eroded gullies and ditches and rock. The government provided minimum maintenance by just digging water bars across some of the steeper sections.

The wooden bridge that crossed the White River just past Mishner's family camp was washed out, so he and Sadie had to cross it by fording the rocky stream bed. The side trails that used to be main thoroughfares back in the day were now grown over with saplings of white birch and alder. They had for the most part of ten years been left unattended and neglected by the Forest Service.

The government did, however, begin a project that bypassed the river crossing and began to cut a new road on the eastern slope of the White River, with the intent to cross the river at a narrow section another mile or so upstream. Carl pondered taking that new route, but it was nothing but a mess of tree limb slash, dozer ruts and stumps.

The devastation angered him. There seemed to be no rhyme or reason behind it, and to what end? He could not fathom any plan they had that included preservation of the forest by building such a wide swath.

It was to be an all-day event to go down and return navigating over twenty miles in total of neglected trail. Up on his own Texas Gap trail, he at least kept it maintained by cutting the deadwood off and recycling it for his firewood and projects; his maintenance included up to a mile in either direction and he was just one man.

The winter was brutal as we mentioned—snow in January and February was deep. Sadie's supplies were short; she was old and lame. Unable to get to her stall because of the snow on a blizzard night with temperatures well below zero, his only companion died there standing up leaning on one side, frozen. Carl Morse mourned for four days, then Catamount appeared at his door one morning, sitting complacent, signifying yet another change.

66 Seer

Elwin arranged most of the supply runs that season with various trusted friends. Carl made the solo trek that spring with a large army-issue backpack of olive green canvas.

The midsummer runs were somewhat of an adventure for the select people involved, with the opportunity to meet the Seer of the mountain, the man who spoke with the animals. Some feared him; others thought he was queer in the sense that he was an oddity and an unsocial individual. Still others thought he was an outlaw of some degree.

Elwin always set them straight whenever he overheard their remarks and comments. He was sure to keep magical factions and mystery of the stories at the forefront of folk's imaginations.

A seer, shaman, or medicine man, was throughout history in all human cultures, the most important and respected person in any clan or tribal community. Gifted with deep connection and knowledge in alternate spiritual dimensions. They provided insights and healing energies that could advise council leaders to make enlighten decisions and take actions to the betterment and wellbeing of the tribe.

The Hermit became known through the whispering's of the declined Granville population as the Seer in the Mountain. They spoke of his ability to see into a person's light body and with a magical touch pull out the disease.

Recounts of select folks who experienced the Hermit's sessions were that his hands became very hot and they had a sensation of lightness along with a dream state of mind during the wordless process. No words were spoken, or needed, even at departure. Some folks had claims of sleeping for two days afterward to awaken completely restored and energized "as if they were never ill," but they all claim to be profoundly changed by the encounter.

There was no fanfare for Carl either prior to, during or after a session, it came to him automatic, he felt an obligation to perform his gift for those who sought him out through Elwin or Lola's coordinations. In his mind set, his charge was as a steward of the forest, its animals and the local tribal members with open minds. The healing sessions always re energized his own body and mind as well, increasing his abilities with ease. Only the open-minded folks were somehow allowed, as if it was "meant to be" by a universal force.

67   Hunters' Wood

It was the second week in November, and the Hermit was up in Deer Hollow hunting for the one elder buck that he would take for his winter meat supply. The bucks were in full rut, with does in full heat.

He could count 12 does in a day, with always one or two six- or eight-point bucks in trail vying for the dominant rite of passage into the harem.

His daily routine was to eat, drink, and sleep the daily hunting routine following the deer herd's feeding and territorial areas. He knew their patterns as nobody else did.

This one morning while on game trail, Catamount appeared, acknowledging him, then walked up in the direction of a knoll, stood and looked back at him, requiring Carl to follow.

Just over the knoll in a small hollow, three does stood alert they charged trotting about 50 yards, stopped, and bleated their calls. Off in the distant hardwood two big bucks were in full battle, racking and locking horns. This lasted all of a minute or so with the 12-pointer emerging as the victor.

They both then charged straight into the does where the whole dominant buck routine took place in a less subtle manner. The 12-point buck mounted the larger doe and they thrashed in wedlock for quite a while. It was a rare sight to witness.

The massive buck had to weigh over 250 pounds, he estimated from its size, and his antler spread was all of two or even three feet with the points on each side webbed from the swamp feed it lived on. This deer could have been "crossbred with a moose," Carl said to himself.

He could not bring himself to take down such a magnificent animal just yet, especially after being witness to the mating ritual with both tough bucks sowing the seed straight of these does for future strength of the herd.

"No, not yet, I'm gonna let 'em go past the rut season. We shall wait till a couple weeks from now for this one," he thought, as he glanced over at his companion Cat for approval.

They charged off, splitting up, with the does heading in one direction out of view, and the bucks heading to another area to service another harem of does.

After everything quieted down, the catamount's ears perked up and with one last glance at Carl, it disappeared into the brush.

The cat's reaction was a clear sign of another presence approaching. Carl's heightened abilities and senses alerted him to the same.

Sure enough, down slope within 100 yards or so he caught the silhouette, another hunter quietly stalking toward his position, Carl would stand still and remain concealed using the knoll and the larger trees and let this man walk on by.

He came close, within twenty yards or so, enough to see his facial features. He was quiet in his footing, obviously tracking the two big bucks in the light snow cover.

Carl sensed he was a man of some skill but not anyone that he knew from town or local. Not many hunters ventured this far back country anymore, so he watched. Suddenly the man stopped and stared in his direction, then just waved to acknowledge his presence. Carl could clearly see his face.

The hunter resumed his stalk and disappeared over the next knoll, as stealthy as he himself would be. No sooner did the hunter go out of sight some thirty yards from Carl's position and within just less than a minute, he turned and there stood the same man—the exact same man who had stealthily walked within ten yards of him. The Hermit was stunned.

The hunter walked right up, looking and scanning the landscape the whole time, "Didn't you happen ta see some big deer come through here?"

Carl stared at him in amazement. It was the same exact fellow he had just seen a few moments ago who had disappeared over a knoll down slope well over 70 yards away. There was no conceivable way that this man could have made up that kind of ground in that short of time in dead silence!

The Hermit's seer abilities kicked in and he could see and feel this man's unique personality.

At that moment this fellow walked up, slung his rifle over his right shoulder, extended his hand and whispered, still scanning the tree line, "I'm Bob, Bob Foster. Didn't mean to disturb your huntin'. I just come up here where the big deer live, didn't expect to find anybody else this far back!"

Carl was so taken by the whole event and his outgoing friendly energy that reminded him of Elwin, it was as if he had known this person for years already. He had no choice but to break his character and stutter out his name. Bob was the first stranger in twenty years or more that he was able to feel comfortable speaking to, brief as it was.

"Huh, huh, how di… di… did ya get from down there to ha… ha… here behind me just now?" Carl asked.

Bob just gave him a sideways smile with a slight chuckle.

"Oh that, that's a deep secret," still smiling both with his face and his eyes.

"Well, good luck today. Hope ya get one. I might shack one back toward ya!" The man had a magnetism, an irresistible personality, that piqued Carl's interest as no one had before. He almost wanted to extend the conversation to where ever it could go in the acquaintance. He felt no fear or apprehension, and he did not want the man to leave!

Then Bob went out of sight as quietly as he had come in behind him. Our Hermit just took a few moments reflecting of these three events—first the appearance of his Catamount animal guide, then the entire mating sequences of the does and bucks, and the monster buck itself. Then the outgoing hunter, Bob, appearing out of nowhere, miles back in no man's land of the Green Mountains, stalking the same buck. He perceived a teaching, a synchronicity to the day's events, something that would somehow unfold.

It energized him to the point that he wrote it out in his journal as soon as he returned to the cabin. He wrote it as a spiritual teaching, nature's energies, the vibrations of living beings and manifestations.

68 Departure

Provisions were brought up to the Hermit's camp on a regular schedule, as organized by Elwin along with two other younger fellows with strong backs. Kelly and Harve Downs were trusted relations, along with Denny Beatty. They all became better acquainted with our Hermit and respected his concepts and skills with woodsmanship.

On one of the fall trips they went on a morning hunt with Carl in the lead to the area that would provide results for the boys. There was only one condition—bucks only, no exceptions. "Take anything else, you drag it out yourself." That's how Elwin relayed it to the boys from Carl's directive.

The Bob Foster hunter experience was truly a teaching for Carl, preparing him himself to open a little better to humans after so many years of solitude. His distrust of strangers prevailed, but he learned to build a comfort level with folks whom Elwin would select to lug the gear and visit. It would be the synchronicity of what was about to be a significant change in the Hermit's life style.

Elwin had just arranged to sell his store down in the valley and finally implement his retirement plan. This turn of events would have an impact on Carl's supply chain. They discussed the implications of Elwin's plan in detail, and how it would affect Carl. All the paperwork for Carl and his estate was in place and protected, along with the accounts and land holdings in his name, which on Carl Morse's direction would all be transferred to the Town of Granville in lieu of taxes and living expenses. His separate interest-bearing account would be also placed in the town's trust to be used strictly for "the needy and the poor."

The general store would move to a new location in a building owned by Pete Dredo. Elwin had already reduced much of the overstock items and large pieces of hardware and display items always out on his front porch.

Feeds and grains were no longer big-selling items, as gas-powered vehicles had long since replaced horses. The highway of Route 100 was constructed straight up through the valley, better connecting Granville with the other towns to the south and the north.

"We got some years and miles on us!" they both agreed. The last winter for Carl had taken its toll. The Hermit conceded to his friend, "I might not sustain another winter up here."

So on that occasion it was agreed—Carl Morse would come off the mountain. Elwin and the boys helped load the essentials of Carl's personal gear in a Willy's Jeep. Most of his effects Carl neatly packed in three canvas sacks by himself. The tools, evaporators, implements and hardware items would all be picked up later and given to Elwin or his sons-in-law to be put to good use.

Carl asked in a letter that his cabin remain intact and be preserved and maintained in repair by the town. Elwin's kin and the helpers, Denny, Harve, and Kelly would be in charge and use it for hunting excursions or summer retreats.

It was such an emotional task for Carl to agree to this transition, not knowing what it would be like to live in another place with other people milling about and getting used to the changes down in town. It was so emotional that he needed a few days alone there to collect himself before moving downhill. They left with the Jeep and most of his supplies. These they placed in the little room at Elwin's boarding house—the same room in which Carl slept in comfort all those years ago before departing to France with the Army Corps.

From there, after a few weeks, arrangements were made for him to live with a woman, Mrs. Boardman, a widower who took over the old Briggs place on Route 100. She had some nursing care background and a small room for board that was similar to his cabin in size, with its own entry door on the same side as he was accustomed.

They returned to Texas Gap five days later to retrieve the Hermit and his grey army-issue pack with his manuscript, forest recipes, pipe, tobacco pouch filled with the natural sweet grass, wool shirts, denim jacket and his simple personal effects, along with his three prized rifles and the small hatchet and long knife that he kept on his belt.

He bid his domesticated wild animal friends farewell and sat up on the top of his favorite ridge with the big cat for an entire afternoon taking in the vistas overlooking the valley below. His aging body was the reality behind the changes desired by the few who cared about him. His spirit, however, had no real wish to leave the quiet wilderness and natural beauty that filled his eyes and senses every day. He didn't mind if he departed the earthly bounds up here; in fact, he planned to do so when the time approached. When his body turned to spirit, it would be on his own terms.

He closed up the cabin, methodically latching the handmade wooden door hinge. On the table inside, he left a wooden note board with simple instructions for anyone who might visit.

Welcome—Morse Cabin:

#1 Replace any dry wood you use.
#2 Fresh water downslope at stone bench spring.
#3 Wash and clean your pots and pans.
#4 Find simple shelter and warmth.
#5 Find peace, harmony, and comfort.
#6 Listen to the quiet and hear its voice.
#7 You now are keepers of secret solace.

The wooden sign hung on the cabin door with its hand-chiseled message was simple: "WHISPER."

69   Town Houses

The Hermit could not speak to anyone on his final trip out of the wilderness. The self-powered Jeep ride was a first for him, and he did not care for the engine noise. Elwin was the only person remotely aware, keeping a close eye.

Traumatic was nothing near the description of his emotions. He motioned for them to stop four times on the trip out to collect himself. Elwin tried to console him to no avail.

With hands shaking, tears running, and breath winding hard he felt a fear of the change unlike any other, even while under fire in France. It was like the helplessness with his horses in the war—trying to save them and protect them from the chaos. He would collect himself each time and get back in the seat.

The younger boys didn't comprehend the old Hermit's actions, and they whispered to themselves once on one of the stops with Carl over by the river embankment.

Elwin stepped up to them holding his index finger up to get their attention. The explanation was that they were to show respect for the Hermit's trauma, and they did because they were briefed prior to being invited to this task. They just needed a reminder.

That afternoon they arrived at Elwin's place—now just a boarding house with three small rooms in the rear, one of which housed Carl's affects. Lola had prepared a nice dinner of chicken pot pie for the evening meal. It would be a short, quiet evening—just the three of them, as it should be. The Hermit retired to the familiar room immediately after dinner to a restless, sleepless night.

So much had changed in Granville village! The biggest was the large front room of El and Lola's building that had once been the general store. It now seemed vacant, with only small corner post boxes for the reduced population of folks.

The Shirleys still performed the town clerk's duties with a quorum of five Select Board members, meeting once per month.

The Bowl Mill employed many of the town folks, producing and distributing high-quality maple bowls and other wooden Vermont Made products and utensils. They also made and milled clapboard siding and cedar shake shingles for roofing and siding applications that shipped throughout New England regularly.

The Shirleys now had a 1942 Chevrolet sedan car and a 1926 Model T pickup truck that Elwin had acquired almost new in 1928. It still had the wooden spoke wheels, and varnished oak bed body behind the cab, intricate top wood slats of oak over the cab head with olive green canvas that could roll back and let the sun and air flow through. "Watch this!" Elwin exclaimed, showing off his truck. He pulled the hand choke out at the front of the bumper, pulled the hand crank through once, reached in the cab, turned a switch on the dash and with one aggressive crank the engine fired up and purred. "See, just like a kitten, Carl!"

He took the Hermit for a ride down to the new store location, then showed him the Briggs place, where he could have his own room to himself to come and go as he pleased. Widow Boardman happened to be out front at her little flower planter, so they pulled up and made a brief introduction. Still intimidated, the Hermit could not find words to utter, but he could sense her kindness, and her loneliness as well.

On Sunday, as was the ritual, they packed a basket. Carl was invited to go on the Sunday drive in the car and stop along a White River meadow and have a picnic lunch. Elwin threw a couple of fly rods in the trunk and a creel, as fishing was now his favorite pastime. One hole quickly produced three 10- to 14-inch or so brookies, released with a smile for another day.

The Hermit was amazed at the new road improvements with this new substance called "macadam," made of tar and fine gravel. He was also intrigued with the speed of the travel these motor cars could attain, compared to riding horseback or walking. These were truly time machines.

He still preferred the pace of a walk each day along the riverside trail to maintain his solitude.

The goings-on at Elwin's place, with folks stopping to collect their post and other business, started to take their toll on the Hermit. Their voices could be heard through the walls all day. The only quiet time he could enjoy was his walks along the river but even then, the drone of car and truck traffic on the road interrupted him from enjoying the stillness he was accustomed to have.

One day he followed the trail down to Mrs. Boardman's and happened upon her again tending her garden. He stood there quiet for a time, unsure as to how get her attention. He somewhat surrendered his apprehension and she suddenly stopped, stood up from her kneeling position, turned and smiled at him.

"Oh, hello there, Mr. Morse! I had a feeling you would be coming over soon."

She set her basket down, walked right up to him, took his hand, and said, "Come, it's time we had some tea.

"Elwin filled me in on all of your particulars, so I'm familiar with some of your intricacies and nature of things. You do not have to feel uncomfortable with my trying to have conversation. You can just smile if you agree with my words. My name is Wilma. I've been alone here for four years now since my Alvin passed." Pouring out more tea, she added, "I'm used to the quiet these days." She looked at his eyes deeply, "I think you know. Let me show you the room you will stay in when you decide to be ready."

She opened the rear side door of the separate bungalow. She walked in first, then Carl stepped into the dark room. It took a moment for his eyes to adjust, just like at his home in the woods. She then reached onto the side wall and turned a switch. The electric light hanging from the ceiling flashed on as bright as the sun. Carl cowered back holding his hands over his face.

"Argh," he moaned.

She turned it off immediately. "I'm so sorry. I forgot that you don't care for artificial light. Please forgive me."

The Hermit was not so much sensitive to the light bulb, although it was unnatural to him. It was more that he could feel the electricity and its surge through the air and in the entire room. He could sense its concentration of current when it surged into the bulb. Carl could almost see its energy emitting throughout the room. It created a high-pitched frequency in his ears and tingled his skin.

Looking at her in apology, he murmured, "My... my oil lamp will be fine." Liking her manner, and his room very much, he nodded his head in approval, with a smile.

The rental was taken care of through Elwin, and was a great help with expenses for Wilma, who retained her quiet living routines in the main house. She prepared one meal per day, usually at dinnertime, that they would sometimes share at her table, but most times during the week she would bring his meal on a tray and set it on the single table for him if he were out walking.

His little wood stove took the chill off most evenings, with split wood that Wilma had delivered and stacked by Forest Beard with his truck from up on Route 125 in Hancock. Carl would brew his own coffee and tea on it, as well as make his breads and cakes occasionally.

But the Hermit still was somewhat restless, unused to the comings and goings of Wilma's friends and kin, the sound of cars on the roadway, and the electricity flowing through the wires mounted even on the telephone poles.

The old telephone had a loud ring. Whenever calls came in, it would take her at least five rings to answer, if not more, and he could always hear her muffled one-sided conversations for eternities of time! The Hermit could not fathom how a person could jibber-jabber on and on for those durations.

When Mrs. Boardman went to call out, she would have to crank the little hand ringer a few times on the side of the apparatus and hold the horn to her ear, asking the operator, Mavis, to connect her to someone on the party line. Her ring was three shorts. Others on the party line would ring in different sequences, so it was a nauseating irritation—the one thing he could and would never get used to.

Close to a year had now gone by since he came off the mountain. Some of the domestic living he had finally settled into. Most of it he found unbearable. His walks down street to the general store were not so rewarding as they had been from the mountain—all new faces, including the proprietor, much less stock on the shelves compared to the old days. Things he used to get in bulk were now packaged in meager portions.

He would still wait, humble and patient, if others were in the store, and he still created a handwritten list of things he wished to purchase, handing it to Pete, the store clerk. Elwin had set up an account there with Pete for Carl Morse, so he had no need to carry paper or coin money with him.

One afternoon after his walkabout on the riverside trail he began to feel out of sorts. A sharp pang in his side sent him into a cold sweat. After a lie-down in the tall grass in a small meadow beside the river, he managed his way back to his room.

The pang subsided, either by his own healing will or by his relaxation. But it was like nothing he had ever felt before. Back in his little room, with lantern lit, he lay in his simple bunk, not touching his tray of dinner Wilma had placed on the table.

That fall morning brought sunshine at its dawn just over the top of Braintree Mountain. Wilma found his one-page letter on the table at her morning entry to tidy up his room, noticing the untouched dinner and his grey army pack gone from its corner. She sat and read the words of thanks for her kindness and wonderful home cooking. He went on to mention that he would cherish her companionship and the simple, quiet conversations that they had shared.

She knew then with those words that he was heading up the mountain to a place where he felt "better communed," his words whispered during one of their Sunday evening conversations and personal shares.

She began to tear up knowing where he was headed and hoping that he would not leave, being accustomed to his quirks and company. Setting the letter down and contemplating its deep meaning, she could sense that he was nearing the end of his time.

Deeply concerned by the untouched dinner, she decided to phone over to Lola and get Elwin to try to retrieve him. Carl would always savor the meals, so she sensed that perhaps he was feeling ill in some way. His coat and sweater and wool pants were all missing, as were the pack and his broad brim hat and walking stick.

Besides the letter meant for her, the only article left wrapped in brown paper and tied with hemp string was the inch-thick manuscript into which he wrote every evening under the oil lamp light. Within its pages, perhaps meant for Elwin, was a separate note:

> *The treasure of gold and silver placed within the stones of a pastured wall, to remain as 'Secret' as is the resting place of poor Burke, revealed when he returns to earth, redeemed only upon his call.*

On its outer paper wrapping it read:

ENTRUSTED INTO THE CARE OF MY FRIEND ELWIN SHIRLEY
"A READING BY CARL LESLEY MORSE"

70 Minds Connect

Carl appeared at the Granville General Store that midmorning. He stood silent and humble in the corner just inside by the door, he waited patiently for the local patrons who were milling about to conclude their business and stay.

The coffee on the pot belly stove in the center of the room filled the air with its aroma. The Hermit handed his list to Pete the clerk and went to the stove pouring the black hot liquid into the heavy paper cup, no one else was present, he went to the candy shelf and took out some black and red liquorice from the open bin and set them on the counter.

Pete was gathering items for him from his list from behind the counter off the upper shelf: pipe tobacco, hard tack jerky, and the sack of beans, canned stew and Campbell's soups of various styles.

At that moment three men and a young boy walked in, ringing the bell on the entry door. Carl immediately retreated to the corner again, averting his eyes to wait for the strangers to leave.

Two of the men were of very outgoing friendly personalities. One was familiar and recognizable; the other was of almost the same spirit. They were all dressed in woolen hunting-type garb with woolen green pants and flannels.

The boy went straight to the candy boxes and retrieved two handfuls of liquorish, one red and one black. He glanced at Carl two or three times, cocking his head inquisitively at the third glance, Carl finally made eye contact with the young man, and found himself intuitively mesmerized by the moment of it.

Somehow the boy reminded him of his own self when he was in the general store with his Pop all those years ago. He felt an immediate connection to him, something of synchronicity.

Then out the blue one of the men just came right up to him and grabbed his hand, shaking it. "Good ta see ya again! I member you from in the woods last year in the way back." The other man of the same stature came up, outgoing as well, and said, "Hi, I'm Dick," and he smiled that crooked smile.

"I think that big buck is still up there somewhere don't you?" the first one said.

Carl stood stunned, starring at both men. They were identical twins. He had no choice but to smile, realizing that's how the first fella, Bob, was able to sneak up on him in the woods last fall! He still stood silent nodding with a half-smile in recognition of the trick. The Hermit took a liking to these two brothers.

Pete handed him his sack and Carl signed his ledger. He sipped the last of the coffee from the paper cup and placed it in the wooden trash barrel. The three hunters, Bob, Dick, and Ralphy, as he was introduced, departed out the door. The young boy of ten or eleven years old lingered inside for no apparent reason.

And so did the Hermit, who resumed his position in silence near the door. He had no real urgency of time. This day his plan was set along with his mind-set.

Intuition told him just to wait there and contemplate this recurring synchronicity, and let it unfold again, feeling and recognizing the same energy as he felt in the woods with these two brothers a year ago last fall.

The olive green Ford station wagon outside started its engine.

Pete looked at the boy and asked if there was anything else he needed.

The young boy grabbed a pack of Beeman's gum from the bin. He pulled another dime out of his pocket placing it on the counter.

"Thanks, son," Pete said. "That's good stuff. It's my favorite too! You goin' huntin?"

The boy nodded. "Yup, with my Dad and my uncle Dick! They're real good hunters."

There was a call, a voice from out at the car, "Come on, we're already out here."

The young fellow felt there was something he'd forgotten or something else he needed to do, but he could not place it—only that it was nothing in the store itself.

"Be right there!" he shouted out the screened door.

He gathered up his brown paper sack from the counter, looked up at Pete just behind it, who was folding his ledger book up and placing it under the counter after ringing up the dime in the old National cash register drawer.

"Thanks, Mister," the boy said, turning to find himself directly in front of the bearded Hermit still standing quietly at the door.

This time the Hermit slowly raised his gaze and with his steel grey eyes locked into the boy's eyes, there was a higher conscious connection from both of them, a communication within a moment's instant—a knowingness from both individuals, a flash of each other's spirit body, beliefs, and old soul wisdom. There was no difference of age and no sense of time in this powerful moment.

Suddenly another call from the car outside broke the silence and the moment, Carl without saying a word the whole time just nodded approvingly to the young man, not breaking his gaze. The boy nodded to him approvingly in return, and without breaking his gaze just voiced out that he was coming.

He reached out and touched the Hermit's right hand with his, just touching only their forefingers. Another surge of knowingness and connection of spirit locked their eyes again.

Then he pushed the screened storm door open, walked out, closing it behind him, and glanced through the window at the Hermit one last time before clambering into the back seat of the Ford.

71   Return to Fade

Devout hunters Ralphy Dewolf, Bob and Dick Foster, and Paul Clancy all drove more than six hours from Connecticut to spend a week up in the Green Mountains in Granville, Vermont, staying at Bob's friends' place at the bottom of Maston Hill. The big white farmhouse with its red shutters and massive dairy barn across the road now belonged to Lawrence Miner.

Larry and Clancy were back at the house waiting for the gang to get back to organize their hunt for the next opening day of deer season. It was the third year that the foursome from Connecticut—avid hunters all—would rendezvous at the Miners' Vermont house in the Green Mountains.

It took skill and stealth to stalk out the big bucks and the herd of deer was plentiful and abundant. They would also visit and enjoy dinners with Larry Maston, who lived in a century-old farmhouse a mile up Maston Hill Road with his wife, Betty. They were full-time dairy farmers and native local pleasant folks.

This particular late afternoon Bob, Dick and Ralph decided to drive up West Hill onto the government road that was recently extended over the ancient town road deeper into the forest.

The folklore of the Hermit was now legend, and his camp location seemed to be a mystery, with only a few locals knowing its actual location. They spoke of the lore in the station wagon driving up towards the forest.

"Well, that was the Hermit standing there at the store this morning," Bob said. "I'm purdy sure of it. Met 'im in the woods last year 'way up back in here," pointing off to his right. "You remember, Dick, that guy with the worn out clothes and the beard hangin' way down. He was way up there when we was chasin' those big ass bucks, I think he was already on 'em when we came through. You remember?"

"Yup, I remember seein' him, but I didn't talk to him. We just waved. Then I swore I could smell coffee up there after that." (Dick was addicted to coffee.) "All I know is that we took one hell of a hike that day!"

They rounded the bend where Alder Brook fed into the beginning of the

White River. A new culvert had been installed by the Forest Service and the roadway had diminished back down to just a rutted log trail with tall grass on either side and in the middle of the wheel tracks.

It was a road hunt, with everybody including the boy scanning each side of the steep mountain woods on their respective sides of the vehicle. Three times so far, with Ralphy driving, they had to stop and back up to check a potential deer silhouette off in the distant wood line.

They would drive up in here again in the early morning to hunt this vast area for the entire day. They would meet back at the car at noontime to regroup and continue on a new section for the afternoon.

So just at idle speed they continued along the old grown-in mountain road seriously scanning the woods.

Suddenly, as they passed a trail on the right that was definitely ancient but grassed in to a view only a length of it up to a rise, Uncle Dick shouted, "Stop the car! Did you guys see that? Back up! Back up! There was a person standing up that tote road there with a big black cat—a mountain lion!"

Ralphy backed the car up ten or twenty feet.

"Oh, here we go! Dick's up ta sumpthin!" They all got out, including the boy, Butch, as they called him.

"He was standin' right there, clear as day, in the tall grass!" Dick pointed to the trail. It was clear and defined, with trees looming over it on either side, but the center was nice lush, knee-high inviting grass.

Bob decided to walk down slope to scan for deer, Ralphy stood next to the car, and Dick walked uphill to the left of the trail in a small meadow to get a view over the rise. "I swear he had a big black cat next to him," he said. "Couldn't have gone too far! I wanna try ta talk to him again!"

The boy decided to walk straight up the old tote trail.

The car doors, all four of them were open. Ralphy walked up the road in front of the car about 50 yards, stopped, and surveyed.

Bob was downslope across from the car about maybe 100 yards by now and heading through the brush towards Ralph in an arc or half-moon direction.

Dick had already made his way up through the meadow near the hardwood tree line and got up onto the old foundation corner—the same homestead Bill Parish had grown up in years ago.

He scanned the uphill sections of the woods, tried to outline the ancient trail over the rise off to his right, looking for any movement.

The tote road had a turn it just over the first rise, went downhill straight into a bit of a dell, then arced in a bend back up to another rise on a knoll with a bit of a straight section beyond.

As the boy rounded the second bend after some ten minutes or so, he saw up ahead in a bit of a mist some movement, just a shadow really, that could have been a tree trunk, stump or a boulder dancing shadows in the dimming sunlight.

He picked up his pace and slightly came over the knoll, slipping on the wet flat stone and landing face down on the ground.

Picking himself upright to a kneeling position, there, clear as day, up on the straight trail section was the silhouette of a man with a grey pack on his back came into view, the staff in his left hand, a grey beard, and the biggest black cat with yellow round penetrating eyes standing in the foreground between the boy and the man.

It was he, the Seer in the mountain—the same man he connected with at the store that morning. The cat's eyes penetrated the boy's soul, in an instant he intuited the Hermit's life story. A clairvoyant, pristine deep voice penetrated his inner consciousness.

"I am home now. I leave you to remember."

Both of them, man and cat, turned with no realistic motion of walking. Just as they had appeared, the Catamount and our Hermit faded like ghosts into the mountain.

A Granville Photo Album

Hotel, Post Office and General Store

Main Street, Granville

Blacksmith and Wheelright shop

Hillside farmstead

Elwin Shirley

Wagon in front of the old hotel

Relaxing at the General Store

Mountain homestead

Headwaters of the White River

Granville Corners

Barnyard in heavy winter snow

Building the Granville Gulf Road, now known as Route 100

Hauling in the sap during sugaring

Bringing in the hay

Sugar shack

Field gate

The Farr Turkey Barn

Logging Operations

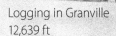

Logging in Granville
12,639 ft

< Logs 16 ft long. Team owned by Frank Petty, driven by R. B. OHea from the Riley district, Granville. 5 miles off the mountain

Diana pulling the log "train"

Saw mill works

Rick's mill, Granville VT DePaul >

Granville Town Historical Papers

VERMONT   ADDISON ss KINGSTON

WHEREAS application has been made to me the subscriber by number
of the free holders of the Town of Kingston in the County of Addison
and State of Vermont to warn a Town Meeting in said Town.
These are therefore to warn the inhabitance of said town to meet
at the dwelling house of Mr. Israel Balls in said Kingston on the
8th day of July at one o-clock P. M. to act on the following articles:

1st.   To chose a Moderator to govern said meeting.
2nd.   To chose a Clerk.
3rd.   To chose Selectmen and other town officiers.
4th.   To act on any other business that they shall think fit when meet.

Kingston, June 26th, 1788   Daniel King, Justice of Peace.

At a meeting of the inhabitance of Kingston warned and convened
at the House of Israel Balls in said Kingston on the 8th day of
July instant agreeable to the above notification:

1st.   Voted and chose Israel Ball Moderator to govern said meeting.

2nd.   Voted and chose Joseph Partick, Town Clerk.

3rd.   Voted and chose Israel Ball, Asa Wood and Moses King Selectmen.

4th.   Chose Gideon Abbott Constable and Collector

5.   Chose Joshua Bechwith, Grand Jurior.

6th.   Chose Joseph Patrick and Joel Rice, Highway Surveyers.

7th.   Voted to ajourn said meeting until September 16th at 3 o-clock
       P. M. to be held at the Dwelling House of Daniel King, Esq.

Sept. 16, 1788   When the inhabitance of Kingston meet at the
       dwelling house of Daniel King Esq. according to above ajournment:

1st.   Voted to petition the General Assembly for a Land Tax.

2nd.   Voted to have said Tax TWO PENCE per Acre.

ATTest: Joseph Patrick, Town Clerk.

Granville (Taken from "Atlas of Addison Co.,
Vermont" published by F. W.
Beers & Co, 1871

      Granville was organized November 7th, 1780 and chartered to
Reuben King, August 7th, 1781, by the name of Kingston. The
name was changed to Granville, November 6th, 1834. Settlements
were commenced soon after the Revolution by Reuben King and
others. At a meeting of the proprietors held at Windsor,
September 28th, 1784, it was decided to give 100 acres of land to
each of the first women who should go with their families and
make a permanent settlement in the town.
      Mrs. Hannah King, wife of Daniel A., Mrs. Sterling and Mrs.
Persis Ball, wife of Israel ball, accepted the offer. The
town was organized July 8th, 1788. First Town Clerk, Joseph
Patrick; first constable, Gideon Abbots; first Selecmen; Israel
Ball, Asa Wood, and Moses King; first Representative, Joseph
Patrick; 1807. November 6th, 1833 a part of Avery's Gore
was annexed to this town.
      The religious denominations were originally Congregationalist
and Baptist. The town is watered by White River and its
numerous branches. The surface of the town is very rugged,
except in the intervales. It is unsurpassed well-adapted
to grazing and agriculture is the chief pursuit.
      The population in 1870 numbered 726.

Granville Town Historical Papers

Granville   (Addison County Gazateer & Directory)

    Granville was granted by Gov. Thomas Chittenden of Vermont
Nov. 7, 1780 and chartered Aug. 2, 1781 toReuben King and
sixty-three others, taking its name "Kingston" from King. This
name it retained till Nov. 6, 1833, when for some local prejudice
on the part of the infabitants, it was changed by the Legislature
to Granville.
    White River ----The overflows, however, sometimes overstep
their bounds and become freshets, when the gentle purling
streams become like a beautiful animal roused to anger, the
master and destroyer. The most destructive of these torrents
occured during the great storm of July 26, 1830. There had been
an unusual fall of rain during the whole season, but on the third
day previous to the flood-Saturday- at about three o'clock, P. Mm,
rain fell with unusual vehemence until Sabbath morning, so that
during the day the streams were forced from their beds upon
soil which had xk slept by their side for ages unmolested.
When at the close of the Sabbath they again began to retreat
slowly and sullenly to their wonted c annels, it seemed that a
short respit was to be allowed the already saturated earth. But
early in the forenoon on Monday the storm broke with redoubled
fury, continuing till far into the night. Houses, barns, bridges,
and everything in the course of the mad torrent were swept before
it, causing an incredible loss of property, though happily,
no lives were lost in this town. The deep gulf at Moss Glen
Falls, lying between the mountain on the west and the hill
on the opposite side, was literally filled up by an immence
mass of earth that had been undermined by the water till it
made a lnad slide, forming a dam that raised the waters above to
a height of seventy-five feet above their normal course, as
was proven afterward by the drift-wood, etc. lodged in the
tops of the trees. At about twelve o'clock this immense mass
gave way, and the waters fromthe mighty reservoir formed by it
came thundering down through the valley, carrying destruction
to all before it. The inhabitants having betaken themselves to
the higher land was all that prevented a great loss of life.
The narrowest escape, perhaps was that ofDavid Wiley, in the
eastern part of the town, whose house was swept away, and he
and his family only escaped death by clinging to a projecting
rock, and under a portion of which they took refuge till morning.

Damage to a river dam after a
freshet

About the Author

Robert S. Foster, known by his nickname, Butch, by his friends and acquaintances, spent the last forty-plus years as an excavation and site development contractor.

His passions over the years have included beekeeping, aviation, woodsmanship, playing guitar and blues harps, song writing, fly fishing and upholding "old school" New England values and traditions.

Along with his wife Mary, he developed a farmstead known as Old Orchard Farm, hosting an antique cider mill, bakery, and sound stage for homespun folk music events—a place where folks can sense the simplicity of old traditions and a small bit of Vermont's serenity.

Today Butch enjoys making music, writing, restoring old things, ancient native Indian cultures along with the quiet natural beauty and energy of Vermont's Green Mountains.